Corporate Models Today

Corporate Models Today

A New Tool for Financial Management

by Peter H Grinyer MA PhD

Professor of Business Strategy,
The City University Business School, London

and Jeff Wooller MSc PhD ACA ACIS AIB

Research Assistant,
The City University Business School
Management Accountant,
United Molasses Co., Ltd

Second Edition

THE INSTITUTE OF CHARTERED ACCOUNTANTS
IN ENGLAND AND WALES
CHARTERED ACCOUNTANTS' HALL
MOORGATE PLACE, LONDON EC2R 6EQ
1978

© 1975, 1978 Chartered Accountants' Trust
for Education and Research

First published 1975
Second edition 1978

ISBN 0 85291 197 1
(1st edition: 0 85291 104 1)

Printed in Great Britain by
The Anchor Press Ltd, Tiptree, Essex

Diagrams and charts by Dahling Dahling, London

Cover and design by Rosemary Claxton

Dedication

To Linda, Sylvia and our Parents

Acknowledgements

No book is written without the authors accumulating a massive debt of gratitude. To list all those who have contributed something of worth is not practicable. None the less we are able to acknowledge some of those who helped us most.

First, we would like to thank the Research Committee of the Institute of Chartered Accountants in England and Wales, without whose financial support the surveys on which much of the book is based could not have been undertaken. Their support, though, was more than purely financial. Ernest Barnes and John Flower, each eminent in his own field, provided very valuable advice.

Second, we offer grateful thanks to the band of stalwarts who read drafts of the book. Their number includes Anne Bolton of the City Polytechnic, Adrian Buckley of Redland, Patrick Frazer of the Inter-Bank Research Organisation, Ken Moss of Midland Bank, Paul Neild of Phillips and Drew, David Pendrill of the London School of Economics, Richard Taffler of The City University and Alan Tapnack of Price Waterhouse Associates. They made a number of good suggestions which we have sought to include in the book. Any shortcomings of the book are, though, entirely our own responsibility.

Third, special thanks are due to those who have produced material actually included in the book. Henry Wilson of Associated Television and Bill Thornley of Baric Bureau jointly provided the example for Chapter 6 on model building. Modellers from Anglia Building Society, Fisons, Lansing Bagnall, Rover and Yorkshire Imperial Plastics kindly provided the case studies for Chapter 8. Gerry Smith, Librarian/Information Officer of The City University Business School, provided valuable support throughout and in particular helped in the compilation of the Select Bibliography.

Fourth, we thank the corporate modellers who assisted us during our survey, spending sometimes hours discussing their work with us, and completing long and detailed questionnaires. Without their support the distinctive element of the book, the information on what UK companies are actually doing, would be absent.

Last, but by no means least, we wish to thank those who have borne the brunt of the turmoil. Sylvia Grinyer, whose supportive rôle is obvious; Barbara Sanderson, who bore our changes with patience and charm, and finally Phyllis Brand, Vera Grey and Margaret McKay, who also provided valuable secretarial support.

Contents

Preface to the Second Edition

Since 1968 an increasing number of companies have been acquiring corporate models. A survey carried out by the authors in 1973 showed that 9 per cent of 'The Times 1,000' had or were developing corporate models then. Since that date, there has been a veritable explosion of corporate modelling, and the figure is probably now in excess of 50 per cent. Moreover, corporate models are not confined to such large companies, but are used by companies of widely differing sizes. Nor are corporate models to be found only in a limited range of industries. Companies with models are to be found in financial services, consumer goods, industrial goods and extractive industries. We use the term 'company' throughout the book in a very loose sense to include organisations such as Anglia Building Society, British Airports Authority, British Rail and British Steel Corporation.

This rapidly growing adoption of models has been accompanied by a minor explosion of articles on corporate models in both the popular management and the technical journals. Many of these articles report briefly the experience of a single company, normally from the point of view of the man responsible for developing the model. They are informative, but highly repetitive, and are characterised by an almost missionary zeal.

There is, therefore, a need for a more general and more objective guide for directors, senior accountants, and planners. They need to have an overview of the different types of model available, how models may be acquired and used, the costs incurred, benefits to be expected, and the sequence of decisions involved in model development. This book is intended to meet this need.

The book consequently starts with a simple introduction to corporate models and with an account of their uses. It progresses to an analysis of the ways companies can acquire corporate models. Then the major alternative features of corporate models are explained as a basis for decisions on the best type of model for the company. Chapters on mode of computer operation and flexibility follow. These lead to a chapter giving broad guidlines to those who wish to develop their own models and a discussion of special services available from computer bureaux to assist them. Chapter 8 provides case studies in which modellers describe their own experiences (including some setbacks).

Chapter 9 analyses the cost of developing corporate models and the factors on which it depends. We believe that this analysis is the most intensive and objective provided in this field to date. Chapter 10 explores conditions for successful development and use of corporate models, the extent to which these conditions exist in UK companies, and the evidence available for success or failure. The final chapter deals with the problem of selection. Drawing upon material presented earlier in the book, it offers a systematic approach to selection, in which checklists and rating methods are used as aids to decision-taking.

Preface

Materials and views presented in the book are based on a number of related sources. A team at The City University Business School started developing corporate models in companies in 1968. The experience this afforded has been extremely valuable. However, much more information has been provided by our survey of 65 companies with corporate models. Most of these companies were visited, several people being interviewed in many of them, and a wealth of knowledge was gleaned from them. Further information was collected in surveys of 100 companies in 'The Times 1,000' and of special facilities applicable to corporate modelling available from computer bureaux, computer manufacturers and consultants. All the surveys were finally sponsored by the Institute of Chartered Accountants in England and Wales.

Prior knowledge of modelling and computers is not required to understand the text. Jargon has been avoided, wherever possible, and only key terms with which the manager should become conversant have been used. In each case, the term is defined at the point at which it is introduced, and also in a glossary at the end of the book. No knowledge of mathematics beyond the simplest algebra is assumed and the manager with only a rusty knowledge of elementary algebra should encounter no difficulties in this respect.

Despite its orientation towards senior managers, including board members, the book should also be of interest to specialists. The text presents material on experience to date in the UK that is made available here for the first time. To aid the specialist, the survey results are given as appendices, in the form in which they were presented at a recent seminar. However, certain of the chapters give additional information, especially the chapter covering the costs of modelling where a detailed break-down of costs is provided.

To enable the manager to skip the more technical chapters, should he wish to do so, and to enable the specialist to dip into the book in a selective fashion, each chapter has been made as self-contained as practicable.

By these means, the book is intended to provide as much information as the individual reader requires to meet his needs, whilst not demanding that he should read the whole book. Ultimately, what is important is that the reader should be sufficiently stimulated to think about corporate models further, and sufficiently informed to make at least initial decisions. Both are very individual matters.

Since the first edition was written, the UK economy has suffered the most severe recession of the post-war era, and companies have often been forced to focus on short-term survival rather than long-term options. Quickening adoption of corporate models has, in part, been a response to the very needs created by these difficulties. Models have been used with greater frequency to provide control over cash flows, sometimes on a daily basis as in the Anglia Building Society (see Chapter 8), but more often on a monthly or quarterly one. Similarly, there has been an increased use of corporate models to provide accurate, fast, relatively cheap financial control by group head-quarters over subsidiaries. As the economy recovers, one may expect a further re-emphasis on long-range planning applications, but we believe that none the less the use of corporate models as a tool for financial corporate control has come to stay.

These changes have led us to review the content of the book since it first appeared in 1975. Were we writing the book for the first time we would adjust the emphasis a little in some of the chapters. For instance, as already suggested, we would now place a heavier emphasis on use of corporate models for financial control in Chapter 1. Similarly, in Chapters 2 and 7, even heavier emphasis would be placed on modelling systems. Use of ready-made models is still as rare as we found it to be in 1973–5. More important, general-purpose languages like FORTRAN are being used less and less for corporate modelling now, for modelling systems are so greatly improved that their superiority is undisputed. These further developments are completely in tune with the text of the first edition, however, and we have chosen to note them here rather than inflate the cost and price of the book by their inclusion in the main text.

xii

In contrast to the main text, Appendix 2 on Financial Modelling Packages in the UK, has been revised completely. Some of the packages which are little used have been dropped, others introduced since 1975 have been included, and entries for those packages which have withstood the test of time have been up-dated to allow for their continued evolution. The information on financial modelling packages was completed in February 1978. One of the gratifying aspects of the success of the first edition has been the large number of practitioners of corporate modelling who have used the book. We gather that they have found the survey of modelling packages available in the UK of considerable value as the only source of such comparative data. This new survey will, we hope, meet a continued need among both new modellers and old hands.

May, 1978

Materials and views presented in the book are based on a number of related sources. A team at the Graduate Business Centre, The City University, started developing corporate models in companies in 1968. The experience this afforded has been extremely valuable. However, much more information has been provided by our survey of 65 companies with corporate models. Most of these companies were visited, several people being interviewed in many of them, and a wealth of knowledge was gleaned from them. Further information was collected in surveys of 100 companies in 'The Times 1,000' and of special facilities applicable to corporate modelling available from computer bureaux, computer manufacturers and consultants. All the surveys were financially sponsored by the Institute of Chartered Accountants in England and Wales.

Prior knowledge of modelling and computers is not required to understand the text. Jargon has been avoided, wherever possible, and only key terms with which the manager should become conversant have been used. In each case, the term is defined at the point at which it is introduced, and also in a glossary at the end of the book. No knowledge of mathematics beyond the simplest algebra is assumed and the manager with only a rusty knowledge of elementary algebra should encounter no difficulties in this respect.

Despite its orientation towards senior managers, including board members, the book should also be of interest to specialists. The text presents material on experience to date in the UK that is made available here for the first time. To aid the specialist, the survey results are given as appendices, in the form in which they were presented at a recent seminar. However, certain of the chapters give additional information, especially the chapter covering the costs of modelling where a detailed break-down of costs is provided.

Appendix 2 on the financial modelling packages available in the UK should also be useful as a source of technical information. This is based on a research paper first issued in October 1973, that has already been widely circulated and used. This has been updated to allow for the rapid rate of development of this area.

To enable the manager to skip the more technical chapters, should he wish to do so, and to enable the specialist to dip into the book in a selective fashion, each chapter has been made as self-contained as practicable.

By these means, the book is intended to provide as much information as the individual reader requires to meet his needs, whilst not demanding that he should read the whole book. Ultimately, what is important is that the reader should be sufficiently stimulated to think about corporate models further, and sufficiently informed to make at least initial decisions. Both are very individual matters.

Chapter 1

Introduction

1.1 *The nature of corporate models*

In 1972 British Steel undertook a major long-range planning exercise which involved a thorough analysis of alternative patterns of investment and divestment. This was complicated by the interdependence of many of the relevant factors. Sources of ore and coal, location of major users of steel, costs of transport, costs of production in existing mills, costs of closure, and other factors bore on the problem of determining the best way in which to meet future projected demand. Nevertheless, plans were submitted to the government for sanction within the time limits imposed, and were approved. Similarly during the negotiations that led to the merging of the computer interests of English Electric into ICL, the future performance of the proposed new company was repeatedly calculated on the basis of a variety of planning assumptions; the results led to a fuller understanding of the merger effects. At Anglia Building Society, Conoco, Lansing Bagnall, London Transport and many other companies, the clerical effort and time taken to prepare long-term financial plans and cash flow forecasts has been slashed. The common feature in all of these cases has been the use of corporate models.

What, then, are corporate models? All models are representations of reality. The architect's three-dimensional model physically represents a proposed building. An Ordnance Survey map represents geographical features by means of symbols; it enables the user to determine where he is, where he should go next, and in what general direction he should head. Accounting conventions provide a framework within which operations of the company, such as buying, manufacturing and selling, are represented in purely monetary terms. Their value lies in the fact that they permit us to understand, plan and control financial aspects of these operations better.

Similarly, corporate models are sets of related expressions that represent the key operations of the company. They vary in sophistication, size, range of applications, and so on, but in their most common form comprise little more than accounting statements linked in a straightforward way. For instance, many models embody routines relating profit after tax to revenue and costs, which may be merely:

PROFIT = REVENUE − COSTS

TAX = PROFIT × 50%

PROFIT AFTER TAX = PROFIT − TAX

An example of a simple model of this kind is shown in *Figure 1.1*. Section (a) shows the sequence of steps, or 'logic', which would typically be used by an accountant, and Section (b) shows the resulting computer print-out.

Figure 1.1 Example of a simple forecasting model

Section (a) – Accounting data and logic (in £000s)

Sales for 1977	=	2,000
Sales for subsequent years	=	Sales for 1977 × growth factor of 10%
Materials	=	Sales × 30%
Wages	=	Sales × 20%
Other charges	=	200 + (sales × 5%)
Depreciation	=	100
Loan interest	=	10
Expenses	=	Materials + wages + other charges + depreciation + loan interest
Net profit before tax	=	Sales − expenses
Tax	=	Net profit × 50%
Net profit after tax	=	Net profit − tax

Section (b) – Computer print-out of results
FORECAST PROFIT AND LOSS ACCOUNTS

	1978	1979	1980	1981	1982
SALES	2200.	2420.	2662.	2928.	3221.
MATERIALS	660.	726.	799.	878.	966.
WAGES	440.	484.	532.	586.	644.
OTHER CHARGES	310.	321.	333.	346.	361.
DEPRECIATION	100.	100.	100.	100.	100.
LOAN INTEREST	10.	10.	10.	10.	10.
PRE-TAX PROFIT	680.	779.	888.	1008.	1139.
TAX	340.	390.	444.	504.	570.
AFTER-TAX PROFIT	340.	390.	444.	504.	570.

It is immediately apparent that the steps of the model could be worked through using pencil and paper. Indeed this is often just what is being done when clerical staff produce accounting reports for future periods. But manual procedures are expensive, slow and liable to arithmetical errors. Consequently, many companies have translated most of such procedures into a form that can be read and followed by a computer, a process known as 'programming'. This involves use of computer readable 'programming languages'. The result of programming is a computer 'program'.

Hence corporate models are usually written as computer programs that direct the computer to execute a series of procedural steps (to follow the logic of the model). In most cases, there is nothing sophisticated or difficult about their logic, and their value lies in the fact that they have harnessed the power of the computer. This permits rapid and often relatively cheap calculation of the results of different planning assumptions. Some of these assumptions are represented by values fed to the computer (input). By changing the input, that is by feeding in alternative assumptions to the computer, a wide range of 'what if' questions may be answered. For instance, by using optimistic, most likely, and pessimistic sales and cost estimates management may gain a deeper insight into the risks inherent in a proposal. Other assumptions may have been written into the expressions in the model. For example, in *Figure 1.1* a growth in sales of 10 per cent per annum has been assumed, as have given relationships between sales and materials, wages, and other charges. To change such assumptions, new 'program statements' must replace the old, for example:

WAGES = SALES × 30%

could replace

WAGES = SALES × 20%.

The effects of the proposed changes may be shown by comparison of the outputs from the amended and unamended models.

Use of corporate models to test alternatives need not necessarily involve computer specialists. The manager with little knowledge of computers or of computer programming can quickly gain sufficient grasp of the mechanics of operating a model to allow him to use it directly himself. At Van den Berghs and Jurgens, for instance, it has been found that managers require no more than a few days to gain sufficient confidence to use the model without technical assistance. Similarly, at British Steel and the International Publishing Corporation accountants run their own models.

Even the development of models may be undertaken by those with no initial command of computer programming; this has been made possible by the advent of special programming languages devised for this purpose. A course of no more than a week is usually enough to allow an intelligent manager to start designing the logic and programming his own corporate models. For example, after very little tuition the Finance Director of Yorkshire Imperial Plastics was able to produce a computer model of his company. It should not be assumed that models built by non-data processing staff are necessarily small or simple. Two of the largest models we have encountered were developed at Lansing Bagnall and London Transport almost entirely by accountants.

1.2 *Applications*

The importance of financial applications may be gauged from *Figure 1.2* which shows the major uses of models. As all corporate models are used for some aspects of financial planning, there is a need for the involvement of accountants, or alternatively, managers with a good working knowledge of the accounting procedures of the company. However, corporate models are also widely used to aid marketing, distribution, production and other major decisions of a primarily non-financial nature. Evaluation of projects requiring capital expenditure is also an important use.

All corporate models produce forecasts of financial reports such as profit and loss accounts, balance sheets or cash flow statements. It can be seen from *Figure 1.3* that a high percentage of them also provide reports on marketing, distribution and production. Moreover, whilst all corporate models give reports for the company as a whole, a large number of them also do so for lower organisational levels. For example, in almost a quarter of companies with a corporate model, reports on operating units such as production plants were produced. This means, of course, that some aspects at least of these units have been represented in the models. Clearly, such models are intended to serve the decision-making needs of marketing, production, and other managers in subsidiaries, divisions and operating units. This is obviously in addition to their use by the board, corporate accountants and corporate planners.

Figure 1.2   Major uses of models

	Application	Percentage of companies %
(A)	*Financial*	
	Financial planning(up to 1 year)	38
	,, ,, (1 to 5 years)	78
	,, ,, (over 5 years)	45
	Cash flow analysis	75
	Financing	14
(B)	*Non-financial planning*	
	Aid marketing decisions	65
	Market share forecasting	8
	Aid production decisions	60
	Aid distributing decisions	38
	Aid purchasing decisions	11
	Manpower planning	12
(C)	*Evaluation of special projects*	
	Project evaluation	45
	New venture evaluation	14
	Acquisition studies	12
	Computer evaluation (rent or buy)	5

Figure 1.3   Output reports produced by models: percentage of companies with each report

Report	Total company %	Subsidiaries %	Divisions %	Operating units %
Profit and loss	98	43	40	22
Balance sheet	79	37	25	12
Cash flow	77	37	28	15
Financial ratio analysis	68	31	23	18
Source and use of funds statement	55	28	20	11
Marketing operations	34	25	31	23
Project evaluation	34	25	12	15
Production	34	22	28	22
Distribution	29	17	20	17

(Figure continued on next page)

Figure 1   continued

Report	Total company %	Subsidiaries %	Divisions %	Operating units %
Purchasing	11	8	8	6
Manpower	9	6	9	6
Financing	8	2	2	2
New venture	3	2	3	2

1.3   *Extent and growth of corporate modelling*

Few companies were modelling in the UK in 1968, even though in the USA 20 per cent had apparently started.[1] However, surveys in 1971[2] and 1972[3] suggested a wider interest. By 1973, our random survey suggested that 9 per cent of the largest UK companies, 'The Times 1,000', had or were developing corporate models. Moreover, corporate models were being used in a wide variety of different industries. *Figure 1.4* shows the distribution between industries of the 65 companies covered by a further survey (see Appendix 1).

Figure 1.4   Classification of companies included in the survey

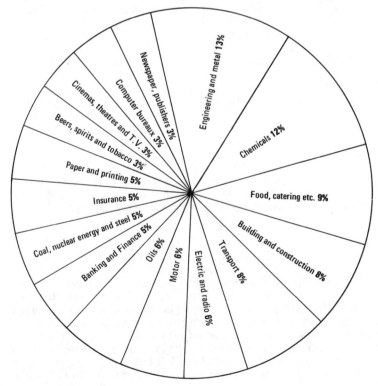

The available evidence therefore suggests that by 1973 corporate models were already fairly widely used in the UK. Many of these corporate models were quite new. As may be seen from *Figure 1.5*, although at least one company in the UK had started to develop its model as early as 1963, the pace of introduction did not quicken much until 1970.

There seems to be no reason why the rate of introduction should fall in the next few years. Indeed, it might be expected to rise, due to increased publicity and the efforts of bureaux to sell their special corporate modelling facilities. The term 'bureaux' is used here, and in the rest of the book, as shorthand for 'computer bureaux, computer hardware manufacturers, and consultants with special corporate modelling software'. The user is referred to the Glossary at the end of this book for definitions of hardware and software.

1.4 Benefits

This spread of corporate models has been accompanied, and no doubt reinforced, by a growing body of literature that stresses their value. Prominent among the benefits claimed are:

- Greater accuracy and speed of forecasting company performance.
- A means of quickly checking on the internal consistency of planning assumptions.
- Reduction of clerical effort involved in evaluating alternative proposals and in preparing long-term financial plans.
- As a result, freedom to explore a wide range of alternatives, as opposed to the few possible with manual calculations.
- Release of management time, by reduction of routine calculations, for thinking about strategic problems and their solution.
- Fuller allowance for links with other aspects of the business when evaluating a proposal.
- Fuller understanding of the internal complexities of the company by decision takers.
- Deeper insight into the risks inherent in proposed projects.
- A means of highlighting the key aspects of both existing business and new projects.
- A tool for showing managers the extent to which reported performances will be affected by errors in estimates.

Although there can be little doubt that many companies have gained these benefits, there are others which have not, and it cannot be assumed that they will necessarily follow introduction of corporate models. Moreover, even where they are most successful, corporate models have limitations that are best recognised at the outset of any serious study of their possible introduction to a company.

1.5 Limitations

- They deal only with quantitative (measurable) aspects. In strategic problems, qualitative (immeasurable) factors are important, and sometimes dominate decisions. Although important, the contribution of corporate models to solution of strategic models can, consequently, be no more than partial.
- They will do only what they have been designed to do. A model which represents the accounting procedures of the company may be extremely useful for long-term budgeting and for working out the financial implications of proposed patterns of investment. However, it can cast no light on how sales will react to a change in

price or on whether the production plant can cope with a projected increase in sales without major new capital investment, unless it embodies expressions representing the response of the market to price changes and the production process respectively.

Figure 1.5 UK modelling starts since 1963

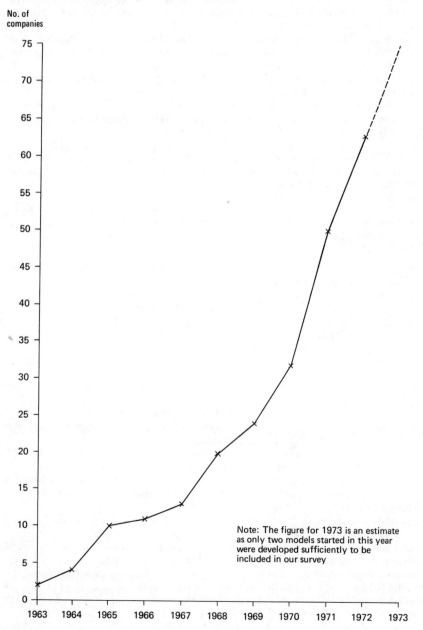

No. of companies

Note: The figure for 1973 is an estimate as only two models started in this year were developed sufficiently to be included in our survey

- Output of most models is highly sensitive to changes in some of the values fed in by the user (input variables). Errors in these variables can lead to serious error in the results produced by the model. Ultimately, therefore, the value of the model must depend on the ability of the company to provide good estimates for at least these critical variables.
- Models may help managers to choose the best of the alternatives tested but they are entirely passive. Only managers can create alternatives put to the corporate model for evaluation. Hence the ultimate quality of strategic decisions still depends on the perception, knowledge of the business and its environment, and innovative flair of management.
- The process by which strategic decisions are reached within companies is political. Participants in this process may sometimes use their corporate model to justify a position already taken rather than to rigorously evaluate alternatives. By careful selection of data for input the model may be used to produce the required report. Even so, use of a corporate model does impose a further discipline within the political process, and should serve to eliminate some of the grosser errors. Where input necessary to justify a course of action is highly unrealistic this may be patently obvious to all concerned.

These limitations are not peculiar to corporate models. They are common to all approaches to evaluating alternative strategies. They can be summed up by saying that corporate models can help good management to make better decisions but cannot prevent poor management from making bad ones.

1.6   *Structure of book*

A number of major questions have remained unanswered in this introduction because they require much fuller treatment. These include:

- How may, and do, companies acquire corporate models?
- What are the main types of models that a company may develop?
- How fully does the user interact with a corporate model?
- How is the computer accessed by him?
- What steps are involved in developing a corporate model?
- What special programming languages and computer routines for corporate models are available from bureaux?
- How successful have corporate models been in practice and what are the conditions for success?
- How much do corporate models cost to develop and run?
- How should management set about choosing the best way to get a corporate model that will meet their particular needs?

These questions are answered in the remaining chapters of the book. The sequence is broken at two points only. Chapter 5 deals with the issue of flexibility of logic, input and output of corporate models and the factors that bear upon it. Chapter 8 is a collection of case studies contributed by companies from widely different industries.

On first reading, the busy manager may choose to skip Chapters 4, 5 and 7, which are somewhat more technical in content. To allow for such selective reading, we have tried to keep each chapter as self-contained as possible, even though this has meant that some points are made in more than one chapter. However, where major repetition would have been involved, cross-reference has been made to other chapters. In addition, to avoid redefining technical terms in each chapter in which they are used, a glossary is provided at the end of the book. The reader may refer to this should he come across a term that was first used, and defined, on a page that he has not read.

Throughout the book we have drawn on the results of surveys, sponsored by the Institute of Chartered Accountants in England and Wales, to provide information on current practice and experience in the UK. Details of these surveys may be found in Appendices 1 and 2. Unless indicated to the contrary, all figures given are based on the survey of 65 UK companies with corporate models (Appendix 1).

References

1.   Gershefski, G. W.; Corporate models: the state of the art.
      Management Science (Application), Feb. 1970.

2.   Wagle, B. V., Jenkins, P. M.; The development of a general computer system to aid the corporate planning process.
      UK Scientific Centre, IBM UK Ltd, Peterlee, County Durham 1971.

3.   Neild, P. G.; Mathematical models as a tool for financial management; Financial modelling in UK industry.
      In: European Federation of Financial Analysts Societies VIIth Congress, Torremolinos, 1972. Proceedings. (A shortened version of the second paper appears in *Journal of Business Policy*, Spring 1973.)

Chapter 2

How companies acquire a corporate model

2.1 *The main issues*

A number of alternatives are open to a company that intends to acquire a corporate model. These are illustrated in *Figure 2.1*. Broadly the alternatives can be stated as:

- Buy a model 'ready-made' from a bureau.
- Develop a 'tailor-made' model specifically for the company by use of:
  - A general purpose programming language or a modelling system (special language for corporate modelling available from a bureau).
  - Consultants and/or own staff.
  - Specialist modellers and/or accountants, managers and other ultimate users, among own staff.

A general introduction to each of these alternatives is given in later sections of this chapter. Chapter 6 gives a more detailed account of construction of tailor-made models and Chapter 7 of ready-made models and modelling systems.

Figure 2.1 Approaches to acquiring a corporate model

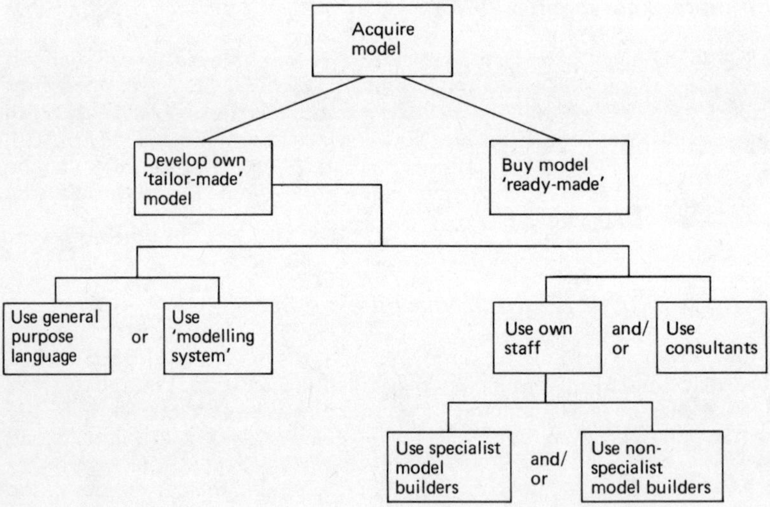

2.2 *Make or buy*

There are basically two ways in which a company can get a corporate model: it may buy one or develop its own. It is easier, quicker and very often cheaper to buy a 'ready-made' model, i.e. one that requires no additional programming by the user. A range of such models is available from bureaux. Virtually all incorporate basic accounting routines, take standard accounting data as input, and produce financial reports as output.

Ready-made models have proved to be valuable, general evaluative tools for consultants and merchant banks. They have often served to introduce companies to corporate models. They put corporate models within the reach of small companies that

10

have not the resources to develop their own. In addition, they possess certain clear advantages, like immediate availability, that are not enjoyed by models built specifically for the company. Consequently, they merit serious consideration.

However, ready-made models have major limitations too. Most important of these is the fact that, because they are designed for general use, they do not include expressions to represent unusual or unique aspects of a company's business. For instance, they rarely extend beyond financial aspects to marketing or production operations. Moreover, even in the financial area they tend to use standard routines, and make little allowance for differences in accounting conventions among companies.

A fuller discussion of these limitations may be found in Chapter 7 where it is indicated that at least one bureau is taking steps to overcome them. Such improvements are certainly necessary if ready-made models are to be used widely. Recognition of their limitations has led to neglect of ready-made models, relative to tailor-made ones, in the UK.

A leading consultant, whose company has its own ready-made models, has estimated that no more than 2 per cent of all corporate models used are ready-made. Certainly, the percentage of large companies using them may be expected to be low. None of a random sample of 100 companies from 'The Times 1,000' used a ready-made model (in Chapter 1 it was seen that 9 per cent had corporate models). On the other hand, one of the bureaux which has specialised in ready-made models has claimed over 60 users, many of them small companies but a number among the largest in their industries.

On the whole, though, evidence available suggests that, rather than use such 'off the shelf' types, companies construct models which represent their own operations and accounting logic more faithfully. Such 'tailor-made' models are by definition series of expressions which describe relationships between constituent parts of the firm and, possibly, its economic environment. Although some of these relationships may be sufficiently general to apply to other companies too, for example tax routines, others are individual to the company.

2.3 *General-purpose languages and modelling systems*

When a model is tailor-made, the expressions comprising the model are almost invariably translated into a form the computer can read and act upon. This process was introduced in Chapter 1 as 'programming'. Programming is largely a technical matter that need not, in detail, concern the manager. However, he does need to understand the basic alternatives open to the company, for the approach adopted influences issues such as the type of staff able to develop the corporate model, the capabilities of the model, the use of an in-house or external computer, and the costs of development, updating and using the model.

Nowadays programming is usually in a 'high-level language', which normally approximates to either a somewhat artificial business English (like COBOL) or to mathematical notation (like FORTRAN). This makes programming much easier than use of 'low-level languages', which are closer to the machine code in which the computer is instructed.

Early corporate models were programmed in those high-level languages, like FORTRAN or COBOL, that are widely available, may be used in a wide range of applications and are transferable between computers. Because they are capable of fairly general application these are sometimes called 'general-purpose' languages. (A fuller account of available languages of this kind appears in Appendix 3 and an example of a program written in such a language is given in Chapter 6.)

In a survey in the USA in 1968 a general-purpose language, FORTRAN, was found to be the most widely used for corporate models.[1] In the UK most of the

Figure 2.2 Percentages of companies using general-purpose languages

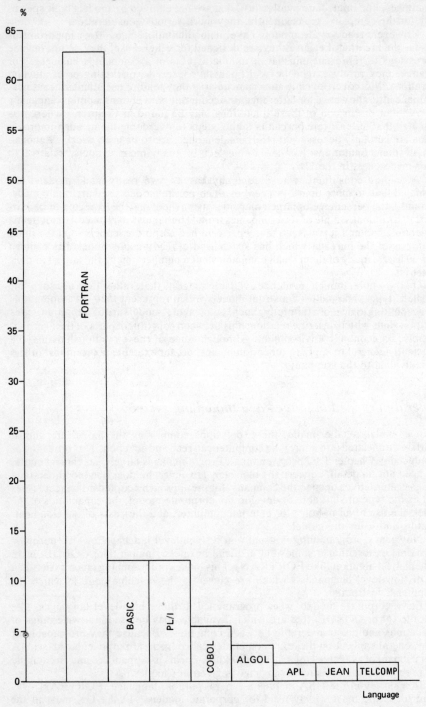

companies that had developed corporate models by 1973 had used general-purpose languages, and most of these, as can be seen from *Figure 2.2*, used FORTRAN. Since 1970, however, an increasing range of 'modelling systems' designed especially for corporate modelling has become available and half of the UK companies with corporate models had used them. Evidence collected suggested increasing acceptance.

Modelling systems are special programming languages devised specifically for corporate modelling, and provide the user with a set of instructions oriented especially to planning. For instance the computer may print out a balance sheet in response to a statement such as 'REPORT B/S'. In so far as it leaves freedom to the user to build his own logic into the model, and to link instructions in a way most appropriate to his needs, the modelling system may best be regarded as a 'tool' to assist the programming of tailor-made models.

The features, advantages and disadvantages of general-purpose languages and modelling systems are considered more fully in later chapters. For the purpose of the manager making an initial study of available approaches to development of a tailor-made model, though, some of the salient differences between the two approaches to model building are summarised in *Figure 2.3*. It is fair to add that there is, at present, no general agreement among specialists on, for instance, the relative costs of using general-purpose languages and modelling systems. In such cases the most widely held view is reported.

Figure 2.3 Summary of major differences between general-purpose languages and modelling systems

Characteristic	General-purpose language	Modelling system	Chapter where further details are given
Computer used	Own or bureau	Own or bureau with greater emphasis on latter	Chapters 4 & 7
Mode of Operation	Batch, conversational, remote batch (historically batch usually)	Batch, conversational, remote batch (greater use of conversational approach)	Chapter 4
Size	Fewer constraints	More constraints	Chapter 7
Need for skilled programmers	Medium to high	Medium to low	Chapter 7
Ability for modeller to more faithfully represent specific relationships	Higher	Lower	Chapters 6 & 7
Speed of programming and model development	Slower	Faster	Chapter 7
Ease of updating	Lower	Higher	Chapter 7

(Figure continued on next page)

13

Figure 2.3 continued

Characteristic	General-purpose language	Modelling system	Chapter where further details are given
Cost of model development	Higher	Lower	Chapter 10
Cost of updating	Higher	Lower	Chapter 10
Cost of operation	Lower	Higher	Chapter 10

2.4 *Own staff and/or consultants*

Companies resolved to develop their own models are soon faced by the problem of who to select to develop, or 'build', the corporate model. A number of alternatives face them, as is clear from *Figure 2.1*. First, they need to decide on whether their own staff or consultants or both should be used. Consultants may bring an outside, objective view to the task, may have specialist knowledge that is lacking within the company, have previous experience of building corporate models to draw upon, enable the company to avoid taking its bright men from other tasks, and have often produced excellent models by stipulated target dates at reasonable costs.

On the other hand, use of internal staff may be much cheaper than paying sometimes high fees to consultants, though one consultant has pointed out that a good systems analyst costs most companies £40 a day even when idle. Moreover, in many companies internal staff may have, or quickly develop, the necessary level of expertise. It can be argued that, especially where modelling systems are used, a detailed knowledge of the accounting conventions of the company is of greater value to the builder of a simple financial corporate model than are data processing skills. Furthermore, when internal staff are used, a group of individuals with intimate knowledge of the model remains in the company after initial model development is completed. This facilitates both updating and extensions to the model to allow for changing circumstances and decision-making needs. In addition, the model building, and subsequent use, should be strengthened by commitment of some at least of the company's staff to its success.

No doubt this general account of advantages and disadvantages of using consultants could be extended. Ultimately, though, the decision in any particular company turns on many factors that are quite specific to it. For example, the availability of staff of the right calibre, skills, experience and personality is a major determinant. There may sometimes be internal political factors that must be taken into account, too. In addition past experience with consultants, and terms on which their services may be obtained, are obviously of major importance.

Available evidence suggests that most corporate models in the UK have been built by companies without external assistance. However, as may be seen from *Figure 2.4,* a large minority had involved use of consultants, often jointly with internal staff. In *Figure 2.4* use of consultants or the company's own staff is related to the approach adopted to programming. If ranked in ascending order of technical difficulty these approaches would be modelling systems, general-purpose languages and optimisation codes (used for optimisation models introduced in Chapter 3). Not surprisingly, the proportion of models on which consultants were used was significantly higher for optimisation codes than for general-purpose languages, reflecting the need for specialist, highly technical outside assistance.

More significant was the difference between general-purpose languages and modelling systems in the manner in which consultants were used. There was a greater tendency, with modelling systems, to use consultants to assist internal staff rather than to build the model themselves. This reflects the fact that many of the companies using their own staff to develop corporate models have employed consultants, frequently from the bureaux, to train their staff in use of a modelling system, to overcome initial teething troubles, and subsequently to deal with difficult problems on an *ad hoc* basis. Many, but not all, bureaux give such initial help free of charge, and most provide a trouble shooting service at normal consulting rates.

Figure 2.4   Approach to construction of 95 models in 65 UK companies

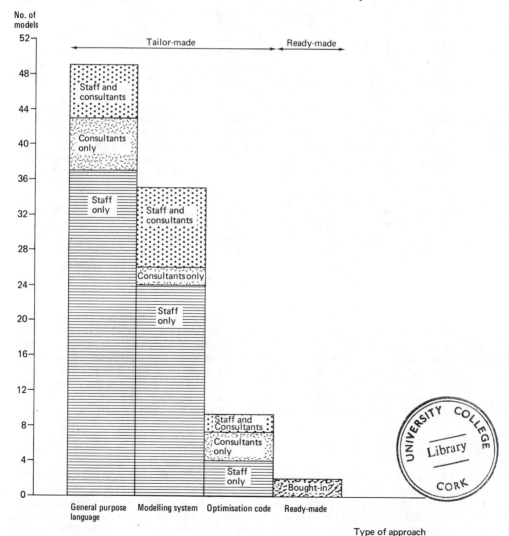

Consultancy charges incurred by this kind of use are in most cases fairly modest, as may be seen in more detail from the chapter on costs, Chapter 10.

2.5 Type of internal staff used

As we have seen, most companies in the UK have chosen to use their own staff to develop corporate models, a process explored more fully in Chapter 6. Clearly, if success is to be achieved, it is important that appropriate staff should undertake this work. The quality of the model, the time taken to develop an initial model, and the ultimate cost all depend on the grade and type of staff employed.

The approach adopted in nearly all early corporate modelling projects was to use operational researchers, mathematicians, systems analysts and other specialist modellers or data processing staff. This was, in large measure, related to the use of a general-purpose language, FORTRAN. FORTRAN uses mathematical notation, requires several weeks to learn thoroughly, and may demand skill in the design of files on which data is held by the computer unless the special data handling facilities of a bureau are used. Consequently, it was more appropriate to use specialist modellers and data processing staff with proficiency in the language. Moreover, many early models were large and complex, sometimes calling for modelling skills of a high order.

The advent of modelling systems has largely changed this situation. Nowadays there are more options open to management when choosing staff for modelling. As indicated in Chapter 1, accountants and others without a specialist knowledge of data processing can now build their own models, and indeed are turning their newly acquired skills to developing models for other functional groups, too. In virtually all of these cases they have used modelling systems, that can be learnt quickly, as a means of entry to the new area.

The extent to which corporate modelling has become the province of non-specialists in data processing may be seen from Figure 2.5. Only half of the modellers in the companies surveyed had been drawn from the ranks of the operational researchers, mathematicians, and data processors. The remainder were accountants, planners, actuaries, economists and other users. Accountants especially have become important as corporate modellers. In the companies where they predominated the models were, as was to be expected, largely financial. Because of their knowledge of the company's accounting routines, and tax calculations in particular, accountants have a strong contribution to make to financial corporate models.

There is no reason, of course, why staff should be drawn from one background alone. Indeed, the advantages of cross-fertilisation of ideas and pooling of specialist knowledge to be gained by multi-disciplinary teams are clear. Recognition of these advantages led to use of staff from more than one background in about half of the UK companies. The background of staff used by companies in their teams are illustrated in Figure 2.6 (page 18). One interesting fact to emerge from Figure 2.6 is that, where a team approach was not used, almost as many companies used accountants alone as used the more traditional model builders alone.

2.6 Trends in the UK

The trends mentioned in earlier sections are, as have been seen, interrelated. Together they amount to an internally consistent pattern.

Nearly all companies have opted for tailor-made rather than ready-made models. On early models, operational researchers, mathematicians and data processing specialists were used to develop models written in general-purpose programming

Figure 2.5 Functional background of model builders

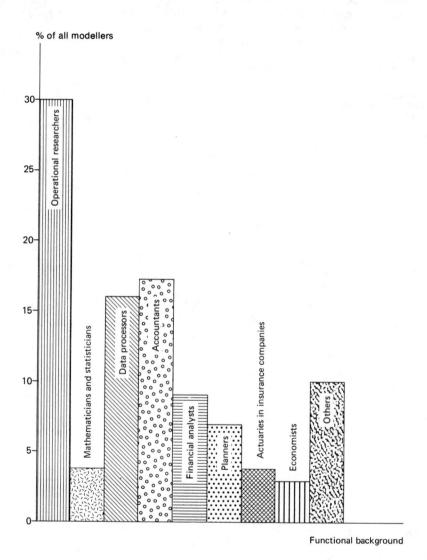

languages. More recently, there has been an increasing use of special corporate model programming languages, called modelling systems. This has been linked to a growth of modelling by accountants, planners and others without an initial specialist knowledge of data processing. Hence the choice of internal staff available for corporate modelling has become much wider where modelling systems have been used.

This entry of accountants, planners, and other ultimate users adopting modelling systems, has not led to a reduction in the proportion of models on which consultants have been used, but it has resulted in a change in the contribution they make. Rather than undertake complete development of the corporate model, their more traditional rôle, they have helped internal staff to construct their own model. They have done this by providing training in the initial stages of model building and use of modelling systems and, in addition, occasional aid in trouble-shooting.

Figure 2.6 Team approach to corporate modelling

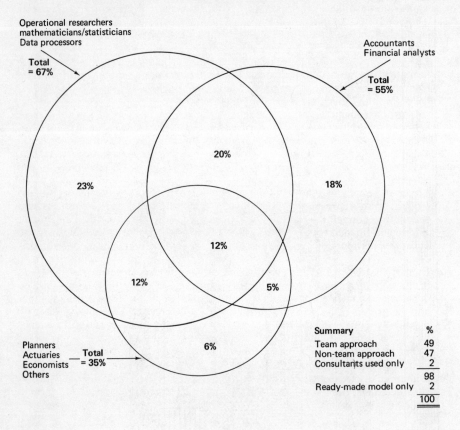

Summary	%
Team approach	49
Non-team approach	47
Consultants used only	2
	98
Ready-made model only	2
	100

Reference

1.   Gershefski, G. W.; Corporate models: the state of the art. *Management Science (Application), Feb. 1970.*

Chapter 3

Types of corporate model

3.1 Main types of model

Models vary widely in their characteristics, capabilities, and hence in the extent to which they meet decision-taking needs. The experience of companies which have retreated from unsuitable corporate models to other more successful ones suggests that choice of type should involve management and not be regarded as a purely technical matter. This choice may be seen as selection between the following alternatives:

- Either to explore implications of possible alternatives by using the model merely to imitate operations of the company or to derive an optimum or 'best' solution from the model by use of special mathematical procedures. The former is called *simulation* and the latter *optimisation*. See Section 3.2.
- Either to use single estimates, for instance a single value for sales in 1980, or to generate multiple estimates for use in the model. The usual approach of management is to use single estimates. Models using this approach are called *deterministic*. Where multiple estimates are used, with a relative frequency that reflects their likelihood of occurrence in practice, the approach is known as *probabilistic*. See Section 3.3.
- Either to represent only accounting conventions of the company within the model, or to represent relationships of a non-financial nature, too. Where accounting conventions alone are represented it is called a *financial* model. Where non-financial relationships, such as those between price and sales volume or between production capacity and output, are also included, the model is said to cover *physical* aspects, too. See Section 3.4
- Either to represent operations of the company at corporate level only or to include in addition expressions representing in more detail the operations of subsidiaries, divisions, and/or operating units such as production plants. Data is usually input into the model for the lowest organisational level represented and consolidated up through the higher levels. For this reason the problem of level of detail is sometimes called the problem of *level of aggregation*. See Section 3.5.
- Either to develop a *single, large, general-purpose* model or to develop *separate models* to meet clearly specified needs of different managers. See Section 3.6.

These alternatives are discussed more fully in the sections indicated. For the convenience of the reader, the main terms are also defined in the Glossary.

3.2 Simulation and optimisation

All models represent reality (see Chapter 1). Consequently, they may be used to imitate behaviour of the reality modelled, this being called *simulation*. For example, models of tall buildings are sometimes tested in wind tunnels by civil engineers, stress gauges being used to measure how the model reacts to different wind conditions. In this way something can be learnt about the way the building, if constructed, could withstand buffeting by wind. Similarly, models of ships are towed in water tanks to find out about their hydrodynamic properties.

Corporate models represent the key operations of companies and can so be used to imitate their behaviour under given conditions. As we have seen, in Section 3.1, corporate simulation models do nothing but this. They are used to explore the outcome of possible, assumed future conditions, but do not derive an optimum or 'best'

(Continued on page 22)

19

Figure 3.1 Cash flow model of the UK Chemical Industry   Case 6

£m	Base 1968	Year 1969	Data 1970	1971	1972
Total Assets (year end)					
Gross fixed assets at cost	2545	2740	3066	3382	3693
Accumulated depreciation	1030	1120	1243	1381	1533
Net fixed assets	1515	1620	1823	2001	2160
Working capital	475	435	505	582	648
Total net assets	1990	2050	2328	2583	2807
Financed by					
Long-term debt	425	438	662	775	881
Equity assets	1530	1617	1666	1808	1926
New loans raised	20	13	224	113	106
New equity raised				59	0
Profit & loss position					
Sales income	2920	3130	3485	3879	4317
Materials & services	1965	2130	2425	2707	3070
Wages & salaries	545	600	675	757	848
Gross trading profit	410	400	385	414	399
Annual depreciation	155	165	178	199	220
Net trading profit	255	235	207	215	179
Interest payments	24	24	25	36	42
Profit before tax	231	211	182	179	137
Profit appropriations					
Tax due less grants payable	44	17	−46	−7	0
Profit after tax	187	194	228	186	137
Gross dividends	103	112	114	110	122
Cash flow					
Tax paid less grants received	28	47	19	−14	−103
Retained profits	100	52	49	83	118
Depreciation	155	165	178	199	220
Total inflow	255	217	227	282	338
Capital expenditure	225	270	381	379	378
Working capital inc.	50	−40	70	77	66
Total outflow	275	230	451	455	444
Cash surplus	−20	−13	−224	−173	−106
Accumulated surplus			0	−173	−279
Ratios					
Return on capital employed	12.8	11.4	8.9	8.3	6.4
Return on equity	12.0	12.0	13.7	10.3	7.1
Self-financing	92.7	94.3	50.3	62.0	76.1
Dividend cover	1.8	1.7	2.0	1.7	1.1
Gearing	21.4	21.4	28.4	30.0	31.4

Types of corporate model

1973	Projections 1974	1975	1976	1977	1978	Total 1971–78
4018	4411	4873	5418	6058	6809	
1699	1880	2079	2298	2542	2814	
2319	2530	2795	3120	3516	3994	
721	802	893	994	1106	1231	
3040	3333	3687	4114	4622	5225	
1064	1166	1291	1440	1618	1829	
1976	2166	2397	2674	3004	3396	
183	103	124	149	178	211	1167
90	320	461	637	854	1117	3538
4805	5348	5952	6625	7373	8206	46505
3481	3948	4477	5077	5757	6528	35044
950	1064	1191	1334	1495	1674	9314
374	336	284	214	122	4	2148
240	261	287	317	352	394	2270
134	75	−3	−103	−230	−389	−122
52	74	81	94	110	129	619
82	1	−83	−197	−340	−519	−741
0	0	0	0	0	0	−7
82	1	−83	−197	−340	−519	−734
129	130	147	163	183	206	1190
−7	0	0	0	0	0	−124
−40	−129	−230	−360	−523	−725	−1807
240	261	287	317	352	394	2270
200	132	56	−44	−171	−331	463
399	473	551	642	748	872	4442
73	81	91	101	112	125	726
473	554	642	743	861	997	5168
−273	−422	−585	−787	−1032	−1328	−4705
−552	−974	−1559	−2346	−3377	−4705	
4.4	2.3	−0.1	−2.5	−5.0	−7.5	0.8
4.1	0.0	−3.5	−7.4	−11.3	−15.3	−2.0
42.2	23.8	8.8	−5.9	−19.9	−33.2	9.0
0.6	0.0	−0.6	−1.2	−1.9	−2.5	−0.6
35.0	35.0	35.0	35.0	35.0	35.0	33.9

(Reproduced by permission of NEDC)[1]

Figure 3.2 Sensitivity analysis produced by cash flow model

	1968	1969	1970	1971	1972
Case 23 (high growth, central cost and price)					
Accumulated surplus £m				−85	6
Return on capital employed %				11.9	13.8
Self-financing %				81.6	120.7
Dividend cover %				2.4	2.3
Gearing %				28.8	23.3
Case 27 (high growth, high cost and price)					
Accumulated surplus £m				−74	49
Return on capital employed %				13.3	16.7
Self-financing %				84.8	125.4
Dividend cover %				2.6	2.7
Gearing %				28.1	21.2
Case 28 (higher growth, central cost and price)					
Accumulated surplus £m				−69	21
Return on capital employed %				12.4	14.7
Self-financing %				85.0	120.3
Dividend cover %				2.3	2.3
Gearing %				24.3	19.0
Case 29 (higher growth, central cost and price)					
Accumulated surplus £m				−73	10
Return on capital employed %				12.2	14.2
Self-financing %				84.3	118.8
Dividend cover %				2.3	2.2
Gearing %				24.4	19.4

solution. Consequently, they merely provide management with information to aid selection among alternatives.

By changing either the input to the corporate model or, where necessary, the expressions comprising the model itself, management may imitate the effect on future performance of a variety of alternatives, for example, introduction of new products, decisions on plant acquisition and shutdown, mergers, and financing. Each change in conditions under the control of management amounts to a new alternative. Normally, when alternatives tested are changed, a number of other figures require adjustment, too. For instance, when the effects of introducing a new product are evaluated, its future sales and its effect on those of existing products must be forecast, and fed to the model. However, most input is generally unaffected by the alternative tested and so remains unchanged between runs of the model. This permits alternatives to be tested

Types of corporate model

1973	1974	1975	1976	1977	1978	Average 1971–78
−16	−320	−625	−961	−1338	−1764	
15.7	16.2	16.3	16.4	16.5	16.7	15.4
95.6	64.9	69.5	70.9	71.6	72.3	75.8
2.4	3.1	3.1	3.1	3.1	3.1	2.9
22.0	26.6	29.3	31.3	32.8	33.9	28.5
84	−170	−392	−611	−828	−1037	
20.2	21.6	22.5	23.3	24.1	24.8	20.8
105.9	75.1	81.8	85.0	87.6	90.0	88.6
3.0	3.8	3.9	4.0	4.0	4.0	3.7
17.8	20.8	21.5	21.3	20.5	19.2	21.3
8	−410	−826	−1288	−1811	−2403	
17.0	17.1	16.7	16.5	16.4	16.4	15.9
97.4	58.7	64.7	66.3	67.3	68.2	71.6
2.4	3.4	3.3	3.3	3.3	3.4	3.1
17.7	25.2	29.4	32.4	34.6	35.0	27.2
−16	−386	−757	−1169	−1633	−2156	
16.3	16.5	16.3	16.2	16.2	16.2	15.5
94.9	60.5	65.9	67.3	68.2	69.1	72.6
2.3	3.2	3.2	3.2	3.2	3.2	3.0
18.5	25.1	29.0	31.8	33.9	35.0	27.2

(Reproduced by permission of NEDC)[1]

on the same set of assumptions as to, say, the rate of inflation, tax rate, and so on.

Use of corporate simulation models is not restricted to evaluating alternatives on the basis of a common set of assumptions. The effect of changes in these assumptions on either the existing or any proposed future business may be explored too. This is done by changing the figure under consideration, say the rate of exchange, in an upward and downward direction around the actual or forecast value. For instance, we could feed into the models the rate with increases of 2, 5, and 10 per cent successively, and examine the effects on reported profits. When this is done systematically for a range of different factors it is called 'sensitivity analysis'.

The 'Neddy Report'[1] on the chemical industry provides a good example of the use of sensitivity analysis. Model runs were made to test the effect of various assumptions regarding growth, costs and prices on the accumulated surplus, return on capital

23

employed, percentage of self-financing, dividend cover and gearing. The report produced by one run is shown, as an example, in *Figure 3.1*. This gives full details for the three base years and eight future projections of the total year-end assets, financing implications, profit and loss positions, profit appropriations, cash flows and key management ratios. *Figure 3.2* is a summary setting out the assumptions fed into the model and giving the key management ratios for each year projected, with average figures for the years 1971–78. The reader is left to judge for himself the value of figures of this kind to senior management.

In contrast to simulation, optimisation models seek the best solution, given any set of assumptions. 'Best' is here defined in terms of measures such as return on capital employed or net present value. Consequently, the approach requires that objectives are stated explicitly and expressed in precise mathematical terms; where there are multiple objectives each must be given an appropriate weight. One or more of a number of different mathematical routines, such as linear programming, may be followed by the computer to converge systematically and efficiently on the 'best' solution.

Despite the apparent advantages of a model which gives a best solution, in the UK most corporate models are of the simulation type. Only 22 per cent of companies with corporate models used the optimisation type and only the oil companies, whose management have had a longer acquaintance with mathematical models, seemed to be particularly happy with them. In contrast, 98 per cent of the companies had simulation models; 78 per cent had only simulation models and 20 per cent had both simulation and optimisation models. Most of the latter made greater use of their simulation than of their optimisation models.

A number of reasons have been advanced for this preference for simulation at corporate level. Managers seem to find simulation models more intelligible. Complex relationships can be represented more easily in simulation than in optimisation models. Top managers often find it difficult, or politically inexpedient, to make objectives explicit, preferring instead to leave them implicit in the alternative chosen. But optimisation models require an explicit statement of objectives whilst simulation models do not. Moreover, because estimates on which strategic decisions are based are liable to such wide errors, there is doubt as to the significance of a mathematical optimum based on them. The emphasis tends, rightly, to be on solutions which will give a satisfactory outcome over a wide range of possible future conditions. Consequently, simulation models which permit the user to explore the outcome of an alternative on the basis of widely different assumed conditions are more appropriate for strategic decision-taking.

For these reasons, and because of their wider use, the emphasis in this book is upon simulation models. Treatment of optimisation techniques can be found in any good text on Operational Research.

3.3 *Deterministic and probabilistic models*

Deterministic models are those which, like most of the calculations of the accountant and the manager, assume certainty. Only one figure is given for, say, sales in each period covered by the model, i.e. up to its 'planning horizon'. Deterministic models so operate on a 'case study' basis and give the answers to 'what if' questions, for example:

What if advertising is cut by 50 per cent?
What if wages increase 5 per cent?
What if interest rates increase to 15 per cent?
What if office rent goes up £1 per square foot?

Any single operation of the model gives no indication of risk. However, insight into the risk inherent in a proposed alternative may be obtained from a deterministic model by repeatedly running it with different values for the input variables beyond the control of management and comparing the results. One of the problems of using this procedure is that, unless all important possible future conditions are varied, management may still not be fully aware of the complete range of possible outcomes. There is a tendency to test only those alternatives which are considered to have a reasonable chance of occurring and, as these are often average or middle values, extreme values may be avoided. But extreme values should be tested too, because they may lead to serious losses.

In contrast to deterministic models, probabilistic models recognise the fact that sales, costs and so on are not certain and that there are many possible values for each. The model is run once for each set of assumptions, but within each computer run the results are calculated many times and each time the figures for sales, costs, etc. are drawn at random from the range of possible values. This is done in such a way that, during the run of the model, each value occurs with a relative frequency that reflects the chance of its occurrence in real life. Consequently, the results produced by the model give an indication of the frequencies, or probabilities, with which different

Figure 3.3 Use of probability distributions

Probability distribution no. 1		Probability distribution no. 2	
Estimated probabilities	*Trading profits* £	*Estimated probabilities*	*Overheads* £
.1	12,000	.3	6,000
.4	8,000	.3	4,000
.4	6,000	.3	3,000
.1	2,000	.1	2,000
1.0		1.0	

Tabulation of possible deterministic runs

Run no.	*Trading profits* £	*Overheads* £	*Net profits* £
1	8,000	6,000	2,000
2	8,000	4,000	4,000
3	8,000	3,000	5,000
4	6,000	6,000	—
5	6,000	4,000	2,000
6	6,000	3,000	3,000
7	12,000	6,000	6,000
8	12,000	4,000	8,000
9	12,000	3,000	9,000
10	12,000	2,000	10,000
11	8,000	2,000	6,000
12	6,000	2,000	4,000
13	2,000	6,000	−4,000
14	2,000	4,000	−2,000
15	2,000	3,000	−1,000
16	2,000	2,000	—

levels of performance may occur given the basic assumptions. This shows the decision-taker the level of risk attached to the alternative tested.

The difference between deterministic and probabilistic models may be illustrated by an example. Let us suppose that different values of trading profit and fixed costs may occur with the probabilities shown in *Figure 3.3*. Probability is a measure of likelihood, or chance of occurrence, and is measured mathematically on a scale from 0–1. Where there is absolutely no chance of occurrence, the probability attached to an event is zero, and where there is absolute certainty the probability is 1. In real life, very few events have a probability of 1, ultimate death being the obvious exception.

The empirical probability of an event is the ratio of the number of occurrences to the number of tests for occurrence, which must lie on the 0–1 scale. Provided events are mutually exclusive, the sum of probabilities calculated for events observed during the tests for occurrence must sum to 1. Consequently, the probabilities estimated for the different possible values of trading profit shown in *Figure 3.3* sum to 1, as do those for overheads.

To test all the possible combinations shown in *Figure 3.3* with a deterministic model would require $4 \times 4 = 16$ computer runs. Thus, an arbitrary decision may be made not to make any computer runs where at least one of the inputs has a less than .2 chance of occurring. Then only six runs, i.e. those numbered from 1–6 in *Figure 3.3* need be made. This tells management that net profits may fluctuate between 0–£5,000. In fact, they have a 72 per cent chance of doing so, as each of the six cases has a probability of 12 per cent. These results give more information to management than a bald figure of £2,900 which is the relevant single value estimate arising from the two distributions – see *Figure 3.4*. However, if management made all 16 possible runs as in *Figure 3.3* it would see that it could make as much as £10,000 in one case but also it could lose up to £4,000 in another.

Figure 3.4 Calculation of the expected value of the distributions

Probability distribution no. 1				Probability distribution no. 2			
Estimated probabilities	Trading profits		Product £	Estimated probabilities		Overheads £	Product £
.1	×	12,000 =	1,200	.3	×	6,000 =	1,800
.4	×	8,000 =	3,200	.3	×	4,000 =	1,200
.4	×	6,000 =	2,400	.3	×	3,000 =	900
.1	×	2,000 =	200	.1	×	2,000 =	200
1.0			£7,000	1.0			£4,100

Estimated net profit is expected value of the trading profit	£7,000
Less: Expected value of the overheads	£4,100
Net single value estimate	£2,900

In the example given, *Figure 3.3*, the chance of a loss of £4,000 is three times as great as that of a profit of £10,000. This information is not to be found in *Figure 3.3*. However, by generating the different values of trading profit and overheads independently with the same relative frequencies as dictated by the probabilities, we may determine the expected relative frequencies of different values of net profit. These may be displayed graphically as in *Figures 3.5* and *3.6,* which show, for instance, that three times in a hundred a loss of £4,000 may be expected, that nine times in a hundred a loss of at least £1,000 will be incurred, that only 14 times out of a hundred will a profit of over £5,000 be made.

Figure 3.5   Histogram of results of probabilistic simulation

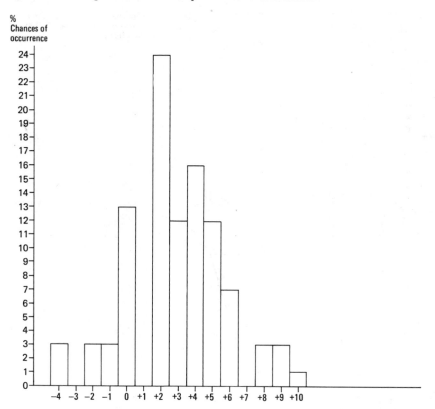

It is clear from the example that probabilistic models give the manager an indication of risk in a way that deterministic models do not. Yet despite this considerable advantage, only 25 per cent of the UK companies incorporated such 'risk analysis' into their models. Few of these companies used probabilistic models for more than half of all runs, the vast majority using them for 10 per cent or less of all runs. Few companies seemed to be particularly happy with their probabilistic models. One reason advanced was the high cost; 500 calculations by the computer are frequently needed for every one of a deterministic model. It should be remembered, though, that a number of runs of the latter are required if any insight into risk is to be gained. Another reason was the difficulty encountered by management in understanding the model and interpreting the output. For instance, the Rover Motor Company found 'that the concept of attaching probabilities to forward estimates of sales volumes, costs and capital expenditure was

Figure 3.6 Cumulative graph of results of probabilistic simulation

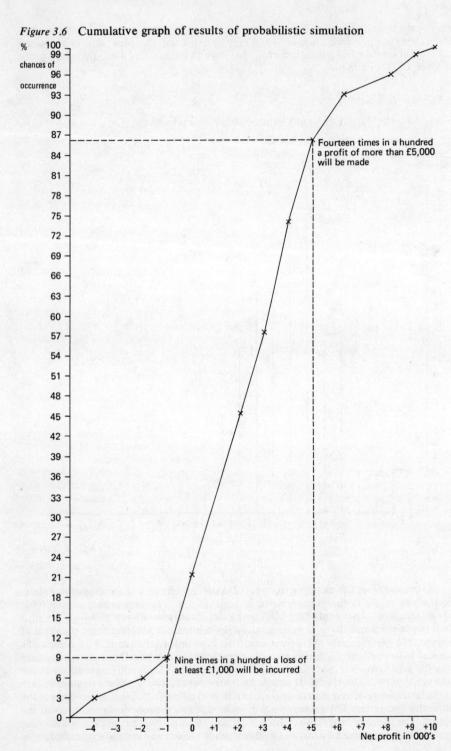

Fourteen times in a hundred
a profit of more than £5,000
will be made

Nine times in a hundred a loss of
at least £1,000 will be incurred

Net profit in 000's

not clearly understood by management, who were unwilling to provide such probabilities and who were unable to attach significant meanings to results'. The probabilistic model was therefore dropped. Similar experience is reported by Wells Fargo in the USA.[2] In addition, in a number of other companies the modellers had failed even to complete their probabilistic model, because they could not get sufficient data to establish empirical probabilities.

Despite these difficulties with probabilistic simulation, it can be worth while when there could be a high risk and major sums are involved, as in the case of the evaluation of the Access credit card venture by the National Westminster Bank. In such cases, probabilistic models can be built on an *ad hoc* basis, and run separately, to avoid the costs of operating a total company model repeatedly. Output from the probabilistic model can then be fed into a deterministic corporate model to see how the proposed investment would affect total company performance.

A greater use of probabilistic models may follow a growing awareness in the accountancy profession and other financial circles of risks and uncertainties prevalent in profit forecasting. The Institute of Chartered Accountants in England and Wales has emphasised 'that profit forecasts necessarily depend on subjective judgements and are, to a greater or less extent, according to the nature of the business, subject to numerous and substantial inherent uncertainties'.[3] Similarly, the City Take-over Panel has argued that it may be appropriate for maximum and minimum forecasts to be given rather than a single figure.[4] The use of probabilistic corporate models would facilitate forecasting in terms of maximum, minimum and average forecast profits, which would be a step towards the provision of more useful information to shareholders. This may well come, as suggested by several of the bureaux we contacted, with greater numeracy and sophistication of management.

3.4 *Representation of financial and physical flows*

The operations of a company may be seen as a series of interrelated flows of materials and services, in other words 'physical flows', which may be represented in its corporate model. For instance, the model may represent physical production as at Van den Berghs,[5] British Steel and Rover. An example is shown in *Figure 3.7*. Such models may be valuable particularly for decisions by lower levels of management. They have been used for decisions on product mix by Van den Berghs and machine capacity utilisation decisions by Yorkshire Imperial Plastics. These physical flows of materials may be converted into financial flows and the latter consolidated in the total model or suite of related models for use at higher levels of management.

Alternatively, whatever the level of the company represented, the model may deal with purely financial flows such as value of sales, of direct costs of production and overheads. Many purely financial models use only accounting routines. A flow diagram of such a model is shown in *Figure 3.8*. This permits consolidation of figures within the model, and the presentation of balance sheets, profit and loss accounts, flow of funds statements and financial ratios, within minutes rather than hours.

Even where the logic of the models is based primarily on accounting conventions, other relationships may be introduced. These relationships are of two main kinds. First, rules are sometimes built into the model which represent the way human decision-takers might proceed, these being known as 'heuristics'. For instance, several models described in the literature have an inbuilt rule to the effect that new finance will be raised by debenture issues up to a maximum gearing ratio and then by equity and debenture in a set ratio. The key values in such rules, for instance maximum permitted gearing ratio, may be subject to adjustment by the model user to allow different policies to be tested. In some other models, used conversationally (see

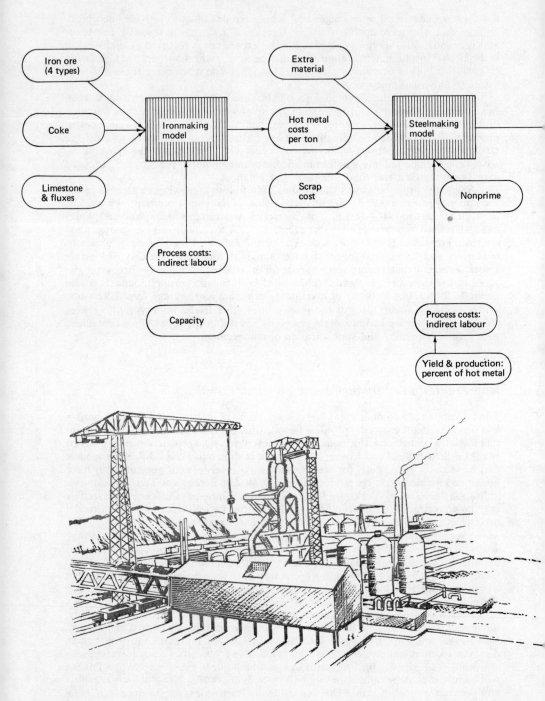

Figure 3.7 Relationships in Inland Steel model – an example of a physical model

Types of corporate model

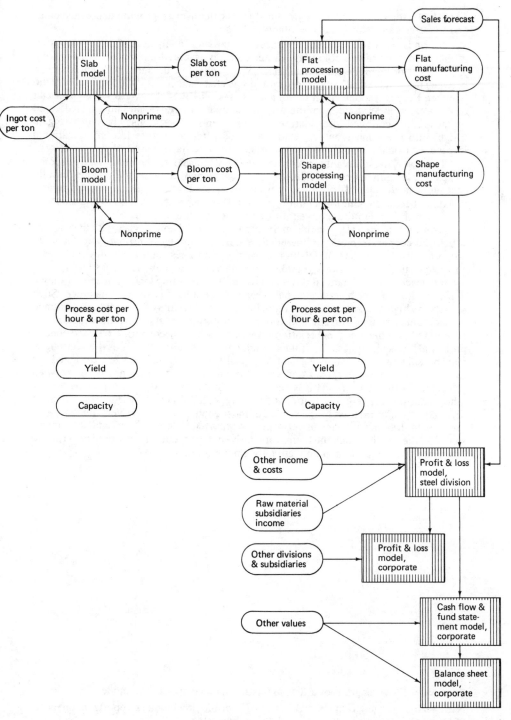

(Reproduced by courtesy of Boulden & Buffa)[6]

31

Chapter 4), the computer is programmed to ask the user to provide necessary data, and the user's decisions replace inbuilt rules.

Second, many relationships are based on statistical analysis or direct observation of the operations of the company, rather than on assumed human decision-making processes. For instance, statistical analysis of available data permitted relationships between price, advertising expenditure and sales to be successfully incorporated in the Van den Berghs' model. Such relationships make the model powerful. The user can gain a greater understanding of the way the company operates, and how it is affected by these often complex interrelationships between its operations. He may also gain insight into the impact on its performance of external factors like gross national income, seasonal demand, and so on, over which he has no control.

However, these advantages can be gained only at a cost. The models may become more complex and hence more difficult for management to understand. They usually cost more to develop. Moreover, they may require more frequent monitoring and updating, because the non-accounting relationships represented tend to change more often than the accounting conventions employed by the company.

The kinds of flow represented in the corporate model tend to vary with the uses for which the corporate model is intended. Where the model is primarily to facilitate corporate decisions, like acquisition of new subsidiaries, launching new products, entry to major new markets, building new factories or new stock issues, models usually describe only financial flows and use only accounting logic. The model shown in *Figure 3.8,* to which reference has already been made, is such an instance. Such models use highly aggregated input data, like financial results of subsidiaries, assumed price/earnings ratios, current and forecast corporate assets, current and forecast corporate liabilities and depreciation rates, and print out corporate balance sheets, profit and loss accounts, flow of funds statements and financial ratios as their output. It may be said that the balance sheet and profit and loss account are designed for statutory and control purposes and are not the best basis for making decisions when projected for future years. This is certainly so, and they need to be supplemented by other data, but it is equally true that future reported financial performance is most certainly of major interest to the boards of most companies. Moreover, top managers are used to thinking in terms of performance reported in this fashion, and are conversant with the way in which the figures are derived. Consequently, it would be wrong to underrate the value of such conceptually simple models.

Figure 3.8 Flow diagram of a deterministic financial simulation model

N.B. – This flow diagram shows a routine for producing financial reports on the basis of forecasts for each year up to a planning horizon.

Types of corporate model

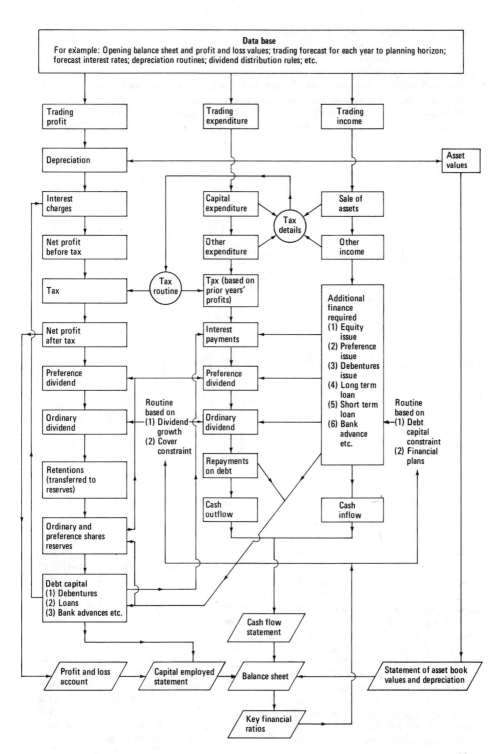

3.5 *Organisational levels included*

As the level of management for whose use the model is designed falls from corporate, to subsidiary, to divisional and ultimately to operating unit level, representation of physical flows becomes increasingly important. In addition, the time periods appropriate to decision-taking become shorter. These relationships are illustrated in *Figure 3.9*. Whilst corporate management is interested primarily in financial annual data, at operating unit level monthly figures relating to physical operations are valuable.

Figure 3.9 Levels of aggregation of detail

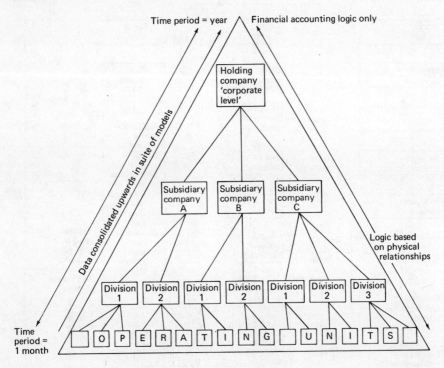

These relationships were found among the sample of UK companies. *Figure 3.10* shows the number with models incorporating expressions for, first, financial and, second, physical relationships at corporate, subsidiary, divisional and operating unit level. All companies had financial models at corporate level but, as expected, the number fell with the level of the company to which the corporate model extended. None the less, 43 per cent of the companies had models which extended down to operating unit level, and aggregated financial data from this to corporate level.

Physical operations were found to be less widely modelled than financial ones. Only 57 per cent of the companies had models representing physical flows in their selling, distribution, production and purchasing operations. Again, this number fell with the level of the company to which the model extended, reflecting the fact that many corporate models did not extend far down from the corporate level in terms of either physical or financial flows. This fact may well be due, at least in part, to recognition of the disadvantages of models extending down to operating unit level (see below). It may also be due to the introduction of simple, purely corporate, financial models in the first instance, modelling being extended to more detailed aspects of the company only later. Incidentally, the reader should not assume from *Figure 3.10*, which deals with corporate models only, that financial models are more prevalent than physical ones in UK industry. The reverse is probably true in view of the number of years for which operational researchers have been modelling stock control, production, distribution and marketing systems.

Figure 3.10   Representation of physical and financial flows (percentages of companies)

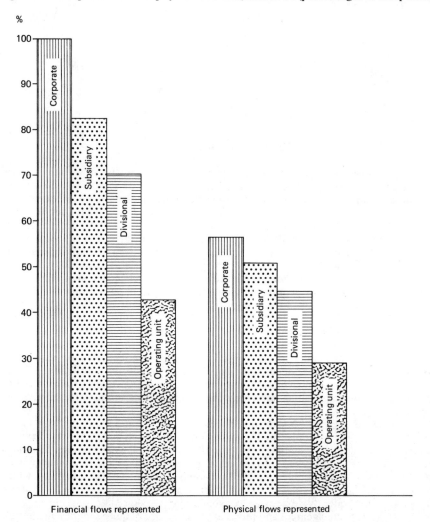

Note: The assumed hierarchy of corporate, subsidiary, divisional and operating unit levels is somewhat arbitrary. Some companies had no subsidiaries. In others there was no sharp distinction between levels. Hence, whilst the two extremes presented no problem, allocation of company models to the 'subsidiary level' and 'divisional level' classes often depended on the subjective judgement of the researchers, and is therefore rather suspect. The figures are given, none the less, because they should have some indicative value.

Figure 3.11 Time periods used in corporate models in the survey companies

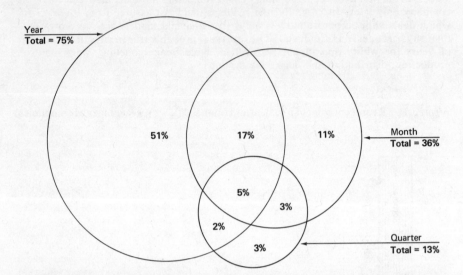

The data on time periods used in corporate models is consistent with the general picture presented by *Figure 3.10*. From *Figure 3.11* it may be seen that, whilst 75 per cent of the companies used years in at least some of their model runs, 13 per cent used quarters, and 36 per cent used months. These latter periods are usually more appropriate for decisions by line managers than for those by the board. As many as 27 per cent used different time periods for different purposes. In some, but not all, of these cases the data for the shorter periods was consolidated within the model for use by higher levels of management.

Several arguments have been advanced in favour of such inclusion of lower levels of the company. First, by representing the relationships between different activities the effects of proposed changes in one part of the company on other parts can be shown. Second, inclusion of different levels of the company may facilitate integration of line management into corporate planning. Managers in subsidiaries, for instance, can use the model to plan their own future operations, the resulting data can be consolidated by the model to corporate level, and the effects can be studied by corporate managers before acceptance or reference back to the subsidiaries. Third, the model may be used on an *ad hoc* basis for tactical decision-taking, for example by functional line managers on material mixtures, maintenance shut downs, or advertising expenditure.

Experience suggests, though, that detailed corporate models are not used in this way in practice. For example, the Unilever Group has found that to permit relevance to lower level decisions, the time period used may be days, weeks or months, whilst years are more appropriate for strategic decision-taking for top management. Moreover, most of the detailed information about operations of.the company, which models of physical flows are designed to provide, is of no relevance to strategic decisions. Consequently, extensive consolidation is required to provide the data necessary for top management and this is expensive. Use of quite separate models for different levels of management has been found preferable.

3.6 *Size and the modular approach*

Development of separate models to meet different needs, a corporate suite rather than a single, corporate model, is a very different approach from that reported in much of the literature.

Early corporate models, particularly in the USA, seem to have been designed to represent detailed operations as well as financial aspects of the company within a single model and were intended as a general tool to aid a wide range of both tactical and strategic decisions. *Figure 3.7* has already illustrated such a monolithic model. Because they were all embracing, some had tens of thousands of program statements, of input variables, and of output variables. Consequently, they were very expensive to develop. It has been estimated that the huge British Petroleum linear programming model has cost well over £200,000 to develop and implement.

Not only are such huge models very expensive, they take a considerable time to develop, and almost as long to get implemented. The fate of the much publicised Sun Oil Model,[7] which took 23 man years to develop and implement, is instructive in this respect. Quite apart from the fact that some of the relationships were probably out of date by the time it was completed, it was overtaken by more climacteric events, for Sun Oil amalgamated with another company to form an organisation different to the one modelled. A great deal of effort would have been required to update the model. Reliable sources suggest that this was never done, and it has never been used![8]

Even if such major calamities are avoided, which might be reasonably expected, the very length of time before heavy expenditure produces results useful to management tends to erode enthusiasm. As we shall see later, management support is a critical prerequisite of success, and its erosion could so prove disastrous. Moreover, once the model is completed it will be used by management only if they understand and have full confidence in it. Although there are some notable exceptions, such understanding is less likely the larger and more complex the model.

The size and complexity of large, monolithic models create problems for computer specialists, too. As tax law, product range, technology, and so on, change, the model must be either updated or discarded as obsolete. Most or all of the original team may have moved to other posts, and updating may have to be done by those not versed in the internal intricacies of the model. The difficulties can be great, and the cost of updating high.

For these reasons, we found a trend towards smaller models. Moreover, rather than all aspects of the company being covered inseparably in each computer run, the majority of companies had developed a modular approach. This permits a model generating financial reports for senior management to be built quickly and relatively cheaply. Some of the companies visited had produced a first working model in less than a week. This gives a quick return to management on a modest investment, gives it a chance to understand a simple model before proceeding to more ambitious ventures, and for these reasons tends to maintain its interest and support. Additional models may be added as thought necessary.

Smaller, separate models have further advantages over large, monolithic ones. They allow closer identification by management with models of more direct value to them, and an easier understanding of their structure and logic. Construction of different models within the corporate suite may be undertaken by different people as long as each separate model is properly documented. Costs of using the models are usually lower because only parts of the suite of direct relevance will be called into use. Models may be more easily updated and maintained because changes in accounting conventions of the firm, or in other relationships described in the model, normally affect only one model of the suite. Perhaps for these reasons only 20 per cent of companies had a single module corporate model.

Moreover, few of these could be said to have large monolithic models, possible exceptions being British Rail and Union Carbide. Mostly, they were companies which were relatively new to corporate modelling and had started, quite rightly, with a model of the entire organisation at a highly aggregative level. The model of ATV which is used as a detailed case study in Chapter 6 is a good example of such a model. We understand that ATV are now working on a more detailed model, which will look at subsidiaries in detail and should be more useful to line managers than the present model which is orientated to top managers only.

This was not the only difference between most of the single module models found in the survey companies and early ones described in the literature. Early models were written in FORTRAN for use on in-house computers, whereas many of the single module models we encountered used modelling systems and were run in conversational mode on bureaux computers. Less than a quarter of the companies were dependent on in-house computers for running their models. If the monolithic model described in American literature was ever the most prevalent in the UK, which is doubtful, it is certainly not so now.

3.7 *Most common features*

Whilst the possible combinations of features of corporate models are numerous, certain characteristics were found to be prevalent in the UK, as indicated in earlier sections of this chapter. These are summarised briefly, in order to underline these features, and to draw the different strands into a coherent whole.

Overall, a picture emerges of use of mainly deterministic simulation models. All these models are financial, being used to aid financial planning and strategic decision taking at corporate level, but often extend down to subsidiary, to divisional or to operating units and frequently describe physical relationships when they do so. Where such detailed operations of the company are modelled, the models may be used for more detailed planning of production, marketing and distribution, too. However, these more detailed operations are represented increasingly in separate models which jointly compose a corporate suite, rather than in a single, large model.

The fact that this is the general picture does not, though, mean that management would be well advised to proceed in the same direction. Ultimately, management must decide on the type of model in the light of their own needs, as well as the experience of others. Chapter 11, which gives guidelines on choice, may be of some help in this respect.

References

1   National Economic Development Office; *Investment in the chemical industry 1972*. A Report by the Investment Working Party of the Chemicals EDC, 1972.

2   Wagner, W. H., Akutagawa, L. T. and Cuneo, L. J.; Telecommunications estimation model (TEEM): an evaluation.
Published in Schrieber, A. N. (ed.); *Corporate simulation models*. University of Washington, Graduate School of Business Administration, 1970.

3   Institute of Chartered Accountants in England and Wales;
Accountants' reports on profit forecasts: Statement S15, 1969.

4   City Take-over Code on Take-overs and Mergers;
Practice Note No. 6.

5   Cooper, J. and Jones, P.; The corporate decision.
Data Processing, March-April 1972.

6   Boulden, J. B. and Buffa, E. S.; Corporate models: on-line, real-time systems.
Harvard Business Review, July-Aug. 1970.

7   Gershefski, G. W.; *The development and application of a corporate financial model*.
Planning Executives Institute, Oxford (Ohio) 1968.

8   Hall, W. K.; Strategic planning models: are top managers really finding them useful?
Iournal of Business Policy, Winter 1972.

Chapter 4

Operation of corporate models

4.1 Operating the model

Although it would be possible to operate a corporate model manually, by working through step by step with pencil and paper, this would be too time consuming and would rob it of most of its advantages. In practice, as we have seen, corporate models are generally expressed as a series of instructions that allows the accuracy, speed and storage capacity of the computer to be harnessed. The extent to which management benefit from the speed of the computer, how closely they interact with the model, and how much it costs to use all depend very heavily upon the mode in which the corporate model is run on the computer. There are three widely used modes of operation, batch, conversational and remote batch. As we shall see in Section 4.2, each has advantages and disadvantages, and what is best for the individual firm depends very largely on its circumstances.

Because most companies do not have conversational facilities on their own computer, the mode of operation is closely related to whether a company uses its own computer, or that of an outside bureau. Advantages and disadvantages to the company of using in-house and external computers are considered in Section 4.3.

As seen in Section 3.6, there are advantages in developing a suite of separate but related models, rather than a single, large one. However, unless these separate models are interlinked (so that output from say a production model is fed into a sales model) they are less powerful in total than a non-modular model. Section 4.5 examines the ways in which models are linked and relates them to both the mode of operation and the computer used.

4.2 Methods of accessing the computer

Batch processing. In most early corporate models the computer was accessed in the batch mode. Batch processing will be familiar to users of computer payroll, accounting, inventory and similar commercial systems. The feature of this method of accessing the computer is that data for input is collected and run on the computer as one complete batch. Where a corporate model is run in batch mode, output is delivered to the planning staff and can be analysed before further data is despatched to the computer as input to another run. Since many planning assumptions remain largely unchanged, and can be stored in a readily accessible form, for example, on discs, drums or magnetic tape, only a limited amount of data may need to be input on each successive run.

Consequently, this method of operating the model is not so laborious as it may appear at first sight. Moreover, because faster line printers are used for batch processing, the mode tends to be more efficient in terms of computer time where the models produce a lot of output data.

Generally, however, batch processing is considered slow as far as the ultimate user is concerned. We found in our main survey that the average 'turnaround' time between despatch of input data and receipt of results among those who batch process was 18 hours. The most commonly quoted figures were 12 hours and 24 hours. In some cases though, where modellers were dependent on the postal service, the time was very much longer. These figures are based, on the whole, on the use of in-house computers. It is important to qualify them by pointing out that a much faster turnaround can sometimes be obtained by use of bureaux. A number of bureaux in

Figure 4.1 Visual display unit

London can deliver output within half an hour of input, for a small model which takes only a few minutes of computer time.

Where the model is used in an annual planning exercise, a longer turnaround time may not matter greatly, but in a major takeover battle it could be a serious disadvantage. However, on such occasions runs of the corporate model could take precedence over more routine work on the in-house computer, and turnaround time could be reduced substantially.

*Conversational mode.*These problems of slow turnaround are overcome by use of conversational models. The user converses with the computer via a terminal. There are many types of terminal currently available which vary greatly in speed and cost. Visual Display Units (VDUs) which resemble television sets in appearance (see *Figure 4.1*) provide a fast response for users not requiring printed output. However, we found that most companies were relying on the much slower, but cheaper keyboard printers which are also known as teletypes (ITT tradename). Such terminals are rather like typewriters (see *Figure 4.2*). They have the same keyboards with alphabetical and numerical characters, plus a few keys to facilitate control. In addition, many have an attachment which permits them to punch and read paper tape. Some sophisticated terminal systems allow input of data on punched cards, magnetic tape, magnetic

41

Figure 4.2   Keyboard printer

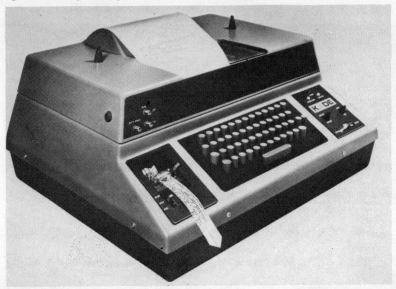

cassette, or by optical character recognition. All terminals may be linked to computers inside or outside the firm by internal or GPO telephone lines. Instructions and input data are given to the computer through the keyboard, paper tape reader, or other input device. Messages from the computer, and output from the model, are returned to the user via the terminal.

Conversational models allow a high degree of interaction between the manager and the model. For instance, during a run of the model the manager may change decision rules used by the model, or alter other planning assumptions. This is achieved by instructing the computer to print out data followed by a request to the user to input further information. For example, in one routine of a model written in BASIC the following statements were used:

110 PRINT 'DO YOU WANT TO CHANGE CASH FLOWS?'
112 INPUT C$
115 IF C$ = NO THEN 400

Statement 110 tells the computer to print, via the terminal, the question shown. The user responds by typing 'YES' or 'NO' at his terminal. This is accepted by the computer as input C$ in statement 112. (C$ is here nothing but a label attached by the computer to the answer typed.) Statement 115 tells the computer to jump to statement 400 if the answer is 'NO'. If the answer is 'YES' the program proceeds to instruct the computer to accept changes in data it already holds.

Some of the general-purpose languages like ALGOL and COBOL are more suitable for batch-run than for conversational models. Others, like BASIC, have been devised to facilitate use of the conversational mode. Even so, as shown by the example, the sequence of questions and appropriate responses to the answers must be written into the program. This complicates its logic. In contrast, modelling systems, to which we referred in Chapter 2 and which are more extensively covered in Chapter 7, have inbuilt instructions for dealing with the 'dialogue' between the user and the computer. This often leads to reduction in the time and effort required to program a model for operation in conversational mode.

The conversational mode is attractive, and was found to be widely used, because of the speed of response and the appeal of the manager sitting at a terminal and rapidly exploring a range of 'what if' questions. Not only does the computer become a computationally powerful extension of the decision-taker's mind, it also permits him to learn about the company, to get a 'feel' for the sensitive features of his business as represented by the model. It is probable that this is the direction in which we will move in the future. Certainly it is the direction in which some firms that were earliest in this field, such as Unilever in the UK, have been moving.

It is only fair to report, though, that the reality may be less than the dream. A survey in the USA by Boulden[1] of 55 of his clients using terminal based models showed that in virtually all cases the ultimate decision-taker chose to test alternatives via his staff rather than directly on a terminal himself. Broadly the same conclusions may be drawn for the UK. For instance, after the first flush of enthusiasm, many line managers and accountants at Van den Berghs have got their secretaries to operate the corporate model rather than sit at the terminal themselves. Secretaries are probably faster at keying in information because of their greater familiarity with the keyboard. Many executives prefer to pore over figures at their desks rather than spend time thinking at computer terminals. As some bureaux charge in excess of £12 per hour for the time the terminal is linked to the computer (connect time), there are good economic reasons, too, for keeping thinking time at the terminals to a minimum. Whatever the reasons, this method of operating a conversational model means the advantages of interaction between the manager and the model are lost.

Because of the questions, answers, and additional logic necessary in conversational models (see the example in BASIC), they are usually more complex and involve more statements than comparable models for batch running. Consequently, they cost more to develop unless a modelling system is used, when they may, in fact, be cheaper. Conversational models can also cost more to operate, especially when modelling systems are used, as it takes the computer longer to follow their more complex logic and keyboard terminals print out reports at much slower speeds than line printers used for batch runs. Moreover, for reasons given in Section 4.3, conversational models may require use of a bureau computer, even if the company's own computer has idle capacity. This, too, may increase the costs of using a conversational model.

Estimates given by both users and consultants were that conversational models cost three to four times as much to operate as otherwise identical batch-run models. However, where the conversational mode is used in the evenings, the relative difference is certainly not so high, because of special terms given by the bureaux for off-peak use of their computers.

Higher costs of operation do not necessarily mean that the use of conversational models is not worth while. In many instances, these additional costs are more than outweighed by the benefits of interaction with the computer, and by the shorter turnaround time. Instead of waiting for hours or even days between successive model runs, as with the batch mode, the user running his corporate model in conversational mode can obtain the results of alternatives he wishes to test in minutes, can inspect them, and then can test other alternatives almost immediately.

Remote batch (including remote job entry). Models may also be run in batch mode by feeding input data through a terminal located away from the main computer installation. Because the normal GPO telephone facilities may be used the terminal may be located any distance from the computer although there may sometimes be problems when an attempt is made to access computers in other countries. For instance, we recently found that it would be both costly and difficult to link a terminal in Madrid to a computer in either London or Paris.

Terminals used for remote batch operation should not be confused with those generally used when the conversational mode is employed. They normally accept cards as input, and read these into a buffer store at the main computer, where the job enters a queue. Once its turn is reached, the job is normally run continuously by the computer (as in the batch mode), and the results are printed out at the computer installation for despatch to the model user or, more usually, may be printed on a line printer located in the user's premises.

A popular alternative is to use, say, a keyboard printer or *VDU* terminal to feed input to the computer. Use of the terminal in this way is called 'remote job entry'. This has the advantage that the input is accepted via a conventional terminal and run in the cheaper batch mode. Where input is accepted in the conversational mode, but run in the batch mode, this is known as *'conversational remote job entry'*. This allows errors to be detected before a run is commenced instead of after a batch run has either proved abortive or produced garbage because of them. On the other hand, it is slow and expensive to type input while connected to the computer. Because of this, input is often punched onto paper tape while the terminal is unconnected to the computer, and then read at the start of the run by the paper tape reader attached to the keyboard printer. This considerably reduces the time the user is connected to the computer, and hence the cost of running the model, but unfortunately paper tape readers on some keyboard printers are notoriously liable to error and most are slower than punched card readers used in remote batch. It is for these reasons that some companies have acquired more expensive but faster and more reliable input devices, such as magnetic cassette readers.

Remote batch and remote job entry are generally both much cheaper than the normal conversational mode in terms of computer run costs. Consequently, where little is to be gained by interaction between the user and the model or a great deal of data is to be processed, they are preferable. Fortunately, most bureaux offer both conversational and remote batch entry services. Consequently, it is often possible to use such a model in either conversational or remote job entry mode, according to the needs of the situation. *Figure 4.3* gives an indication of the extent of such savings that may be made, but details are best obtained direct from bureaux.

Figure 4.3   Typical costs of a modelling system used on a bureau computer

Cost of time connected to computer (per hour) / Mode of operation	£8	£5	£3
Computing	Conversational	Conversational	Batch
Printing	Conversational	Batch	Batch

Both remote batch and remote job entry are usually more expensive than conventional batch processing. As already pointed out, they often involve use of a bureau computer and this may involve additional costs. Terminals must be bought or rented, too. A decision must be made, therefore, on whether the advantages accruing to the user warrant the additional cost involved.

Operation of corporate models

Modes of operation in use. The way in which the corporate models of the companies in our survey were operated is illustrated in *Figure 4.4*. This shows that 60 per cent of the companies were accessing the computer conversationally, 52 per cent were using the batch mode of entry and 28 per cent remote batch. It is immediately apparent that a number of companies were operating models in more than one mode. Although this situation arose mainly where a company had models specifically for use in separate modes, other companies ran the same model in different modes. This highlights the fact that more and more companies are seeing the different modes as complementary to each other, recognising the benefits of each one and using whichever appears most attractive for a particular application.

Figure 4.4 Modes of operation

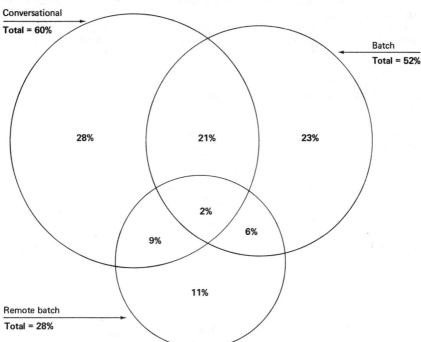

Models built in general-purpose languages tended, as we anticipated, to be run in batch or remote batch mode. Modelling systems, with the conversational facilities they afford, were associated with a fuller use of the conversational mode and with remote job entry.

4.3 Company or bureau computer

As we have seen, batch processed models may invariably be run on the company's own computer, whilst this is not true of conversational models. Most companies do not yet have facilities which permit terminal access to their own computer. In addition, conversational models may require too much internal storage capacity in the computer, i.e. 'core store', to allow use of the company's computer. Consequently, the choice of company or bureau computer depends very much on whether the company prefers batch or conversational models.

The advantages of use of the company's own computer are, perhaps, obvious. If it has idle capacity, the true cost of running the model amounts to little more than the paper consumed, and this is largely incurred on use of a terminal anyway. Of course, when the computer is fully loaded, the cost is much higher, because of the delay and disruption attendant on forcing other computer work to queue. Where large amounts of data are to be input, to set up 'files' on magnetic tape or discs at the start of a series of runs of the model, it is normally more efficient to input the data direct to the computer via tape or punched card readers at the computer installation. This presents no problems with the company's own computer. With a bureau computer, it can usually be done but special arrangements must be made, and there may be fears about security of the data in transit and at the bureau. Consequently, data is normally input expensively via the terminal.

Talk about security of data at bureaux is frequent. During June 1973, there were reports of electronics graduates in the USA tapping files of company data. There is

Figure 4.5 Extent of use of company or bureaux computers

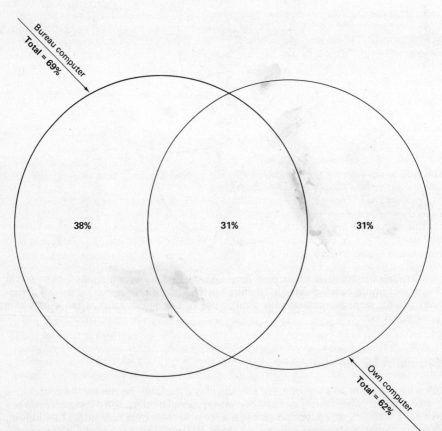

little doubt that it is possible to successfully carry out such an exercise in 'industrial espionage'. However, it is very difficult, takes very considerable skill and probably a little luck too, and we doubt whether it would be the most economic way available to a competitor seriously intent on obtaining confidential information. Most bureaux have code systems to prevent unauthorised access to computer files. To increase security, many bureaux regularly change both the code names of customers and the system by which the code name gains access to files. In some cases, such changes are made every 24 or 48 hours, which means that the electronic 'eavesdropper' has little time to break the code.

Some bureaux provide an additional security safeguard in the form of automatic 'scrambling' facilities. This means that data retained on files at the computer centre is deliberately 'jumbled' or 'scrambled' so as to appear incomprehensible; the scrambling is applied to all headings, figures, etc. Should an eavesdropper be successful in gaining access to the file, he will still be unable to understand it.

Wise management would, though, enquire about security arrangements before dumping data on file at a bureau. A simple rule is for its own computer experts to ask themselves whether the brightest specialist they know could break the code in the time between changes. One might also ask whether it is easier for an outsider to gain access electronically to confidential data stored on discs or to punched cards, tape, or printed output in the company's own computer room, in waste paper baskets, or just by talking to staff.

Certainly, few of those we spoke to during our visits to companies with corporate models regarded security of data as an important problem of use of a bureau computer. Costs were seen to be a greater deterrent. Even so, the advantages of using modelling systems, most of which are tied to operation on a bureau computer, were thought by many to outweigh these. As can be seen from *Figure 4.5,* roughly equal numbers of companies used their own computer only, used a bureau computer only, and used both.

·4 *Interlinking*

In Section 3.6 of the last chapter it was shown that most of the UK companies have preferred to develop corporate suites of separate models rather than single, large, all embracing, general-purpose, monolithic models.

Such suites of models may be little more than a collection of tools for decision-taking by production, marketing and financial management separately, unless they are interlinked. Some form of automatic linkage between the models is desirable if they are to be used jointly, as a representation of the corporate whole. It is surprising, therefore, that over half the UK companies with suites of models had at best manual links between the models (see *Figure 4.6).* Thus, output from one model had to be prepared afresh, for example punched on to cards, before being used as input to another.

Obviously, such manual interlinks are laborious and inefficient, but a case may sometimes be made for them. For example, in the suite of models used by ICL for its own planning, there is both a seven-year long-range planning corporate model, and a forecasting model. The latter is not directly linked with the former, as forecasts are carefully checked against more subjectively determined estimates of sales management, and differences reconciled. It is, quite rightly, recognised that a computer routine does not have the predictive ability of an intelligent and experienced human mind.

This case for manual interlinking is weakened, though, by the fact that changes in the output from one model may be made before its use as input to another where interlinking is by means of disc-held files. Output from one model may be dumped on magnetic disc in a format suitable for direct input to other models. By printing the contents of the file via the keyboard printer terminal or the computer's line printer, its contents may be scrutinised by the user, and changed if necessary before being input to other models. The advantages of using magnetic discs in this way are such that all the companies with automatic interlinking of models (just under half of those with suites of models) had adopted the approach (see *Figure 4.6*).

Figure 4.6 Linking between models

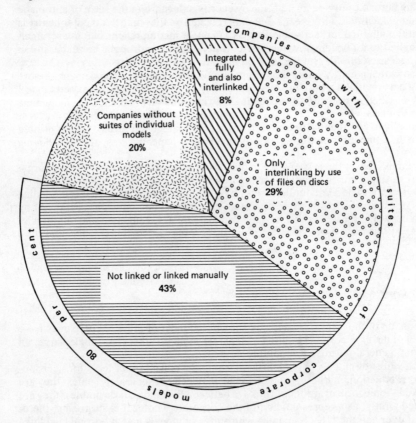

Most of these companies had used modelling systems with facilities for interlinking models, often on bureaux computers. Many of the bureaux offering conversational mode have routines which permit use of, say, forecasting packages to set up files of data on magnetic discs at the computer centre, which can then be called on quickly. These may also be used where a general-purpose language, like BASIC, is used in the conversational mode on a bureau computer. Interlinking via discs does not presuppose use of a bureau computer, though, for most modelling systems intended for operation mainly on in-house computers have this facility, too.

Use of files on magnetic discs is not the only means of interlinking models automatically. Models in some suites may be integrated fully, and run together on the computer as a single model, but still used separately when required. By feeding appropriate control parameters into the computer at the beginning of the run, it is directed to by-pass certain parts of the suite, and go to others. When used separately, the output from a single model may be printed by the line printer, but can also be stored on disc for use by other models in the suite. Hence, interlinking via disc files is not incompatible with full integration.

In many respects these models with integration capabilities may be seen as an interim stage between the old-style monolith and the more loosely linked suites now favoured. They are certainly computationally more efficient if the models in the suite are normally used together rather than separately. They tend, though, to be computationally less efficient if the models are normally used individually, because the computer must follow a sometimes complicated logical path in detecting which parts of the suite are to be used in the run and which are not. Moreover, their size and complexity make them more expensive and time consuming to build, and more difficult to understand and update, than the non-integrated suite. For these reasons, most companies saw no advantage in full integration, and only 8 per cent of companies chose to integrate fully as well as using files on magnetic discs.

4·5 *Summary of trends*

As the use of modelling systems has become relatively more important, since about 1970, there has been an increasing use of bureaux computers to which many of them are tied. Similarly, because nearly all of them may be used in conversational mode, the batch-run model has lost its first place to the conversational one. However, to avoid the high costs of running models in conversational mode, an increasing use is being made of the remote batch mode for operation of corporate models written in a modelling system and capable of accepting conversational input.

This increasing use of bureaux is linked to the trend towards development of suites of separate models. Some of the earlier ones were capable of full integration into a single computer run but increasingly the linkage seems to be via disc files of data to which access may be made by the different models. Such interlinking is possible where general-purpose languages are used but is much simpler with modelling systems. For this reason, the growth of interlinking via disc files has been largely related to the use of modelling systems, which as we have already seen is related to use of the conversational (or remote batch) mode of bureaux computers.

The trend towards suites of smaller but interlinked models means, as we have seen, easier updating of the model. In other words, the logic of the model is more flexible, and the trends we have discerned are related to the important subject of flexibility, too. We turn to this subject in the next chapter.

Reference

Boulden, J. B.; Computerised corporate planning.
Long Range Planning, June 1971.

Chapter 5

Flexibility

5.1 Types of flexibility

The versatility of corporate models varies greatly. Versatility, or flexibility, is a rather imprecise concept, and its use has contributed to confusion rather than enlightenment on the subject. This is unfortunate because the flexibility of a model has a direct bearing on the ease with which it may be used, the extent to which the model may be made to meet the varying needs of different managers, and the speed and cost of updating it. In an attempt to overcome confusion, four kinds of flexibility are defined in *Figure 5.1*, each in terms of characteristics that would be associated with inflexibility and flexibility.

Each of these kinds of flexibility has advantages but these tend to be gained at a cost. Consequently, as will be seen in subsequent sections, many companies have chosen not to make their models as flexible as is technically possible.

Figure 5.1 Kinds of flexibility

Type of flexibility	Section in which discussed	Characteristics of inflexible model	Characteristics of flexible model
Structure	5.2	Individual models in suite must be run sequentially	Individual models in suite may be run in any order
Logic	5.3	Major changes in company structure necessitate reprogramming	Major changes in company structure may be accommodated by model without reprogramming
Input	5.4	(i) Each input variable must be expressed in one specified unit of measurement	(i) The user may input a piece of information in any one of a number of units of measurement
		(ii) Format of input is 'fixed'	(ii) Format of input is 'free'
		(iii) Data must be input only at the start of a run	(iii) Data may be input, e.g. changes made, during a run
Output	5.5	(i) The items included in reports produced by the model are fixed	(i) The user can determine the items included in reports produced by the model
		(ii) The format of output reports is fixed	(ii) The user can determine the format of output reports
		(iii) The reports are produced by the model in a fixed order	(iii) The user is free to choose the order in which reports will be produced

5.2 *Flexibility of structure*

Flexibility of structure is closely related to the interlinking of models which was dealt with in the last chapter. A corporate model has structural flexibility if its modules, the individual models of the suite, can be run individually in the order requested by the user. This is obviously not possible if one module is dependent upon another to such an extent that the input of the second cannot be provided except by running the first.

For example, a company may have a marketing model, production model, and corporate accounting model within its corporate suite. In normal planning, the marketing model may be run to determine sales, which are then input to the production model. Where production capacity constraints are broken, this may be made clear and the marketing model may then be re-run to allow for this fact. Outputs from the marketing and production models may then be input to the corporate accounting model. Hence the normal sequence is marketing, production and corporate accounting. If this sequence cannot be changed the suite is inflexible. On the other hand, if the three models may be run independently, and therefore in any sequence, the corporate suite has structural flexibility. The highest level of structural flexibility would be where interruption of model runs, to allow other models in the suite to be used, does not mean that they must be started again.

Though this final degree of structural flexibility may be difficult to gain, it is normally fairly easy to allow an optional sequence of complete runs of the separate

Figure 5.2 Degree of structural flexibility

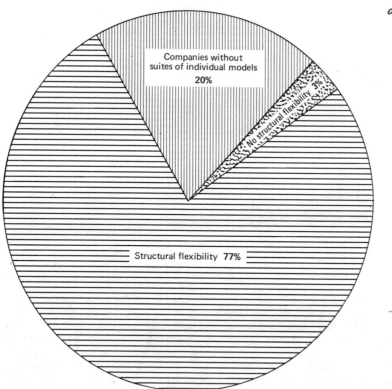

o

Companies without
suites of individual models
20%

No structural flexibility 3%

Structural flexibility 77%

models, the use of random access to disc-held files allowing the uncoupling of models to a high degree. This is reflected in the fact that virtually all of the UK companies with suites of models had this kind of structural flexibility (see *Figure 5.2*). These companies are able to run individual models in the suite as and when they please, although in many cases they choose to run them in a natural sequence.

5.3 *Flexibility of logic*

Modellers can design the logic of a model so that it is able to accommodate major changes in the company without the need for the model to be reprogrammed. The extent to which this is possible determines the degree of 'flexibility of logic' of the model. Ability to quickly accommodate these changes in the business is obviously important if the corporate model is to be used to evaluate alternative strategies which involve major departures from existing business.

Figure 5.3 shows that 61 per cent of the UK companies had corporate models with such inbuilt flexibility. It is instructive to see the means by which this was achieved. In a few companies flexibility was gained by means of redundant items. These may be thought of as spaces in the model deliberately left blank for use at some time in the future. For instance, a firm with three existing subsidiaries might program for four, so that, if acquisition of another subsidiary should be considered, it is necessary to provide only appropriate input data, and the model can be run without undue delay.

Figure 5.3   Flexibility of model logic

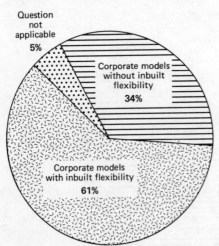

Question
not
applicable
5%

Corporate models
without inbuilt
flexibility
34%

Corporate models
with inbuilt flexibility
61%

Redundant items tended, on the whole, to be used where the model was written in a general-purpose language. This is largely due to the fact that changes are more difficult to cope with in a general-purpose language, although where a company has good programmers there is usually no problem. One prominent consultant told us that redundant items are used only by lazy programmers, and should be unnecessary. The issue is, though, not quite so clear cut. There is a trade-off between reprogramming time saved by the redundant item in a possible future contingency and the usually slight increase in computer run time whenever the model is used.

When a modelling system is adopted, a new division normally involves only another set of inputs in most instances, because the consolidating routines of the system automatically cope with integration of its accounts into the corporate whole. Most of the companies which claimed inbuilt flexibility for their models gave this as a reason. They recognised, though, that new business could be incorporated into the model in this way only if it had no interconnections with activities already represented in the model. Where complex transfers between existing and new divisions, say, might be expected, they could be represented in the model only if additional programming were undertaken. This is, of course, just as true of the general-purpose language model using redundant items as of the modelling system model.

Further reference to *Figure 5.3* reveals that 34 per cent of companies had no inbuilt flexibility of logic, and any new subsidiary, division, or major business would have involved some reprogramming. To establish how serious a drawback this really was, modellers in these companies were asked how long it would take to make the changes necessary to allow for a new subsidiary or division, their answers being summarised in *Figure 5.4*. The number of man-hours required was, in fact, surprisingly low in most instances. Only 5 per cent of companies thought that more than 50 man-hours would be necessary. It was recognised by one multi-national company, though, that any integration of physical operations with existing business would involve time-consuming changes. It was said that an additional two man-years would be required if the Dutch factory was integrated with the British one.

The low number of man-hours required to change models without inbuilt flexibility should not lead us to underrate the limitations of such models in some situations of great strategic importance. Fifty man-hours of programming may mean three or four weeks, at least, of elapsed time, and in a fast-moving merger situation this may make the corporate model useless.

In some companies, lack of flexibility may not matter, because no major change in business seems to be possible. Five per cent of the companies suggested that the question about inbuilt flexibility was not applicable to them for this reason. For instance, the Anglia Building Society told us that no new kinds of business ventures were possible given the strict legislation governing its operations.

In other companies, however, flexibility of logic can be of great importance, and both senior management and modellers are well advised to ensure that the degree of flexibility appropriate to the intended use of their corporate model is built into it.

5.4 *Flexibility of input*

Three kinds of flexibility of input were introduced in Section 5.1.

(i) *Choice of unit of measurement*. This is the extent to which the user has freedom to input data in a number of different units of measurement. At first sight, this kind of flexibility looks attractive, because the manager using the model can choose to adopt the unit most convenient to him. Particularly useful in this respect is the facility, built into one of the models of a large financial institution, to input absolute figures for some years and either absolute changes or rates of change for others. For instance, a manager might forecast sales as £300 million for 1975, £335 million for 1976 and then stipulate a 5 per cent per annum growth from 1976 onwards.

Flexibility of input can be achieved in a number of ways. In some cases, the magnitude of figures expressed in different units is so great that a simple rule can be built into the computer program (where a general-purpose language is used) to ensure conversion to a basic unit. For example, the program can contain statements telling the computer to accept all figures below 100 as annual percentage growth rates, and to use these to calculate annual, absolute figures.

Figure 5.4 Man-hours required to allow for major changes in business

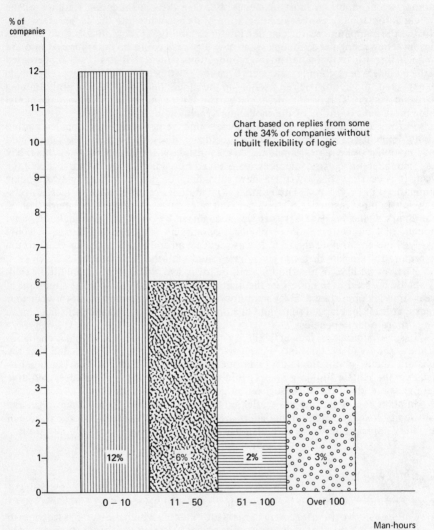

Chart based on replies from some
of the 34% of companies without
inbuilt flexibility of logic

Such routines are fairly simple technically, but inevitably increase the cost and complexity of the model, and could lead to serious errors unless great care is taken. It is therefore wise to avoid using this kind of device, unless there is absolutely no danger of input being converted into the wrong unit by operation of the routine. Perhaps for this reason only 5 per cent of the companies had such routines (see *Figure 5.5*), and it is interesting to note that all were designed by experienced teams of operational researchers. In so far as we could ascertain, the routines were not likely to lead to errors in any of these cases, however they had added further complexity to models that were already large and complex.

An alternative that is normally safe is to use control parameters to direct the computer to either follow or by-pass routines to convert input into the basic unit

Figure 5.5 Companies with flexibility of input units

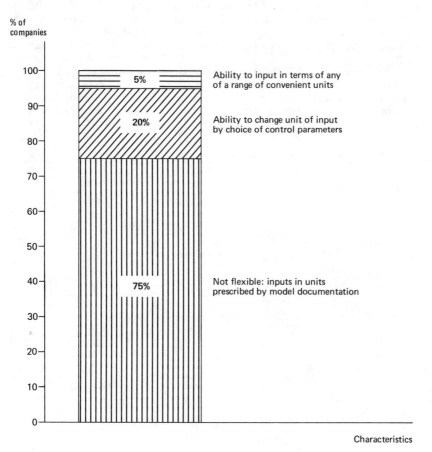

% of
companies

Ability to input in terms of any
of a range of convenient units

Ability to change unit of input
by choice of control parameters

Not flexible: inputs in units
prescribed by model documentation

Characteristics

used within the corporate model. However, the use of control parameters involves additional logic in the model, and perhaps for this reason they were used by only another 20 per cent of the companies.

Consequently, only a quarter of the companies gave the user any choice as to the unit in which data was input. Thus, three-quarters of the companies thought the added cost did not justify the benefits derived from this form of flexibility of input, and required the user to adopt the unit of measurement prescribed in the model documentation. A number of them argued, in fact, that freedom of choice of unit of measurement would be a very mixed blessing anyway. By use of a clearly specified unit, a discipline was imposed on the user, and preparation of input data therefore became more routine.

(ii) *Free or fixed format.* Another aspect of flexibility of input is the ability to punch the data onto cards or tape for reading into the computer in the right order but without attention to precise spacing. This, in the jargon of the computer specialist, is known as 'free format'. The alternative to free format is 'fixed format'. Fixed format means that a given space on the punched card, for instance, is reserved for a particular piece of information, and care must therefore be taken to ensure that spacing of characters is right. Where a general-purpose language, like FOR-TRAN, is used the model may be programmed to accept one or the other. There is no difference in programming difficulty or cost. However, by increasing the complexity of the program, a choice could be afforded the user, who could instruct the computer on the input format statements to be used by means of control parameters.

Free format has the advantage of reducing errors in input. Where fixed format is used, if an error of spacing is made in punching cards or tape, the computer will either reject the information or, worse, accept wrong data. As long as there is a space, of any size, between figures input in free format, this will not happen. On the other hand, some computer specialists argue that mistakes are

Figure 5.6 Characteristics of changes to data base during computer runs

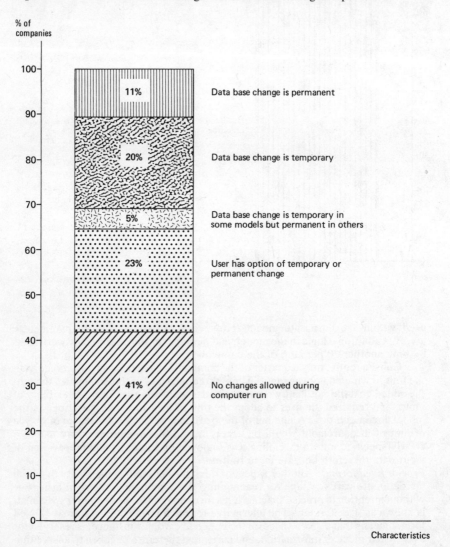

less likely with fixed format, because the format itself imposes a discipline on both the punch operator and on the user who records his data on pre-prepared forms. With fixed format it is also easier to see if an entire item has been omitted.

Modelling systems do not normally give flexibility of input format. However, if used in the conversational mode they do provide the much more important type of input flexibility discussed next.

(iii) *Input changes.* On occasions the user may wish to change input data during a computer run of the corporate model. Conversational mode gives him the means to do so but the batch mode does not. The importance of this kind of flexibility of input is reflected in the fact that 59 per cent of the UK sample companies, virtually all of those using the conversational mode, made changes to their data bases during computer runs (see *Figure 5.6*).

Where the data base is changed during a computer run, the change may be temporary or permanent, and in some cases the user has the option of making it either. This is achieved, in conversational mode, by the model using a temporary duplicate of a more permanent file held on disc by the computer. The user can then change the file used by the model run without changing the more permanent record. Alternatively, he can change the permanent file, if he wishes, either during or after the computer run. In the latter case, he does not have to key data in again, he merely instructs the computer to replace the permanent by the altered temporary file.

Users having the option of making temporary or permanent changes to their data bases totalled 23 per cent. A further 20 per cent could make only temporary changes, and had to change the permanent file outside the run. More seriously, another 11 per cent could make only permanent changes, and 5 per cent had some models in which changes were permanent and others where they were temporary. This meant that in 16 per cent of companies the original data base was distorted by any temporary changes made during the run. Hence, the original data had to be input again after the model run, if the permanent file was to be restored to its original state. This is both tedious and inefficient.

Changes to data bases, whether temporary or permanent, may be made in one or both of two ways. Many models run in conversational mode, and particularly those using modelling systems, interrupt their calculations at stipulated points to ask the user whether he wishes to make changes and to accept any he makes. In addition, some bureaux have 'break' facilities, which permit the computer run to be halted at any stage to change input data. This can be useful if, say, a report is being produced and the user realises that something has gone wrong or merely wishes to try other alternatives.

5.5   *Flexibility of output*

Flexibility of output is important. Different users, say, planning staff and directors, have different needs. The planning staff require detailed output over which to pore. Directors normally demand more summary data supported by explanations from those who have studied the detail. Similarly, different situations lead to changing emphasis on the importance of both different reports and the items they include.

(i) *Choice of reports.* The importance of flexibility of output is reflected in the fact that 80 per cent of the companies allowed choice of output reports. From *Figure 5.7* it may be seen that control parameters, fed to the computer at the beginning of the run, were used in 38 per cent of companies to indicate the reports to be printed. This approach is used in models developed with general-purpose languages and modelling systems alike when run in the batch mode. However, when the models are run in the conversational mode a different approach is common. The computer prints via the terminal a request for information on the reports required. Then the user keys, on the terminal, the output required. Choice of output report was achieved in this manner by 22 per cent of the companies. A further 18 per cent called required reports during operation in conversational mode on some occasions, and used control parameters on models run in the batch mode at other times.

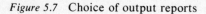

Figure 5.7 Choice of output reports

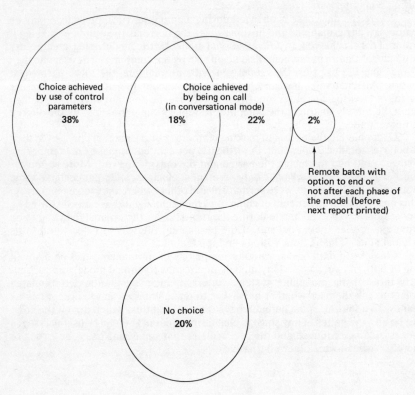

One of the companies, the Butterfield-Harvey Group, had a different approach to choice of output reports. The model was run in remote batch mode. At the end of each phase of the output routines, when a further report had been generated and printed, the operator was given the option to continue or to terminate the run.

(ii) *Report formats.* By contrast with choice of report, most companies thought format of report to be relatively unimportant, and only 34 per cent of companies gave the user some choice in this respect. In most of these cases, the computer had been programmed to produce alternative forms of the same report, for instance a summary for top management and a detailed account for planners. Some of the modelling systems provide even more variety by enabling reports to be printed with either a horizontal or a vertical time scale. This might be useful if reports are wanted for different departments who have traditionally had reports specially tailored to their requirements.

(iii) *Sequence of reports*. Choice of the sequence of reports can be valuable when a particular document is required urgently by top management. Required sequence can again be communicated to the computer either by means of control parameters or via the terminal where the conversational mode is used. Many modelling systems, particularly where use in the conversational mode is intended, give options for the sequence of reports. This is, no doubt, the reason why nearly all the companies whose corporate models allowed different sequences of output reports were using modelling systems. In exactly 50 per cent of the companies in the UK sample at least some of the models gave the user choice of sequence of reports. The remainder, virtually all using only batch mode, had a completely fixed sequence (see *Figure 5.8*).

Figure 5.8   Choice of sequence of output reports

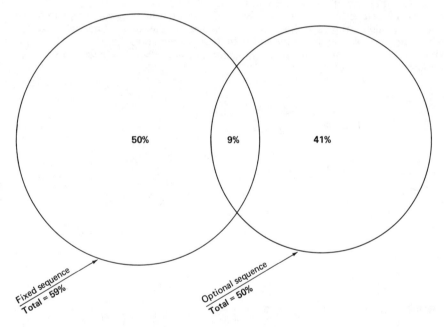

5.6   *Concluding points on flexibility*

It is apparent from what has been said about flexibility of logic, input and output that there are important differences between general-purpose languages and modelling systems in this respect, which are related to a large extent to whether batch or conversational mode is used.

In practice the most flexible of corporate models are those built with modelling systems and run in conversational mode. These allow the user to change the logic quickly and relatively cheaply. The data base may be changed, either temporarily or permanently, during computer runs. A full range of output reports is usually available, and the user has some freedom of choice between them. He can often also program the computer to produce a non-standard output report if he wishes.

In theory tailor-made models written in a general-purpose language should be as flexible as the user wants them to be. There is nothing that a modelling system can do which cannot be done by a general-purpose language, whereas the reverse is not always true. Unfortunately this flexibility does not extend into practice; we found that tailor-made models written in general-purpose languages, and run in batch mode, are usually the least flexible of all models. Changes in logic can involve tedious and expensive reprogramming to such an extent that they are not encouraged. None the less some useful flexibility can be gained by use of 'redundant items'.

Modelling systems in the batch mode and general-purpose language models in the conversational mode fall between the above extremes. It is difficult to say which of these is, in practice, the more flexible. The former loses the flexibility associated with conversational mode whilst the latter gains it. Which system is preferable must depend ultimately on the individual requirements of each company.

Nothing has been said about ready-made models in this chapter. This is because they are not widely used and are usually inflexible in terms of logic, input and output. Moreover, they are discussed fully in Chapter 7.

The advantages of flexibility of logic, input and output are readily apparent. In general, the higher the degree of flexibility the greater the range of applications, the greater the ease of using, and the lower the cost of updating the model. These are gained at a greater cost of model development, in some cases, and higher cost of use in others.

Chapter 6

Building corporate models

6.1 The stages of model building

As seen in Chapter 2, almost all of the sample of UK companies had developed their own corporate models (only 2 per cent were purchased ready-made), hence there is a very high likelihood that newcomers to the field will choose to do the same. It is consequently important that managers interested in corporate models should have some knowledge of what is involved in model building.

Over the years, experience has led to a fairly standard approach to development of models, which is illustrated in *Figure 6.1*. This approach was followed by, for instance, Gershefski[1] when he developed his Sun Oil model using a general-purpose language, but is equally applicable where a modelling system is used. The same approach has also been followed in the corporate model building with which we have been directly associated.[2] Whilst for convenience the stages may be described separately, and in practice the sequence shown in the figure is followed broadly, they almost always overlap. As new information is gathered, and further problems emerge, the model builder is frequently forced to revert to earlier stages. This is shown in *Figure 6.1* by broken arrows. Consequently, development of a corporate model is in practice an 'iterative' process.

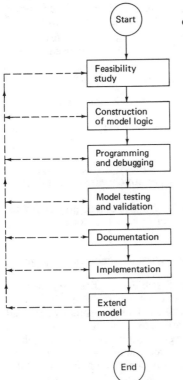

Figure 6.1 Flow chart depicting the stages of model building

6.2   *The feasibility study*

The first stage of model construction should be a feasibility study intended to determine whether it is worth proceeding with development of the model, and the best way of doing so. Decisions that the corporate model is intended to aid must be identified. In too many cases, the apparently basic questions about intended users and their decision-making needs are not put. Even models with inbuilt flexibility are unlikely to be of much use for applications for which they are not specifically designed.

Answers to these basic questions permit initial decisions on the nature of the model, the way in which it might be developed, and the mode of operation. The feasibility study should cover a number of related points: whether the model should extend down to subsidiary, to divisional or to operating unit level, whether an optimisation or simulation, deterministic or probabilistic, conversational or batch-run model is to be built by consultants, internal staff or both using general-purpose languages or modelling systems. A feasibility study cannot proceed without initial decision on these issues.

These early decisions are followed by a study of technical feasibility. Obviously the application must be within the limits of available technology and resources. The nature of the model envisaged, the complexity of the relationships to be described in the model, the expected size of the model and the computer facilities required are just some of the factors which should be considered. As far as deterministic, financial corporate simulation models are concerned technical feasibility does not usually present a problem. Also where it is intended to use probabilistic or optimisation models, the necessary technology and computer facilities are normally adequate, but there may be difficulties in getting sufficient data to establish realistic relationships reflecting adequately, say, random, seasonal and cyclical fluctuations in sales.

A second aspect of the study is what has been called 'operational' feasibility.[3] Here the question being asked is 'If the model is developed, will it be used successfully?' Several issues are involved:

- Will managers understand the model, have confidence in it, and make full use of it, or will they ignore it?
- Will data necessary for operation of the model be collected, collated, filed and updated or will it be thought that the expected benefits do not warrant the additional work?
- Can a procedure for collecting and updating the required data be designed and integrated into the normal routines of the company relatively easily or is this likely to cause even more problems?
- Can use of the model be integrated into the normal planning process of the company, or will it be used on a few *ad hoc* decisions and forgotten?

The over-enthusiastic, or hasty, may brush aside these issues too quickly, not giving them the consideration they deserve.

The McKinsey Report (1968),[3] dealing with feasibility studies from a more general point of view, places heavy emphasis on 'economic' feasibility. It urges that a full analysis of financial benefits and costs be undertaken. This is absolutely right and an attempt should be made from the outset to quantify costs and benefits as fully as possible. A bland assumption that, because others are developing corporate models, it must be worth while, amounts to a dereliction of management duty.

There are, however, major difficulties in such a full economic feasibility study. Cost estimates can, and should be made, but even this can be difficult. However, the experiences of others is a useful guide and initial estimates of the likely range of costs of development and operation can normally be made. Financial measurement of benefits presents a much greater problem. The gains resulting from a current strategic decision may be realised in periods far in the future and many unforeseen, and often unforeseeable, circumstances can affect the final outcome. Moreover, a strategic decision rarely binds the firm for all time, but establishes a direction and a disposition of resources, which will be modified subsequently by further decisions as the future unfolds. How can a value be placed on any one of the series of decisions? This problem is compounded by the fact that it is impossible to ascertain whether the decision would have been any different if a corporate model had or had not been used.

For these reasons, it is extremely unlikely that any objectively based estimate of financial benefits likely to stem from a corporate model can be made. What is possible, and very valuable, is that management should receive a statement of the information the corporate model could give them, how it might be used, and the expected costs of development and operation. Management can then decide whether the likely benefits justify the investment.

Studies of technical, operational and economic feasibility should lead to a decision on whether or not to proceed with model development. Moreover, where it is recommended that a corporate model should be developed, the feasibility study should involve an initial specification of the model to be developed, of its intended use, of resources required, and of the programme of work to be undertaken. It must be accepted, though, that such initial specifications are unlikely to be final, and that reassessment may be necessary as fuller information becomes available at later stages of development of the model.

6.3   *Construction of the logic of the model*

The next stage following the feasibility study is the construction of the logic of the model. This involves:
- Deciding on the structure of the model in more detail than in the feasibility study.
- Developing logical and mathematical expressions to represent accounting conventions and other relationships within the company.
- Using these expressions to relate the required output to the available inputs.

Each of these stages draws upon answers to some key questions, first put during the feasibility study, which must be asked repeatedly and which largely shape the logic of the model. These are:
- What are the major decisions taken by those for whom the model is to be built?
- What major alternatives, or types of alternatives, are open to them when confronting these decisions and how are these related?
- What performance measures do they take into account, or would they wish to take into account, in choosing between alternatives?
- What relationships exist between these alternatives, other factors, and the performance measures? How best might they be expressed?
- What data would be required by the model if these relationships were built into it? Is such information already available or could it be provided easily and economically?

These questions can be answered at various levels of detail. First, by use of fairly general, qualitative questions the modeller may obtain an outline that is more detailed than that produced in the feasibility study, but is still too general for actual operation. Then once the modeller is satisfied that this framework is sound, it may be filled in with successively greater detail. The best ultimate level of detail is dependent on a variety of factors specific to the individual company, and is largely a matter of judgement, but it is worth noting that the general tendency has been towards too great rather than too little detail in initial models.

Where the logic is mainly accounting, it will help if the model builder proceeds backwards from the forecast balance sheets, profit and loss accounts, and financial ratios produced towards inputs which embody the alternatives to be tested. Naturally, a detailed study of the accounting conventions and procedures of the company are a central feature of this process. For this reason a senior accountant, with a detailed knowledge of the company's accounting procedures, should be a member of the modelling team or at least readily available to provide the relative information.

Once detailed operations of a company are represented, in the model or suite of models, statistical analysis becomes particularly important. For example, sales volume may be related to changes in price, advertising expenditure, and other pertinent factors to determine some key relationships to be incorporated into the model. In such cases, the emphasis moves to the relationships between actions the manager can take, factors beyond his control, and key variables like sales and costs.

Results of this detailed study of logic may be expressed in a number of forms. Some model builders prefer to list relationships merely as a series of written logical steps, whereas others start with very general diagrams (flow charts), showing major relationships and refine these in successive steps. Such a graphical approach shows major relationships and any gaps more clearly. Also, flow charts aid discussion with management whose involvement in development of the logic is normally imperative. Detailed logical, and mathematical, operations can then be listed in sequence as a basis for programming.

The general approach discussed above can best be illustrated by an example. One of the first companies to contact us to volunteer assistance with our survey was Associated Television Management Services (ATV). ATV decided that the best method of starting to model was to computerise the existing manual system. This allowed the first working model to be produced in a mere two days.

In the case of ATV, the logic was already well established, and was passed to the consultant as a sequence of expressions. However, had this not been so, development might well have started with a diagram like that shown in *Figure 6.2*. The operations in each of the boxes shown there would then be studied in detail. This would have involved, if at all typical, discussion with accountants, examination of available statements of procedures, study of calculation sheets used in manual calculations, and collection of information on tax and other charges thought possible as well as on the options the management would wish to explore. The results of this labour could have been expressed in the more detailed flow chart given in *Figure 6.3*. It will be readily apparent that this very much resembles *Figure 6.2* on which it is based. The main difference is, of course, that detailed logic has been added. The headings are more concise and are consistent with the lines of the accounts produced later in Figures 6.8 and 6.9.

Figures 6.2 and *6.3* show that there are four main stages in the logic. Trading profit before interest and depreciation is calculated first. Then cash flows are computed. Receipts include new loan stocks and profit before depreciation and interest. Outflows include expenditure on plant and equipment, interest, tax, loan repayments and dividends. Overdraft is used as the balancing factor. From the cash flow calculations, a figure for interest is produced which is then used in producing the profit and loss account in the third stage. This is reasonably straightforward, but an unusual feature is that the net earnings per share ratio is calculated in this section. Dividends, taxation on trading profit, loan stock and profits carried to reserves calculated in earlier sections are all used to produce the balance sheet in the final stage.

The detailed logic is usually listed before it is programmed, that for the ATV model being given in *Figure 6.4*. The expressions are so ordered that every figure required is produced before it is needed for use in a later statement of the program. This allows the computer to work through the statements in sequential fashion.

Figure 6.2   General flow chart – ATV model

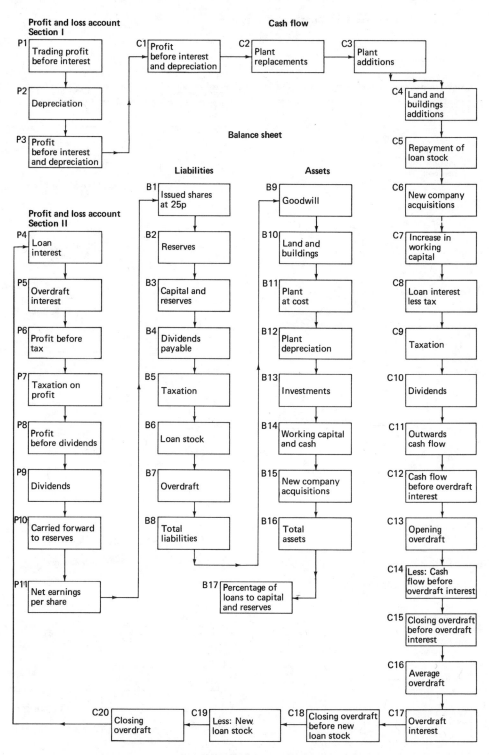

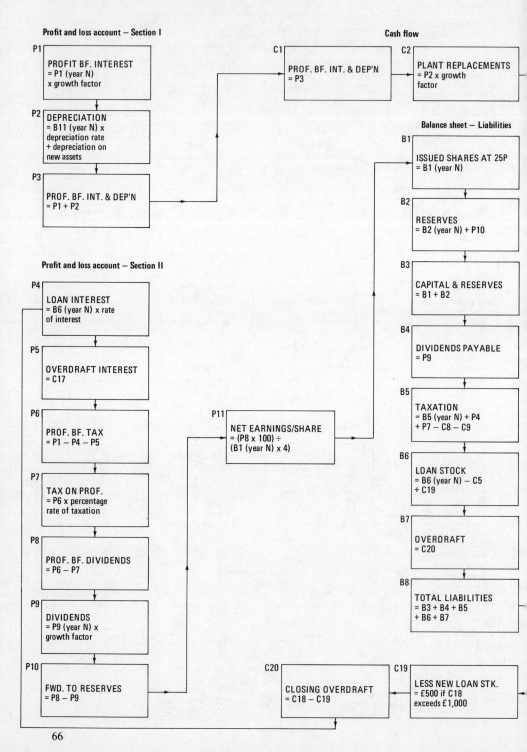

Figure 6.3 Detailed flow chart – ATV model

Profit and loss account – Section I

P1
PROFIT BF. INTEREST
= P1 (year N)
x growth factor

P2
DEPRECIATION
= B11 (year N) x
depreciation rate
+ depreciation on
new assets

P3
PROF. BF. INT. & DEP'N
= P1 + P2

Profit and loss account – Section II

P4
LOAN INTEREST
= B6 (year N) x rate
of interest

P5
OVERDRAFT INTEREST
= C17

P6
PROF. BF. TAX
= P1 – P4 – P5

P7
TAX ON PROF.
= P6 x percentage
rate of taxation

P8
PROF. BF. DIVIDENDS
= P6 – P7

P9
DIVIDENDS
= P9 (year N) x
growth factor

P10
FWD. TO RESERVES
= P8 – P9

P11
NET EARNINGS/SHARE
= (P8 x 100) ÷
(B1 (year N) x 4)

Cash flow

C1
PROF. BF. INT. & DEP'N
= P3

C2
PLANT REPLACEMENTS
= P2 x growth
factor

Balance sheet – Liabilities

B1
ISSUED SHARES AT 25P
= B1 (year N)

B2
RESERVES
= B2 (year N) + P10

B3
CAPITAL & RESERVES
= B1 + B2

B4
DIVIDENDS PAYABLE
= P9

B5
TAXATION
= B5 (year N) + P4
+ P7 – C8 – C9

B6
LOAN STOCK
= B6 (year N) – C5
+ C19

B7
OVERDRAFT
= C20

B8
TOTAL LIABILITIES
= B3 + B4 + B5
+ B6 + B7

C20
CLOSING OVERDRAFT
= C18 – C19

C19
LESS NEW LOAN STK.
= £500 if C18
exceeds £1,000

66

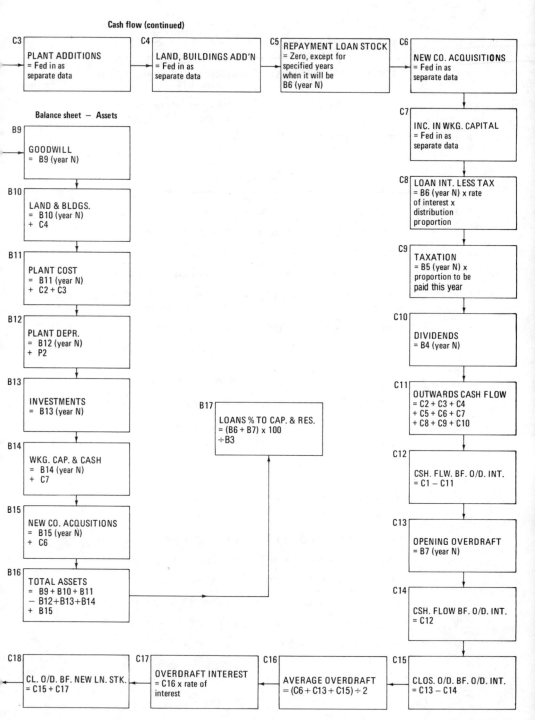

Figure 6.4 Basic logic of ATV model

Code		**B** Balance sheet
Year Z	This year	**C** Cash flows
Year N	Year Z–1	**P** Profit and loss account

| | | **III** Detailed accounting logic (see flow charts also) |
I No.	**II** Steps (see flow charts)	Profit and loss account-Section I
P 1	PROFIT BF. INTEREST	=P1(year N)×growth factor (fed in as separate data)
P 2	DEPRECIATION	=B11(year N)×depreciation rate+ depreciation on new assets
P 3	PROF. BF. INT. & DEP'N	=P1+P2
		Cash flows
C 1	PROF. BF. INT. & DEP'N	=P3
C 2	PLANT REPLACEMENTS	=P2×growth factor
C 3	PLANT ADDITIONS	=Fed in as separate data
C 4	LAND, BUILDINGS ADD'N	=Fed in as separate data
C 5	REPAYMENT LOAN STOCK	=Zero except for specified years when it will be B6(year N)
C 6	NEW CO. ACQUISITIONS	=Fed in as separate data
C 7	INC. IN WKG. CAPITAL	=Fed in as separate data
C 8	LOAN INT. LESS TAX	=B6(year N)×rate of interest× distribution proportion
C 9	TAXATION	=B5(year N)×proportion to be paid this year
C10	DIVIDENDS	=B4(year N)
C11	OUTWARDS CASH FLOW	=C2+C3+C4+C5+C6+C7+C8+C9+C10
C12	CSH. FLW. BF. O/D. INT.	=C1−C11
C13	OPENING OVERDRAFT	=B7(year N)
C14	CSH. FLOW BF. O/D. INT.	=C12
C15	CLOS. O/D. BF. O/D. INT.	=C13−C14
C16	AVERAGE OVERDRAFT	=(C6+C13+C15)÷2
C17	OVERDRAFT INTEREST	=C16×rate of interest
C18	CL. O/D. BF. NEW LN. STK.	=C15+C17
C19	LESS NEW LOAN STK.	=£500 if C18 exceeds £1,000
C20	CLOSING OVERDRAFT	=C18−C19

IV Equivalent logic using symbols

V Equivalent in JEAN programming language

$P(1,Z)=P(1,N)\times D1$ (see *Figure 6.5*)

$P(2,Z)=B(11,N)\times(D2\div100)+D3(Z)$

$P(3,Z)=P(1,Z)+P(2,Z)$

$C(1,Z)=P(3,Z)$

$C(2,Z)=P(2,Z)\times D4$

(See *Figure 6.5* item D5)

(See *Figure 6.5* item D6)

$C(5,Z)=0$ except for year D7 when it will be B6(year N)

(See *Figure 6.5* item D8)

(See *Figure 6.5* item D9)

$C(8,Z)=B(6,N)\times(D10\div100)\times D11$

$C(9,Z)=B(5,N)\times(D12\div100)$

$C(10,Z)=B(4,N)$

$C(11,Z)=C(2,Z)+C(3,Z)+C(4,Z)+C(5,Z)+C(6,Z)+C(7,Z)+C(8,Z)+C(9,Z)+C(10,Z)$

$C(12,Z)=C(1,Z)-C(11,Z)$

$C(13,Z)=B(7,N)$

$C(14,Z)=C(12,Z)$

$C(15,Z)=C(13,Z)-C(14,Z)$

$C(16,Z)=(C(6,Z)+C(13,Z)+C(15,Z))\div2$

$C(17,Z)=C(16,Z)\times(D13\div100)$

$C(18,Z)=C(15,Z)+C(17,Z)$

$C(19,Z)=500$ IF $C(18,Z)>1000$

$C(20,Z)=C(18,Z)-C(19,Z)$

(Figure continued on next page)

Figure 6.4   Basic logic of ATV model – *continued*

Code   B   Balance sheet
Year Z   This year   C   Cash flows
Year N   Year Z–1   P   Profit and loss account

I No.	II Steps (see flow charts)	III Detailed accounting logic (see flow charts also) Profit and loss account-Section II
P 4	LOAN INTEREST	= B6(year N)×rate of interest
P 5	OVERDRAFT INTEREST	= C17
P 6	PROF. BF. TAX	= P1−P4−P5
P 7	TAX ON PROF.	= P6×percentage rate of taxation
P 8	PROF. BF. DIVIDENDS	= P6−P7
P 9	DIVIDENDS	= P9(year N)×growth factor
P10	FWD. TO RESERVES	= P8−P9
P11	NET EARNINGS/SHARE	= (P8×100)÷(B1(year N)×4)

Balance sheet

B 1	ISSUED SHARES AT 25P	= B1(year N)
B 2	RESERVES	= B2(year N)+P10
B 3	CAPITAL & RESERVES	= B1+B2
B 4	DIVIDENDS PAYABLE	= P9
B 5	TAXATION	= B5(year N)+P4+P7−C8−C9
B 6	LOAN STOCK	= B6(year N)−C5+C19
B 7	OVERDRAFT	= C20
B 8	TOTAL LIABILITIES	= B3+B4+B5+B6+B7
B 9	GOODWILL	= B9(year N)
B10	LAND & BLDGS.	= B10(year N)+C4
B11	PLANT COST	= B11(year N)+C2+C3
B12	PLANT DEPR.	= B12(year N)+P2
B13	INVESTMENTS	= B13(year N)
B14	WKG. CAP. & CASH	= B14(year N)+C7
B15	NEW CO. ACQUISITIONS	= B15(year N)+C6
B16	TOTAL ASSETS	= B9+B10+B11−B12+B13+B14+B15
B17	LOANS % TO CAP. & RES.	= (B6+B7)×100÷B3

IV Equivalent logic using symbols	**V** Equivalent in JEAN programming language

$P(4,Z) = B(6,N) \times (D10 \div 100)$

$P(5,Z) = C(17,Z)$

$P(6,Z) = P(1,Z) - P(4,Z) - P(5,Z)$

$P(7,Z) = P(6,Z) \times (D14 \div 100)$

$P(8,Z) = P(6,Z) - P(7,Z)$

$P(9,Z) = P(9,N) \times D15$

$P(10,Z) = P(8,Z) - P(9,Z)$

$P(11,Z) = (P(8,Z) \times 100) \div (B(1,N) \times 4)$

$B(1,Z) = B(1,N)$

$B(2,Z) = B(2,N) + P(10,Z)$

$B(3,Z) = B(1,Z) + B(2,Z)$

$B(4,Z) = P(9,Z)$

$B(5,Z) = B(5,N) + P(4,Z) + P(7,Z) - C(8,Z) - C(9,Z)$

$B(6,Z) = B(6,N) - C(5,Z) + C(19,Z)$

$B(7,Z) = C(20,Z)$

$B(8,Z) = B(3,Z) + B(4,Z) + B(5,Z) + B(6,Z) + B(7,Z)$

$B(9,Z) = B(9,N)$

$B(10,Z) = B(10,N) + C(4,Z)$

$B(11,Z) = B(11,N) + C(2,Z) + C(3,Z)$

$B(12,Z) = B(12,N) + P(2,Z)$

$B(13,Z) = B(13,N)$

$B(14,Z) = B(14,N) + C(7,Z)$

$B(15,Z) = B(15,N) + C(6,Z)$

$B(16,Z) = B(9,Z) + B(10,Z) + B(11,Z) - B(12,Z) + B(13,Z) + B(14,Z) + B(15,Z)$

$B(17,Z) = (B(6,Z) + B(7,Z)) \times 100 \div B(3,Z)$

Figure 6.5 Planning assumptions supplied for each run
in order of appearance in Figure 6.4

		Year 1	Year 2	Year 3	Year 4	Year 5
1. Growth rate of trading profit before interest	D1 = 1.2 (i.e. 20%)					
2. Percentage rate of depreciation on cost of plant and equipment	D2 = 10%					
3. Depreciation of plant and equipment of new company acquisitions to be entered for each year	D3	15	35	65	105	115
4. Multiple of depreciation on plant and equipment for replacement (there is an assumption here that a proportion of the amount depreciated will be used for replacement of the assets as they wear out)	D4	1.0 (i.e. 100% replacement)				
5. Amount of additional capital expenditure on plant and equipment for each year	D5	100	100	100	100	100
6. Amount of additional capital expenditure on land and buildings for each year	D6	50	50	—	—	—
7. Year number in which to repay existing loan stock	D7	2				
8. Cost of new company acquisitions each year	D8	300	400	600	600	200
9. Increase in working capital to be entered for each year	D9	30	30	40	40	50
10. Interest rate on loan stock	D10	10%				
11. Loan interest distribution ratio after tax	D11	0.7				
12. Percentage of year-end taxation as following year's payment	D12	50%				
13. Interest rate on overdraft	D13	8.5%				
14. Percentage rate of taxation	D14	50%				
15. Growth rate of dividends	D15	1.1 (i.e. 10%)				

The first three columns of *Figure 6.4* are reproduced directly from the detailed flow chart (*Figure 6.3*). From the detailed accounting logic in Column III, an equivalent logic can be produced in Column IV using symbols, for example:

$$P\,(1,Z) = P(1,N) \times D1$$

where P simply represents profit and loss items, as opposed to cash flow and balance sheet items; 1 is the number appearing in Column I which is a list of consecutive numbers for each section of the model; Z represents this year and N last year; D implies data fed in separately and D1 specifically refers to a growth factor of 1.20. (All data, prefixed D, fed into the model separately are shown in *Figure 6.5*.) The whole expression simply means that the trading profit before interest is the previous year's figure plus 20 per cent. This symbolic language will be extremely useful when we come to complete Column V which we shall do in the next section.

6.4 *Programming and 'debugging'*

Programming is the translation of the logic of the model into a language which the computer can 'understand' and execute, such a language being general purpose or special purpose. What are termed 'modelling systems' may best be regarded as special languages, and supporting routines, designed specifically for company planning. Further details of the most commonly used languages and some special simulation languages are given in Appendix 3, whilst modelling systems are dealt with more fully in Chapter 7.

Whatever the type of language used the general process tends to be similar. This process may be illustrated by returning to the example of ATV. The logic of the model was set out in Section 6.3. We now look at the programming involved using JEAN. This conversational general-purpose language is not one of the better known, but is the one actually used for the ATV model. It suffers from not being widely available and has limitations, but it is useful as a beginner's guide to programming, because it is very much like what is often described as 'business' English.

First, let us consider how data is fed into the model. Data requirements, as can be seen from *Figure 6.4*, include balance sheet, profit and loss account, and cash flow items for a base year. In addition, for each run a number of planning assumptions are input, these being listed in *Figure 6.5*. *Figure 6.6* shows how the profit and loss account line descriptions and the figures for base year 0 are input, lines 3.01 to 3.11 in Part A give the descriptions of the profit and loss items. In Part B the conversational abilities of the computer are seen, with each line of the profit and loss account being printed out automatically via the terminal. The computer waits until the operator types in the required values before proceeding to print out the next line. Part C prints out the values held by the computer. Similar procedures are followed for balance sheet and other items.

Once base year data and planning assumptions are input, the computer proceeds to follow step by step the logic written into the program. *Figure 6.7* shows the program for the logic given in *Figure 6.4*. Many of the statements remain unchanged, and others change only slightly, for example:

- the multiplication sign is $*$ instead of $\times$
- the division sign is / instead of $\div$.

The standard rules of mathematics apply as to the order in which calculations are completed, for example, brackets operate before multiplication and division, followed by additions and subtractions. One exception is that there are no implied multiplications, for example, $2(a + b)$ must be programmed as $2*(a + b)$. Line C5 may not be clear to those new to programming. This statement sets repayment of loan stock to nil, except when $D7 = Z$, as it will when $Z = 2$ in year 2; then the nil value will be overruled and amended to the value of loan stock outstanding in the previous year's balance sheet. Likewise statement C19 specifies that new loan stock will be nil unless the bank overdraft exceeds £1,000. We hope that *Figure 6.7* will show that programming is not as difficult as some imagine.

Figure 6.6 Examples of input to ATV model

Part A   Profit and loss account line descriptions

3.0 TYPE 'PROFIT AND LOSS ACCOUNT FOR YEAR 0'
3.001 N = 0
3.002 LINE , 2 TIMES
3.01 DEMAND P(1,N) AS 'PROFIT BF. INTEREST'
3.02 DEMAND P(2,N) AS 'DEPRECIATION'
3.03 DEMAND P(3,N) AS 'PROF. BF. INT. & DEP'N'
3.04 DEMAND P(4,N) AS 'LOAN INTEREST'
3.05 DEMAND P(5,N) AS 'OVERDRAFT INTEREST'
3.06 DEMAND P(6,N) AS 'PROF. BF. TAX'
3.07 DEMAND P(7,N) AS 'TAX ON PROF.'
3.08 DEMAND P(8,N) AS 'PROF. BF. DIVIDENDS'
3.09 DEMAND P(9,N) AS 'DIVIDENDS'
3.10 DEMAND P(10,N) AS 'FWD. TO RESERVES'
3.11 DEMAND P(11,N) AS 'NET EARNINGS/SHARE'

Part B   Assigning values in conversational models

PROFIT AND LOSS ACCOUNT FOR YEAR 0
PROFIT BF. INTEREST – 325
DEPRECIATION – 150
PROF. BF. INT. & DEP'N – 475
LOAN INTEREST – 40
OVERDRAFT INTEREST – 45
PROF. BF. TAX – 240
TAX ON PROF. – 120
PROF. BF. DIVIDENDS – 120
DIVIDENDS – 70
FWD. TO RESERVES – 50
NET EARNINGS/SHARE – 3

Part C   Print-out of input values held in computer

$P(1,0) =$	325
$P(2,0) =$	150
$P(3,0) =$	475
$P(4,0) =$	40
$P(5,0) =$	45
$P(6,0) =$	240
$P(7,0) =$	120
$P(8,0) =$	120
$P(9,0) =$	70
$P(10,0) =$	50
$P(11,0) =$	3

Figure 6.7 Basic logic of ATV model

Code		B Balance sheet
Year Z	This year	C Cash flows
Year N	Year Z–1	P Profit and loss account

I No.	II Steps (see flow charts)	III Detailed accounting logic (see flow charts also)

Profit and loss account-Section I

I No.	II Steps (see flow charts)	III Detailed accounting logic
P 1	PROFIT BF. INTEREST	$=$P1(year N)$\times$growth factor (fed in as separate data)
P 2	DEPRECIATION	$=$B11(year N)$\times$depreciation rate$+$ depreciation on new assets
P 3	PROF. BF. INT. & DEP'N	$=$P1$+$P2

Cash flows

I No.	II Steps	III Detailed accounting logic
C 1	PROF. BF. INT. & DEP'N	$=$P3
C 2	PLANT REPLACEMENTS	$=$P2$\times$growth factor
C 3	PLANT ADDITIONS	$=$Fed in as separate data
C 4	LAND, BUILDINGS ADD'N	$=$Fed in as separate data
C 5	REPAYMENT LOAN STOCK	$=$Zero except for specified years when it will be B6(year N)
C 6	NEW CO. ACQUISITIONS	$=$Fed in as separate data
C 7	INC. IN WKG. CAPITAL	$=$Fed in as separate data
C 8	LOAN INT. LESS TAX	$=$B6(year N)$\times$rate of interest$\times$ distribution proportion
C 9	TAXATION	$=$B5(year N)$\times$proportion to be paid this year
C10	DIVIDENDS	$=$B4(year N)
C11	OUTWARDS CASH FLOW	$=$C2$+$C3$+$C4$+$C5$+$C6$+$C7$+$C8$+$C9$+$C10
C12	CSH. FLW. BF. O/D. INT.	$=$C1$-$C11
C13	OPENING OVERDRAFT	$=$B7(year N)
C14	CSH. FLOW BF. O/D. INT.	$=$C12
C15	CLOS. O/D. BF. O/D. INT.	$=$C13$-$C14
C16	AVERAGE OVERDRAFT	$=$(C6$+$C13$+$C15)$\div$2
C17	OVERDRAFT INTEREST	$=$C16$\times$rate of interest
C18	CL. O/D. BF. NEW LN. STK.	$=$C15$+$C17
C19	LESS NEW LOAN STK.	$=$£500 if C18 exceeds £1,000
C20	CLOSING OVERDRAFT	$=$C18$-$C19

IV Equivalent logic using symbols	**V** Equivalent in JEAN programming language
$P(1,Z)=P(1,N)\times D1$ (see *Figure 6.5*)	$P(1,Z)=P(1,N)*D1$
$P(2,Z)=B(11,N)\times(D2\div100)+D3(Z)$	$P(2,Z)=B(11,N)*(D2/100)+D3(Z)$
$P(3,Z)=P(1,Z)+P(2,Z)$	$P(3,Z)=P(1,Z)+P(2,Z)$

$C(1,Z)=P(3,Z)$	$C(1,Z)=P(3,Z)$
$C(2,Z)=P(2,Z)\times D4$	$C(2,Z)=P(2,Z)*D4$
(See *Figure 6.5* item D5)	
(See *Figure 6.5* item D6)	
$C(5,Z)=0$ except for year D7 when it will be B6(year N)	$C(5,Z)=0;\ C(5,Z)=B(6,N)$ IF $D7=Z$
(See *Figure 6.5* item D8)	
(See *Figure 6.5* item D9)	
$C(8,Z)=B(6,N)\times(D10\div100)\times D11$	$C(8,Z)=B(6,N)*(D10/100)*D11$
$C(9,Z)=B(5,N)\times(D12\div100)$	$C(9,Z)=B(5,N)*(D12/100)$
$C(10,Z)=B(4,N)$	$C(10,Z)=B(4,N)$
$C(11,Z)=C(2,Z)+C(3,Z)+C(4,Z)+C(5,Z)+C(6,Z)+C(7,Z)+C(8,Z)+C(9,Z)+C(10,Z)$	$C(11,Z)=C(2,Z)+C(3,Z)+C(4,Z)+C(5,Z)+C(6,Z)+C(7,Z)+C(8,Z)+C(9,Z)+C(10,Z)$
$C(12,Z)=C(1,Z)-C(11,Z)$	$C(12,Z)=C(1,Z)-C(11,Z)$
$C(13,Z)=B(7,N)$	$C(13,Z)=B(7,N)$
$C(14,Z)=C(12,Z)$	$C(14,Z)=C(12,Z)$
$C(15,Z)=C(13,Z)-C(14,Z)$	$C(15,Z)=C(13,Z)-C(14,Z)$
$C(16,Z)=(C(6,Z)+C(13,Z)+C(15,Z))\div2$	$C(16,Z)=(C(6,Z)+C(13,Z)+C(15,Z))/2$
$C(17,Z)=C(16,Z)\times(D13\div100)$	$C(17,Z)=C(16,Z)*(D13/100)$
$C(18,Z)=C(15,Z)+C(17,Z)$	$C(18,Z)=C(15,Z)+C(17,Z)$
$C(19,Z)=500$ IF $C(18,Z)>1000$	$C(19,Z)=0;\ C(19,Z)=500$ IF $C(18,Z)>1000$
$C(20,Z)=C(18,Z)-C(19,Z)$	$C(20,Z)=C(18,Z)-C(19,Z)$

(Figure continued on next page)

Figure 6.7 Basic logic of ATV model – *continued*

Code   B   Balance sheet
Year Z This year   C   Cash flows
Year N Year Z–1   P   Profit and loss account

I No.	II Steps (see flow charts)	III Detailed accounting logic (see flow charts also) Profit and loss account-Section II
P 4	LOAN INTEREST	$=$ B6(year N) $\times$ rate of interest
P 5	OVERDRAFT INTEREST	$=$ C17
P 6	PROF. BF. TAX	$=$ P1 $-$ P4 $-$ P5
P 7	TAX ON PROF.	$=$ P6 $\times$ percentage rate of taxation
P 8	PROF. BF. DIVIDENDS	$=$ P6 $-$ P7
P 9	DIVIDENDS	$=$ P9(year N) $\times$ growth factor
P10	FWD. TO RESERVES	$=$ P8 $-$ P9
P11	NET EARNINGS/SHARE	$=$ (P8 $\times$ 100) $\div$ (B1(year N) $\times$ 4)

		Balance sheet
B 1	ISSUED SHARES AT 25P	$=$ B1(year N)
B 2	RESERVES	$=$ B2(year N) $+$ P10
B 3	CAPITAL & RESERVES	$=$ B1 $+$ B2
B 4	DIVIDENDS PAYABLE	$=$ P9
B 5	TAXATION	$=$ B5(year N) $+$ P4 $+$ P7 $-$ C8 $-$ C9
B 6	LOAN STOCK	$=$ B6(year N) $-$ C5 $+$ C19
B 7	OVERDRAFT	$=$ C20
B 8	TOTAL LIABILITIES	$=$ B3 $+$ B4 $+$ B5 $+$ B6 $+$ B7
B 9	GOODWILL	$=$ B9(year N)
B10	LAND & BLDGS.	$=$ B10(year N) $+$ C4
B11	PLANT COST	$=$ B11(year N) $+$ C2 $+$ C3
B12	PLANT DEPR.	$=$ B12(year N) $+$ P2
B13	INVESTMENTS	$=$ B13(year N)
B14	WKG. CAP. & CASH	$=$ B14(year N) $+$ C7
B15	NEW CO. ACQUISITIONS	$=$ B15(year N) $+$ C6
B16	TOTAL ASSETS	$=$ B9 $+$ B10 $+$ B11 $-$ B12 $+$ B13 $+$ B14 $+$ B15
B17	LOANS % TO CAP. & RES.	$=$ (B6 $+$ B7) $\times$ 100 $\div$ B3

$*$ Multiplication *in JEAN programming language*

$/$ Division *(in JEAN programming language)*

IV Equivalent logic using symbols	V Equivalent in JEAN programming language
$P(4,Z)=B(6,N)\times(D10\div100)$	$P(4,Z)=B(6,N)*(D10/100)$
$P(5,Z)=C(17,Z)$	$P(5,Z)=C(17,Z)$
$P(6,Z)=P(1,Z)-P(4,Z)-P(5,Z)$	$P(6,Z)=P(1,Z)-P(4,Z)-P(5,Z)$
$P(7,Z)=P(6,Z)\times(D14\div100)$	$P(7,Z)=P(6,Z)*(D14/100)$
$P(8,Z)=P(6,Z)-P(7,Z)$	$P(8,Z)=P(6,Z)-P(7,Z)$
$P(9,Z)=P(9,N)\times D15$	$P(9,Z)=P(9,N)*D15$
$P(10,Z)=P(8,Z)-P(9,Z)$	$P(10,Z)=P(8,Z)-P(9,Z)$
$P(11,Z)=(P(8,Z)\times100)\div(B(1,N)\times4)$	$P(11,Z)=(P(8,Z)*100)/(B(1,N)*4)$

$B(1,Z)=B(1,N)$	$B(1,Z)=B(1,N)$
$B(2,Z)=B(2,N)+P(10,Z)$	$B(2,Z)=B(2,N)+P(10,Z)$
$B(3,Z)=B(1,Z)+B(2,Z)$	$B(3,Z)=B(1,Z)+B(2,Z)$
$B(4,Z)=P(9,Z)$	$B(4,Z)=P(9,Z)$
$B(5,Z)=B(5,N)+P(4,Z)+P(7,Z)-C(8,Z)-C(9,Z)$	$B(5,Z)=B(5,N)+P(4,Z)+P(7,Z)-C(8,Z)-C(9,Z)$
$B(6,Z)=B(6,N)-C(5,Z)+C(19,Z)$	$B(6,Z)=B(6,N)-C(5,Z)+C(19,Z)$
$B(7,Z)=C(20,Z)$	$B(7,Z)=C(20,Z)$
$B(8,Z)=B(3,Z)+B(4,Z)+B(5,Z)+B(6,Z)+B(7,Z)$	$B(8,Z)=B(3,Z)+B(4,Z)+B(5,Z)+B(6,Z)+B(7,Z)$
$B(9,Z)=B(9,N)$	$B(9,Z)=B(9,N)$
$B(10,Z)=B(10,N)+C(4,Z)$	$B(10,Z)=B(10,N)+C(4,Z)$
$B(11,Z)=B(11,N)+C(2,Z)+C(3,Z)$	$B(11,Z)=B(11,N)+C(2,Z)+C(3,Z)$
$B(12,Z)=B(12,N)+P(2,Z)$	$B(12,Z)=B(12,N)+P(2,Z)$
$B(13,Z)=B(13,N)$	$B(13,Z)=B(13,N)$
$B(14,Z)=B(14,N)+C(7,Z)$	$B(14,Z)=B(14,N)+C(7,Z)$
$B(15,Z)=B(15,N)+C(6,Z)$	$B(15,Z)=B(15,N)+C(6,Z)$
$B(16,Z)=B(9,Z)+B(10,Z)+B(11,Z)-B(12,Z)+B(13,Z)+B(14,Z)+B(15,Z)$	$B(16,Z)=B(9,Z)+B(10,Z)+B(11,Z)-B(12,Z)+B(13,Z)+B(14,Z)+B(15,Z)$
$B(17,Z)=(B(6,Z)+B(7,Z))\times100\div B(3,Z)$	$B(17,Z)=(B(6,Z)+B(7,Z))*100/B(3,Z)$

The computer has to be given instructions before it is able to print out reports in the required layout (format). Suitable instructions would be given to produce the reports shown in *Figures 6.8* and *6.9*. These show the profit and loss accounts, cash flows and balance sheets for base year 0 and the forecasts for the next five years produced by the model.

Given the base year data shown in these figures and the data given in *Figure 6.5*, the newcomer to corporate modelling can learn a lot by working through the logic sequences of the model. If he can follow the logic and programming of this example from ATV he need have no fears as to his ability to develop his own simple financial corporate model.

Figure 6.8 Output reports from ATV model

Profit and loss account

	Year 0	Year 1	Year 2	Year 3	Year 4	Year 5
PROF. BF. INT. & DEP'N	475	555	680	834	1024	1214
DEPRECIATION	150	165	212	273	350	405
PROFIT BF. INTEREST	325	390	468	562	674	809
LOAN INTEREST	40	40	40	50	100	150
OVERDRAFT INTEREST	45	59	109	134	138	106
PROF. BF. TAX	240	291	319	378	436	553
TAX ON PROF.	120	145	159	189	218	276
PROF. BF. DIVIDENDS	120	145	159	189	218	276
DIVIDENDS	70	77	85	93	102	113
FWD. TO RESERVES	50	68	75	96	115	164
NET EARNINGS/SHARE	3.00p	3.63p	3.98p	4.72p	5.45p	6.91p

Cash flow

	Year 0	Year 1	Year 2	Year 3	Year 4	Year 5
PROF. BF. INT. & DEP'N	475	555	680	834	1024	1214
PLANT REPLACEMENTS	150	165	212	273	350	405
PLANT ADDITIONS	0	100	100	100	100	100
LAND, BUILDINGS ADD'N	50	50	50	0	0	0
REPAYMENT LOAN STOCK	0	0	400	0	0	0
NEW CO. ACQUISITIONS	0	300	400	600	600	200
INC. IN WKG. CAPITAL	20	30	30	40	40	50
LOAN INT. LESS TAX	28	28	28	35	70	105
TAXATION	40	50	104	137	171	209
DIVIDENDS	70	70	77	85	93	102
OUTWARDS CASH FLOW	358	793	1400	1270	1424	1172
CSH. FLOW BF. O/D. INT.	117	−238	−721	−436	−400	−42
OPENING OVERDRAFT	502	430	727	1058	1127	1165
CSH. FLOW BF. O/D. INT.	117	−238	−721	−436	−400	42
CLOS. O/D. BF. O/D. INT.	385	668	1448	1493	1527	1123
OVERDRAFT INTEREST	45	59	109	134	138	106
CL. O/D. BF. NEW LN. STK.	430	727	1558	1627	1665	1229
LESS NEW LOAN STK.	0	0	500	500	500	500
CLOSING OVERDRAFT	430	727	1058	1127	1165	729
AVERAGE OVERDRAFT	444	699	1288	1575	1627	1244

Figure 6.9   Output report from ATV model

Balance sheet

	Year 0	Year 1	Year 2	Year 3	Year 4	Year 5
ISSUED SHARES AT 25P	1000	1000	1000	1000	1000	1000
RESERVES	1000	1068	1143	1239	1354	1518
CAPITAL & RESERVES	2000	2068	2143	2239	2354	2518
DIVIDENDS PAYABLE	70	77	85	93	102	113
TAXATION	100	207	275	341	418	531
LOAN STOCK	400	400	500	1000	1500	2000
OVERDRAFT	430	727	1058	1127	1165	729
TOTAL LIABILITIES	3000	3480	4060	4800	5540	5890
GOODWILL	700	700	700	700	700	700
LAND & BLDGS.	700	750	800	800	800	800
PLANT COST	1500	1765	2077	2449	2899	3404
PLANT DEPR.	500	665	877	1149	1499	1904
INVESTMENTS	100	100	100	100	100	100
WKG. CAP. & CASH	500	530	560	600	640	690
NEW CO. ACQUISITIONS	0	300	700	1300	1900	2100
TOTAL ASSETS	3000	3480	4060	4800	5540	5890
LOANS % TO CAP. & RES.	41.5%	54.5%	72.7%	95.0%	113.2%	108.4%

Debugging is the process of removing mistakes or 'bugs'. This can be a very time-consuming process especially where the model is run in the batch mode, and if the error reporting facilities are poor. There are many types of bugs that arise but they fall mainly into three categories:
● Punching errors or card errors.
● Errors in logic.
● Compiler errors.

Punching errors are a prolific source of errors on batch-run systems. Keying mistakes on terminals used with the conversational approach are easier to spot and correct because the user can see immediately what has been typed and the computer will reject certain of the errors anyway. Card errors arise where the cards in the pack get out of sequence or are inadvertently misplaced. Punching and card errors may lead the computer to stop execution of the program before its end and consequently other errors later in the program may not be discovered until subsequent runs. This multiplies the number of computer runs necessary to debug the model and so increases the time and effort required to develop the model.

Errors in logic are often more difficult to find. The computer run may come to an end without errors being reported but the printed results may be absurd. Full stops and commas omitted or put in the wrong places can lead to wrong results. The programmer must then work through the program meticulously to find the error. Fortunately, many languages have good error reporters which pinpoint statements in which some kinds of logic error are made. This can save hours of tedious checking.

Very occasionally, problems arise because of inadequacies of the compiler (the software used to translate the program into the machine code that the computer executes). However, because such snags occur only infrequently, a great deal of time can be spent in trying to find non-existent errors in the program, before a faulty compiler is suspected. Few companies have the expertise, or access to details of the compiler, to allow them to undertake a check themselves. Consequently, at this point the computer manufacturer or bureau is normally called in, and usually undertakes the necessary work free of charge.

6.5 *Model testing and validation*

Once the model has been debugged, tests are carried out to ensure that the model really does simulate the accounting logic and other company operations adequately. This process is commonly known as 'model validation'. Where models are deterministic and based exclusively on accounting logic there are usually few problems, but as soon as other more complex relationships are introduced the problems multiply. Certainly, use of probability distributions in models compounds this difficulty.

There are four common approaches to model testing. Because no single one, or even all jointly, can guarantee the validity of the model, all four are often followed. First the model may be run with historical data to see if the model produces actual past results with sufficient accuracy. The definition of 'sufficient accuracy' depends on the company and the kind of model. Where the model is deterministic, especially where accounting logic is used, some of the companies known to us have used 'within ±0.5 per cent of the actual results'. Others allow variation of up to 1 per cent or more from the actual data. Once probabilistic models are used, the problem is much more difficult, and it is wise to turn to the specialist operational researcher or statistician who can apply appropriate mathematical tests.

Second, the model may be run with variations in input data, and management can be asked if it responds in the way to be expected. Such tests can be enlightening when unlikely values are inserted as this may reveal oversights by the model developer. Adjustments to take account of unlikely events to which the manual operator would respond might not be allowed for in the logic. For instance the model may calculate tax on losses and come up with negative tax payments!

The ATV model provides a further example in this respect. The results of using the input shown earlier in this chapter had been calculated and agreed completely with the figures prepared manually. However, when input variables were changed it was found that the logic was defective. Cash flow line C19 (*Figure 6.7*) of the model calculates transfers to loan stock by specifying that £500 should be transferred to loan stock, when the bank overdraft exceeds £1,000; the intention was to set a ceiling of £1,000 on bank overdraft, but to issue loan stock in multiples of £500 only. When the bank overdraft exceeds £1,500, only £500 is transferred to the loan stock, which leaves the overdraft in excess of the desired limit. This part of the program has, we understand from ATV, been amended so that blocks of £500 are transferred until such time as the bank overdraft is £1,000 or lower.

A third approach is to discuss particular relationships with informed managers and technical specialists. Even in financial accounting-based models this can be important, since rules reflecting decision-making behaviour may be included. For instance, the model may assume that additional finance is obtained by new loan stock until the gearing ratio reaches a maximum acceptable value, after which new equity is raised. We have examined several models in which this device is used without reference to stock market prices and in which other alternatives, such as leasing or cutting back on capital expenditure, are ignored. Many pragmatic managers, shown such logic, would regard it as inappropriate to their situation.

Clearly, unless managers agree with the way the separate parts of the model operate, there is little chance that they will have confidence in the results of the total model. On the other hand, even where it is difficult to prove scientifically that a relationship is valid, there are good arguments for its incorporation in the model if experienced and well-informed managers think it reasonable. For example, a relationship in one model at Esso Petroleum represents the behaviour of salesmen in the event of divergences from sales targets. No way of testing this adequately by statistical means was found. A number of area sales managers in the company, though, have independently agreed that it adequately represents the way their men respond. As a result the relationship is being used in the model.

Finally, where relationships based on observed data rather than accountancy logic are used, it is often possible to test their validity statistically. This is a large subject which is too technical for inclusion here. Where this is the appropriate approach, there is much to be said for employing the services of operational researchers or statisticians with the necessary expertise. However, the aspiring model builder should not be deterred by lack of such specialists, because most corporate models are based purely on accounting logic and do not require testing of this kind.

.6 Documentation

One of the major headaches in model building is to get the modellers to document the model as they go along rather than putting it off until the model is completed. Documentation should always be treated as a vital part of model development because it serves as the basis for communication between the people involved in the modelling process. In fact one advantage of using consultants is that they produce good documentation – they have to because their fee is at stake.

Several models were running well without documentation, but in these cases both runs and updating of the model were in the hands of the original model building team, and management should ask itself what the position would be if the key modeller or modellers left the company. Would the replacement be able to work the model in the same efficient manner? It may be extremely difficult for even a competent programmer to grasp completely the intricacies and capabilities of the corporate model. The more sophisticated and complex the model, the more this rings true and the greater the need for documentation.

We came across a number of models which had been shelved because the model builder had left suddenly without adequately documenting the model. In one case, the model was finished, validated, and had even been used for planning purposes. Later it was found that the oral briefing given to the model builder's successor, though extensive, was not sufficient to make him familiar with the internal intricacies of the model and its full capabilities. In all these cases it was found easier to start from scratch than to try and unravel the mysteries of the existing model. The cost of such wasted work in terms of time and money can be considerable, certainly far in excess of the cost of documentation. Furthermore, management and their specialist advisors are liable to find the need to explain, yet again, the basic fundamentals of the company's operations immensely irritating.

To avoid such occurrences, full and comprehensive documents should be kept throughout development of the model, including systematically recorded notes on interviews, dated and numbered flow charts, lists of logical statements, and so on. When the model is programmed, full use should be made of facilities given by most languages to embed 'comment' statements in the program itself, so as to allow anybody turning to the program for the first time to understand its structure and logic more easily. Comment statements are merely explanatory text written in plain English. By use of the appropriate symbols, for example in FORTRAN by the use of 'C' at the very start of the line, the computer is directed to ignore the statement. Hence the use of comment statements does not affect execution of the program at all.

Records should, likewise, be kept of work done to validate the model. Once the model is validated, operating manuals should be prepared which show not only the way in which the model may be used, but give the user some insight into its structure and how it works. In addition, once procedures have been designed to assemble and update the data needed by the model, and to integrate its operation into the normal planning procedures, these too should be properly documented.

6.7 *Implementation*

Many of those who build corporate models for the first time believe that their troubles are over once the model has been programmed, debugged, validated and documented. They may then find that the major hurdles are still to be crossed, particularly when the company is not accustomed to computer models. To allow full and regular use of the model, procedures must be designed to ensure that the data required by the model is updated. Moreover, once designed, operation of such procedures usually involves extra work for divisional or corporate staff. This additional burden will not be willingly carried, unless management can see clear advantages stemming from use of the model.

Except where the intention is to use the corporate model on an *ad hoc* basis, for example in merger analysis, steps should be taken to integrate use of the model into the total planning system. This is less a matter of formal systems design than one of education. Management and planners involved may either choose, or not choose, to use the model to evaluate alternatives. In our experience, managers will use models only when they understand how they work, at least in general terms, and the way in which they can make a contribution to decision-making.

Hence a continuing emphasis in implementation must be on educating and involving management. Obviously, management involvement enters at a number of stages of model building. A sponsor in senior management is desirable before even a feasibility study is undertaken. Certainly, on completion of the feasibility study, the decision to proceed is normally taken by senior management. Management is also approached for its views on particular relationships to be built into the model and may, as we have seen, also take part in validation. Throughout this process, management understanding of and identification with the model is likely to grow, hence it is important that the involvement should be other than perfunctory. Sometimes, it helps to have the whole project overseen by a small committee of representatives from the various departments affected. Others have found that the development of the model is best done by a team drawn from subsidiaries, divisions or departments represented in the model and from the corporate planning group.

Once the model has been developed, presentation can be made to the board and line managers affected. Common sense and knowledge of the people involved dictate the structure and content of such presentations. For instance, it is normally wise to work through a number of possible uses of the model and to show the way it would contribute further information of value to the decision-taker. Such presentations should, of course, avoid jargon and technical detail.

Ultimately, successful implementation is complete only when the model is used in earnest. If the educational process has been effective, management should be turning to the model for assistance. Old habits die hard, though, and it is important that offers to run the model on their behalf be made on the first few occasions, at least. Some models may, of course, always involve operation by specialists.

A powerful sponsor in management, who will remind his colleagues of the value of the model, is again a considerable asset. Experience suggests that, provided output reports are in a form to which they are accustomed and are properly edited, management may be expected to see quickly the gain to be made by use of the model. Presentation of only key figures supported by concise explanations in English is most important. A quick route to disfavour is to deposit a thick wad of detailed computer print-out on the desks of the directors!

.8   *Updating and extension*

Once implemented, it is tempting to think that the exercise of developing a corporate model is over, and that those involved may rest on their laurels. Where the model incorporates purely accounting logic, this may be largely true, although even in this case changes may be needed to allow for tax changes or other unforeseen contingencies. However, where non-accounting relationships are described within the model, their validity must be regularly monitored because they can change markedly over time.

This regular monitoring should extend beyond the validity of relationships in the model to its use. Checks should be made on the use to which information produced by the model is put, in order to identify additional information required, redundant information that could be eliminated, and further potential uses. Such further uses often require extensions to the model or to the corporate suite. The major advantage of the modular approach, whereby a suite of models is built, is the flexibility that permits this piecemeal extension as specific decision-needs demand it. Modelling systems, too, facilitate such growth.

Consequently, the corporate model or suite of models is likely to evolve over time, becoming larger and more complex in the process, a tendency strengthened by the natural desire of modellers to improve the accuracy of output and internal efficiency of their models. We noted this tendency in the majority of the users in our main survey, particularly where the first model built was simple, deterministic, and purely financial. But it was also found among the many who said that, were they to start again from scratch, they would develop a much simpler model initially.

Care must be taken, though, to avoid evolution of the model or corporate suite of models to a point at which it is too elaborate for management to understand or requires information not easily available on a routine basis. In either event it is likely to be shelved. The ultimate criterion for success of a corporate model is not its internal efficiency or sophistication, but the positive contribution it is seen to make in the process of management decision-making.

References

1   Gershefski, G. W.; *The development and application of a corporate financial model.* Planning Executives Institute, Oxford (Ohio) 1968.

2   Grinyer, P. H. and Batt, C. D.; Some tentative findings on corporate financial simulation models. *Operational Research Quarterly,* March 1974.

3   *McKinsey and Company Inc.,* 1968, pp. 1–38. Reprinted in McRae, T. W. (Editor), *Management information systems.* Penguin Books 1971.

Chapter 7

Bureaux packages

7.1 Importance of packages

In Chapter 2 we saw that bureaux offer packages of two distinct kinds. First, a number offer 'ready-made models', which require no programming before being put into use, but which are not widely used. These are discussed more fully in Section 7.2.

The second kind of package is the so-called modelling system, which falls between a general-purpose language such as FORTRAN and a ready-made model. Like the general-purpose language, it is used to develop tailor-made corporate models for the company, but provides special routines to facilitate this exercise. Availability and sophistication of these modelling systems have grown rapidly since 1970. Before that time, most corporate models were built in general-purpose languages, but even so, over half the companies included in our survey had used modelling systems. As many of the models covered by the survey were built before 1970, when few good modelling systems were available, it is apparent that the majority of models built since then have used modelling systems.

In Section 7.3 examples are given of such systems; their general advantages and disadvantages are discussed and differences for which prospective users should look are analysed.

7.2 Ready-made models

Ready-made models are available from a number of bureaux. A ready-made model is a single program or a suite of programs to which the user has access, on agreed financial terms, either via a terminal to a bureau or on his own computer. Frequently, the user is not given details of the logic of the programs, or model, and hence cannot modify it to meet his particular needs. Even when details of the program are available, the costs of mastering it and making appropriate modifications are normally so great that it is preferable to write a new tailor-made program.

So, ready-made models are virtually 'black boxes' into which data is input in the stipulated form and from which reports are generated in an equally fixed, pre-prescribed format. Because of this the ready-made model must have logic, inputs and outputs which are fairly generally applicable to companies. This restricts ready-made models, in most cases, to the mapping of financial flows by use of accounting logic. Furthermore, many of them are restricted in their range of applications to situations where their logic, inputs and outputs are appropriate.

This may be illustrated by reference to the suite of one bureau. Its simplest model focuses on revenue and costs. A company may be broken down into a number of groups, or divisions, each containing a number of products. Revenue, costs and stocks are input for each product, and results are aggregated to corporate level. This model is appropriate for preparing profit plans, analysing mixes of products and showing the effects of changing costs, prices and market sizes.

A separate model produces a complete financial forecast for a company from aggregate income and expense figures. Relevant profit and loss account and balance sheet items are considered and interrelated, and flows of funds are netted out to give the cumulative funds requirement or surplus in each period. Additional reports show cash flows, source and use of funds and financial ratio analyses. The model so enables financial requirements to be identified and permits extensive analysis of alternative strategies provided they can be expressed in aggregate financial terms. A variant of this model takes input of the most important factors as triple estimates (most likely, optimistic and pessimistic). Instead of specific financial statements, the output is a report showing the odds of reaching certain profits and financial positions, which gives management some indication of risk inherent in the alternatives tested.

A further model is available to consolidate financial results produced by these forecasting models or, indeed, independent estimates. By repeated operation of the model, consolidation to subsidiary and then holding company level may be undertaken, if required, and inter-company activity may be eliminated as necessary. This

Figure 7.1 Example of an input form for a ready-made model

COMPANY NAME: _____

DATA FILE NAME: /_____/

1 QUARTERS OF OUTPUT DESIRED   – –A01
How many quarters of output do you want?
(Use 2 digits in response; e.g. normally all
five years would be required, so the answer
would be 20.)

2 FIRST YEAR OF STATEMENTS   – – – –A02
What is the first year of the output reports,
e.g. 1980 is entered as 1980.

ASSETS

		N/O Ent.	Code	First Quarter	Second Quarter	Third Quarter	Fourth Quarter
3	CASH	–	A03	01 .	02 .	03 .	04 .
	What are the *ratios* of			05 .	06 .	07 .	08 .
	Cash to Net Quarter's			09 .	10 .	11 .	12 .
	Sales?			13 .	14 .	15 .	16 .
	(e.g. if ratio was 20% of			17 .	18 .	19 .	20 .
	this quarter's sales,						
	enter .20)						
4	DEBTORS	–	A04	01 .	02 .	03 .	04 .
	What are the *ratios* of			05 .	06 .	07 .	08 .
	Debtors to Net Quarterly			09 .	10 .	11 .	12 .
	Sales?			13 .	14 .	15 .	16 .
				17 .	18 .	19 .	20 .
5	PREPAID EXPENSES	–	A05	01 .	02 .	03 .	04 .
	What are the *ratios* of			05 .	06 .	07 .	08 .
	Prepaid Expenses to			09 .	10 .	11 .	12 .
	Total Assets?			13 .	14 .	15 .	16 .
				17 .	18 .	19 .	20 .

6 RAW MATERIALS STOCKS – OPENING _____ A06
What is the opening balance of Raw Materials Stocks?

model can also be used for cross-functional analysis. For example, divisions may be consolidated by country and by function.

Although there is a limited amount of flexibility of logic in some of these models, it is still true that, like all ready-made models, their basic features are fixed logic and standard form of inputs and outputs. To illustrate this, *Figure 7.1* shows the way the user may write input, *Figure 7.2* the output reports he might expect from a 'typical' ready-made model and *Figure 7.3* a list of output reports which might be received from a more sophisticated ready-made model. *Figure 7.4* shows examples of output reports for one of the models.

Figure 7.2   List of output reports received from a 'typical' ready-made model

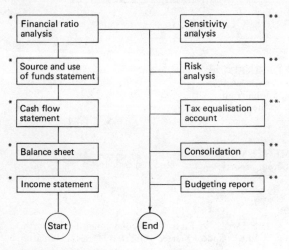

*Produced automatically

**Can be suppressed at option of user

From these it may be seen that ready-made models are suitable for use by accountants or managers without programming experience. Indeed, although rarely more than figure consolidators or 'crunchers', they can provide a useful tool to companies so small that they do not even boast an accountant. Their use is not, though, restricted to small companies. One of the more sophisticated ready-made models has users in the £50 million-plus turnover bracket.

Ready-made models are often relatively cheap because the fixed cost of development may be spread between users. Fairly typical charges for a ready-made model for use on a time-sharing computer are £1,500 for introduction or access, and £100 per day for consultancy, as may be seen from Appendix 2 on financial modelling packages. Estimated operating costs quoted to us varied, £125 per month was fairly typical, but we heard of small companies with annual costs below £500.

A further advantage is immediate availability where time is of the essence. If a company sees a takeover threat or opportunity looming, a ready-made model may be 'Hobson's choice'.

Those very features which give ready-made models their distinctive advantages also limit their value. The inflexibility that makes programming unnecessary is restrictive. It may not be economic to adapt the standard logic of the model to reflect accurately any unusual operations and accounting conventions of the company. Similarly the model may be unable to accommodate changes in tax or company law. A number of applications thought important by the company may be beyond the scope of the model. Inflexible input requirements may create difficulties or otherwise unnecessary costs of data collection may be incurred. The layout of output reports, and indeed in some cases their content, may be unfamiliar to management and so increase difficulty of use. Finally, even where there is a certain amount of flexibility of logic, for example, the number of subsidiaries or divisions for which figures are consolidated may be varied, there are inevitable limitations on the number of inputs and outputs. Size restrictions may, therefore, be important. *(Continued on page 94.)*

Figure 7.3   List of output reports received from a sophisticated ready-made model

1   *Short-range planning*

Part	1	Profit and loss analysis
	2	Balance sheet analysis
	3	Sources of capital employed
	4	The pricing record
	5	Marketing efficiency
	6	Production – Productivity
	7	Overhead controls
	8	Management performance
	9	Investment and liquidity standards

Summaries

A	Profit and loss analysis
B	Balance sheet analysis
C	Management performance
D	Liquidity controls
E	Investment and liquidity standards

2   *Long-range planning*

3   *Monitoring accounting* (budgeting)

Figure 7.4 Typical output reports from ready-made models

Example Group Limited Illustrative Projections Income Statements Pounds 000s	**Income Statements**					
	1980	**1981**	**1982**	**1983**	**1984**	**1985**
1 Sales	65172	70910	77150	80310	84750	89140
2 Direct materials	33556	37582	40504	42163	44494	46799
3 Direct labour	11651	13827	15430	14456	15255	16045
4 Manufact overheads	3947	4184	4435	4701	4983	5282
10 Depreciation*	5117	5649	6269	6597	6970	7360
13 Cost of goods sold	54271	61243	66638	67916	71702	75486
14 Gross profit	10901	9667	10512	12394	13048	13654
20 Selling expense	1273	1385	1507	1569	1655	1741
21 Admin expense	1541	1618	1699	1784	1873	1967
22 R & D	675	734	799	832	878	923
24 Operating profit	7412	5930	6507	8210	8642	9023
33 Investment income	824	824	824	824	824	824
36 Royalties	312	339	369	384	406	427
47 Interest payable	1612	1499	2166	2275	1938	1717
48 Pretax profit	6312	4915	4796	6374	7122	7703
50 Tax	2197	1636	1589	2220	2519	2752
54 Net profit	4115	3279	3207	4154	4603	4951
60 Minority interests	215	170	167	216	239	257
61 Exceptional items	200	100	−197	0	0	0
92 Disposals−P/L	0	50	−45	0	0	0
62 Preference dividend	40	40	40	40	40	40
63 Earnings	4060	3218	2758	3898	4323	4654
65 Ordinary dividend	2710	2710	2710	2710	2860	3042
66 Retentions	1350	508	48	1188	1463	1612
11 * Depn plant etc.	4920	5452	6072	6400	6758	7133
12 * Depn land & buildings	197	197	197	197	212	227

Example Group Limited **Financial Ratios**
Illustrative Projections
Financial Ratios

	1980	**1981**	**1982**	**1983**	**1984**	**1985**
1 Gross profit + depn/sales	0.246	0.216	0.218	0.236	0.236	0.236
2 Gross profit/sales	0.167	0.136	0.136	0.154	0.154	0.153
3 Operating profit/sales	0.114	0.084	0.084	0.102	0.102	0.101
4 Pretax pft + int/sales	0.122	0.090	0.090	0.108	0.107	0.106
5 Gross op asset/sales	1.266	1.273	1.287	1.295	1.306	1.303
6 Depn/gross op asset	0.062	0.063	0.063	0.063	0.063	0.063
7 Pretax pft + int/av cap empl	0.124	0.094	0.094	0.111	0.117	0.123
8 Pretax pft + int/av tot asset	0.103	0.079	0.079	0.093	0.097	0.101
9 Curr asset/curr liab	1.796	1.896	1.946	1.967	1.893	1.848
10 Curr asset − stock/curr liab	0.772	0.796	0.816	0.792	0.802	0.781
11 Working capital/sales	0.208	0.209	0.210	0.227	0.213	0.210
12 Sales/debtors	6.780	6.780	6.780	6.780	6.780	6.780
13 Cost goods sold/stock	4.046	4.049	4.049	3.704	4.049	4.049
14 Cred/cost goods sold + inc stock	0.171	0.171	0.171	0.171	0.171	0.171
15 Fixed asset/total asset	0.699	0.692	0.693	0.671	0.671	0.654
16 Equity cap/total asset	0.631	0.589	0.540	0.547	0.584	0.601
17 Equity cap/cap employed	0.757	0.703	0.641	0.657	0.707	0.740
18 L debt+pref cap+minrty/cap empl	0.233	0.215	0.236	0.237	0.214	0.221
19 Overdraft + def funds/cap empl	0.000	0.072	0.113	0.097	0.071	0.032
20 Equ cap + pref cap +l debt/l debt	4.833	4.872	4.149	4.223	4.931	5.046
21 Pretax profit + int/int	4.916	4.278	3.214	3.801	4.674	5.486
22 Ret + depn/inc op ass + inc wkg cap	0.856	0.529	0.470	1.187	1.317	1.476
23 E.P.S.I (incl excpt itm)	0.189	0.150	0.128	0.181	0.190	0.205
24 E.P.S. II (excl excpt itm)	0.180	0.143	0.140	0.181	0.190	0.205
25 E.P.S. III (II fully diluted)	0.170	0.140	0.137	0.177	0.190	0.205
26 Div cover (on E.P.S. II)	1.424	1.132	1.107	1.438	1.512	1.530
27 Earn incl excpt itm/av equ cap	0.083	0.065	0.055	0.077	0.082	0.084
28 E.P.S. II growth	0.000	−0.205	−0.022	0.299	0.051	0.076
29 Div per share growth	0.000	0.000	0.000	0.000	0.000	0.063

Figure 7.5 A sophisticated ready-made model

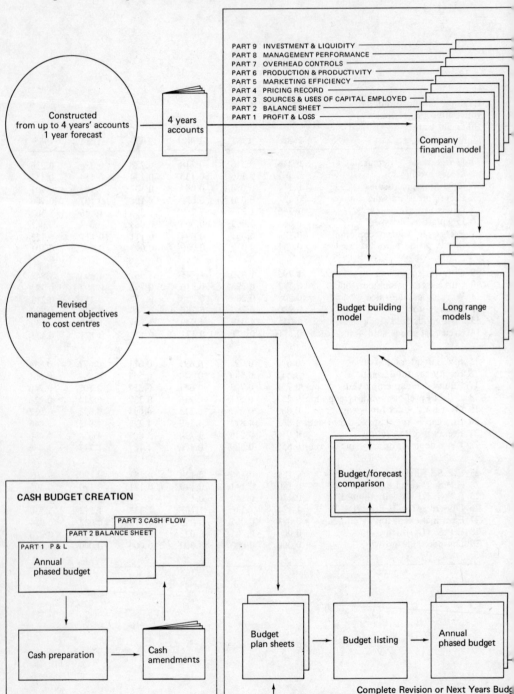

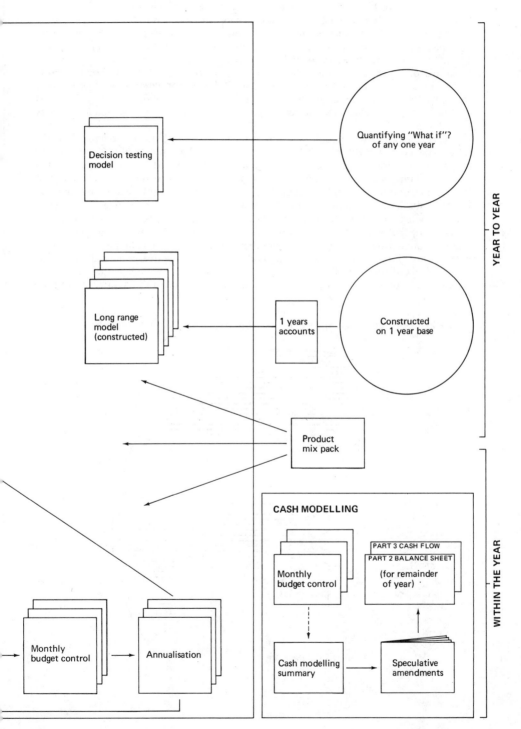

A number of bureaux have sought to overcome these disadvantages of inflexibility, to some extent at least, by building greater flexibility into their models. Some permit a degree of flexibility of logic, input, and output by use of redundant items and control parameters. For example, in the ready-made model illustrated in *Figure 7.5*, sets of alternative routines are available for most accounting operations. For instance, a number of alternative methods for calculating depreciation, contribution to profit, and so on are available in the model. By use of the appropriate control parameters, those routines which represent the accounting conventions of the company most faithfully may be selected, and a ready-made model closer to a tailor-made one may be obtained.

It is generally true, though, that the provision of these kinds of flexibility greatly inflates the cost of developing the ready-made model. An estimate of £160,000 to date has been given for development of the model mentioned in the last paragraph. This means that charges made to companies using it must necessarily be higher than for a less flexible and much simpler model. In addition, user company accounting routines must be studied, and the set of options that best represent them selected. Consequently, consultants from the bureau or internal staff are required to undertake much of the work that would have been involved in developing the logic for a tailor-made model, though programming by the user company is avoided. The limitations inherent in the inflexibility of many ready-made models can, then, be overcome only at a cost.

To find out why so few companies had used ready-made models we asked them to allocate 100 points between possible reasons, and calculated the average rating for

Figure 7.6 Aspects deterring modellers from use of ready-made models

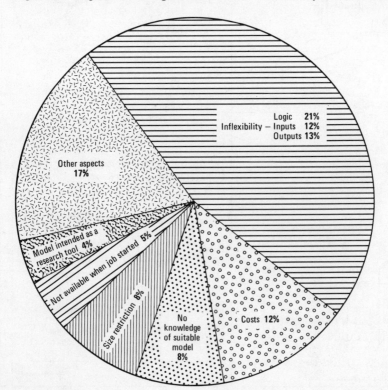

each reason. The results are shown in *Figure 7.6*. They indicate that inflexibility and costs were the major deterrents. This emphasis on costs might be partly explained by the fact that some of the costs of developing a tailor-made model are often hidden. For example, an accountant working part-time on a corporate model may not have any of his salary charged to the development project. However, this can be no more than a very partial explanation as many modellers were fully aware of the costs of building tailor-made corporate models, but still regarded ready-made models as expensive for what they would do. We have insufficient objective evidence to either support or refute this view and can only report that it seemed to be fairly widespread. Three per cent of the survey companies used ready-made models and did not consider them expensive. However, it is difficult to say whether or not they were representative of all users. In each case we were put in touch with the user by the bureau concerned. Unfortunately, our random survey did not produce any users of ready-made models.

The importance of these disadvantages is suggested by the very fact that so few companies use ready-made models. None the less, it would be unreasonable to reject them out of hand, for there are many situations where they could be the best choice. Small companies in particular may find them preferable to developing their own model, with the attendant demands on staff time, skill and patience. Moreover, now that ready-made models with considerable inbuilt flexibility are available, the limitations of the old-style inflexible packages are greatly reduced. They may still be unsuitable on technical or cost grounds for any particular company but are certainly worth considering.

·3   Modelling systems

Modelling systems are special programming languages which use computer routines designed specifically for planning applications. For instance, one system has routines which permit different items of data to be summed, differences between consecutive years to be calculated, and present values to be obtained. The way each of these, respectively, is called into use is illustrated below:

```
190    DIRECT COSTS = SUM (COST OF MATERIALS, LABOUR COSTS)
200    MATERIAL COST INCREASE = DIFF (COST OF MATERIALS)
210    NPV = PV (CASH FLOW, 10.0)
```

In statement 210, in which the net present value is calculated, CASH FLOW refers to data held on files by the computer, and 10.0 is the discount rate.

A notable feature of these examples is that there is no mention of time. Yet these simple statements lead to operations being performed for each of a previously specified number of periods. This highlights one of the most useful features of modelling systems, the automatic handling of time, which makes their use simpler than that of general-purpose languages. To illustrate the differences, the examples given above are programmed in FORTRAN. In the FORTRAN version, the lines of the program instruct the computer to perform an operation for only one period of time, T, and statement 180 leads the computer to execute all the statements between it and statement 220 for periods 1 to 6 consecutively.

```
180    DO 220 T = 1,6
190    DIRECTCOST (T) = MATERIALCOST (T) + LABOURCOST (T)
200    IF (T.EQ. 1) GO TO 220
210    MATERIALCOSTINCREASE (T) = MATERIALCOST (T) −
       MATERIALCOST (T-1)
220    NPV(T) = CASHFLOW (T)/(1+0.10) ** T)
230    CONTINUE
```

95

Comparison of this with the modelling system version reveals how dealing with time has added a further degree of complexity. This becomes even more important when the model is large and complicated.

Nearly all modelling systems have inbuilt arrangements for dealing with time and all give access to sets of standard routines which may be used by the modeller in his model of the company's operations. As has been seen from the examples, some of these routines perform calculations that may be required at a number of different points within the logic of a corporate model, and are analogous to the standard mathematical routines available in general-purpose languages like FORTRAN. Other widely available routines fall into four broad categories:

- Those to help the user prepare forecasts and input data.
- Those to consolidate data and produce standard financial reports.
- Those to print out these reports.
- Others that control the manner in which the model operates.

The way these standard routines are related in one of the systems is illustrated, as an example, in *Figure 7.7*.

Aids to preparation of data include standard forecasting routines. Many of the modelling systems give their users a comprehensive armoury of mathematical and statistical techniques for extrapolating trends from past data. A detailed account of what each of the main systems offers is to be found in Appendix 2. Such statistical 'packages' are also, it should be noted, available to users of models programmed in general-purpose languages but run on bureaux computers.

So long as the user recognises their limitations, there is no doubt that these aids to forecasting can be useful. The conditions that shaped the past are always liable to change in the future and a forecast based on nothing more than extrapolation may prove to be worthless. Automatically produced forecasts must therefore be scrutinised carefully by those who understand the business conditions that underlie patterns of past data and how these might change in the future. The fact that this is rarely necessary for short-term forecasts for production or stock control purposes, unless there is a major and persistent deviation from forecast, should not blind us to the fact that judgement is more important than mathematical sophistication or precision where long-range forecasts are concerned.

Not only do modelling systems provide aids to forecasting input data, they have inbuilt routines for reading input into files held by the computer and its peripheral storage facilities (such as discs). Such routines are available, too, to users of bureaux computers with general-purpose language models. The importance of routines of this kind can be seen by examining the ATV example in Chapter 6. Even in this simple model, a considerable amount of programming was necessary to deal with input, so it is not difficult to imagine the size and complexity of general-purpose language routines to read several thousand input variables.

Once files of input data have been established, they need to be corrected, modified and updated, to allow for errors, changed assumptions as new alternatives are tested, and further information available with the passage of time. Those systems run in conversational mode normally have editing facilities to aid this process. The user can call for the contents of any file to be shown on his terminal, and can then correct, modify or update items as he wishes. For instance, in one modelling system 'DELETE: 20, 33, 41 TO 60' would instruct the computer to remove line 20, line 33, and lines 41 through 60. Similarly, 'MODIFY: 30 (2, 1983, 3000, 1984, 4000)' would lead to the two values 3,000 and 4,000 replacing those already on file for 1983 and 1984 respectively in line 30 of the file. At the option of the user, in most systems, these changes may be temporary, the original file remaining intact throughout the whole of the computer run, or may be made permanent. In the latter case the file held on disc, drum or other suitable storage medium for the next run of the model is modified and the old data is lost. Again, like forecasting and data inputting routines, these editing

Figure 7.7 The structure of a modelling system

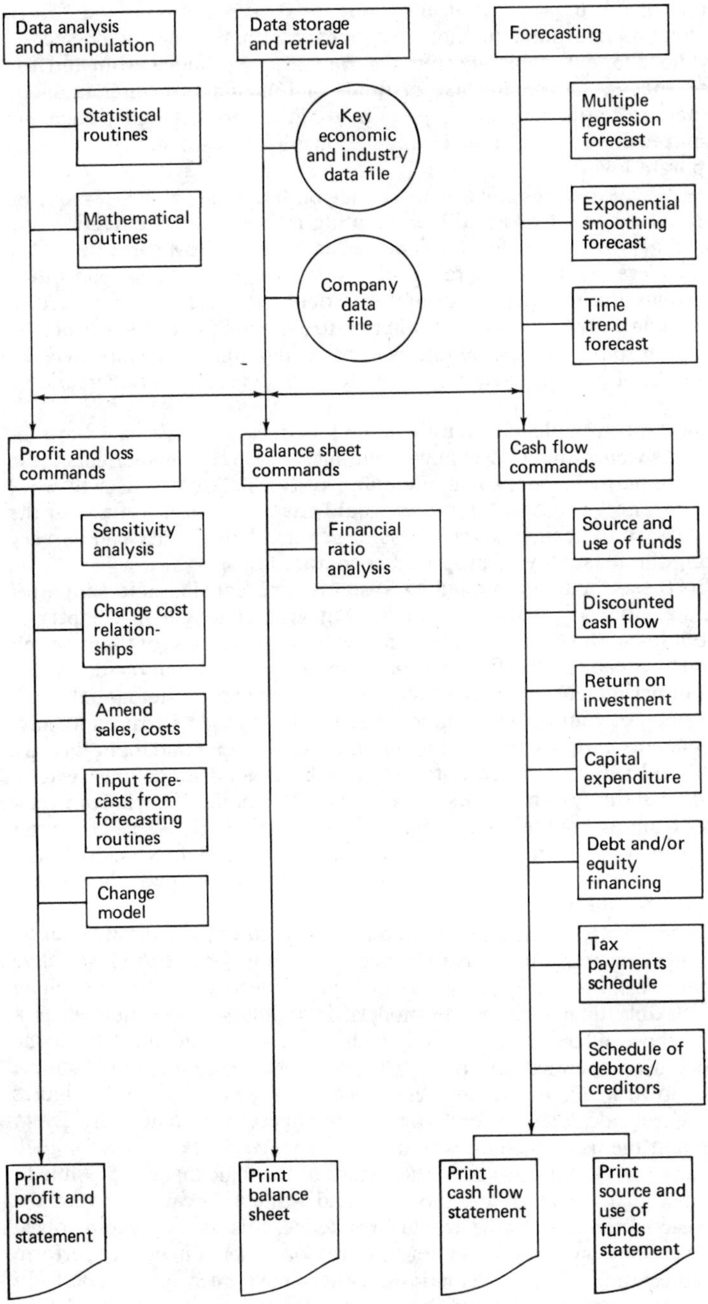

facilities of modelling systems are normally available where general-purpose language models are used on a bureau computer.

The value of these aids to preparation and input of data is perhaps obvious. Even so, they are matched in importance, in most instances, by the routines in the second category, namely those for automatically *consolidating* data to produce profit and loss accounts, balance sheets, source and use of funds statements and other financial reports. These standard routines remove a great deal of the detailed logic design and programming required in a model that involves consolidation of data from, say, divisional to corporate level.

The third category of routines can greatly reduce both the time and cost required to develop a corporate model by virtually eliminating the tedious specification and programming of *output content and format*. The better systems allow some flexibility of output format to users, who can program their models to produce any report they require. All the systems give the user choice of the particular reports to be produced on any given run. This is achieved by means of either control parameters which direct the computer to the output routines it should follow or by responding to questions via the terminal. The latter is, of course, used only when the model is run in conversational mode.

The most important example of a routine in the fourth category is 'backward' or 'reverse iteration'. As well as allowing changes in input data, to see what effects these would have on future performance, some modelling systems allow the user to work 'backwards'. For instance, backward iteration would enable the user to find out the levels of sales necessary to achieve given levels of profits. This facility can be very useful for exploring the feasibility of proposed corporate objectives.

In addition to these facilities, modelling systems give considerable scope for interlinking separate models, a subject dealt with at greater length in Chapter 3. Though the capabilities of the different modelling systems vary, most of them permit models to be linked by means of disc files. Output from one model is put on file, which may be temporary or permanent, and this is then used as input to the other model. Such interlinking is possible, of course, with a tailor-made suite of models written in, say, FORTRAN. It demands care in ensuring that the format of output and input files are the same, though, and this is handled automatically by a good modelling system. Moreover, with some of the systems the user may, where the model is run in conversational mode, move from one model to another and back again in the same computer run; for instance, from a profit and loss model to a cash flow model. No model built without use of a modelling system has, to the best of our knowledge, given this facility to the user. The cost would be prohibitive.

Against these advantages must be set a number of attendant disadvantages. Reasons why a number of companies have rejected modelling systems are instructive in this respect. They are shown in *Figure 7.8*. Although it is recognised that modelling systems are more flexible than ready-made models, inflexibility is still quoted as a weakness. Some of those interviewed referred to difficulties that stemmed from the way the system they used operated on only a 'row' basis. For example, in the simple forecasting model shown in *Figure 1.1* and reproduced as *Figure 7.9* the sales figures for all the years were calculated before any of the figures for materials. Every accountant knows that the usual method would be to produce all the figures for 1978 before calculating any for 1979. In this case, the nature of the logic made it possible to operate on a row basis. If, however, the modeller had wanted to carry forward the profits from one year to the next, as he would in practice, this would have involved 'column' operations. Some systems have, for this reason, been unable to perform straightforward depreciation or tax calculations. Others have been able to perform them only by complex manipulations of the system. Fortunately, some modelling systems work on the more acceptable 'column' basis, whilst a few can use either at the option of the user.

Figure 7.8 Aspects deterring modellers from use of modelling systems

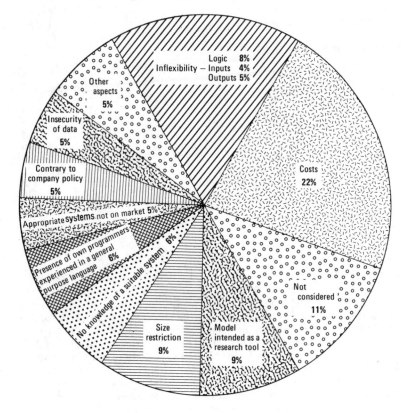

Figure 7.9 Example of a simple forecasting model

Section (a) – Accounting data and logic (in £000s)

Sales for 1977	=	2,000
Sales for subsequent years	=	Sales for 1977 × growth factor of 10%
Materials	=	Sales × 30%
Wages	=	Sales × 20%
Other charges	=	200 + (sales × 5%)
Depreciation	=	100
Loan interest	=	10
Expenses	=	Materials + wages + other charges + depreciation + loan interest
Net profit before tax	=	Sales − expenses
Tax	=	Net profit × 50%
Net profit after tax	=	Net profit − tax

(Figure continued on next page)

Figure 7.9   continued

Section (b) – Computer print-out of results

FORECAST PROFIT AND LOSS ACCOUNTS

	1978	1979	1980	1981	1982
SALES	2200.	2420.	2662.	2928.	3221.
MATERIALS	660.	726.	799.	878.	966.
WAGES	440.	484.	532.	586.	644.
OTHER CHARGES	310.	321.	333.	346.	361.
DEPRECIATION	100.	100.	100.	100.	100.
LOAN INTEREST	10.	10.	10.	10.	10.
PRE-TAX PROFIT	680.	779.	888.	1008.	1139.
TAX	340.	390.	444.	504.	570.
AFTER-TAX PROFIT	340.	390.	444.	504.	570.

    High costs of access and computer use were also heavily stressed as a disadvantage of modelling systems. In some instances, a high access fee may be charged. In others no initial charge is made, but operation of the system is tied to use of a bureau computer, and a higher computer cost of operating the model may be incurred for this reason alone. Furthermore, a number of users have suggested that some bureaux increase the computer 'run time' charges to users of modelling systems to recover their development costs. Unfortunately, an assessment of the extent of such increases, if any, and relative costs of operating available modelling systems, can only be gained by experimental development of models in a number of modelling systems. A few companies have done this, at fairly considerable cost, but are unwilling to have the results published. Such experiments are welcomed by many bureaux who will often render considerable assistance and also waive access fees in the hope of getting future business.

    Even where no additional charge is levied in this disguised form by the bureau for use of the modelling system, it is still true that computer run time is usually greater than for a model programmed efficiently in a general-purpose language, and the costs of operation tend to be higher for this reason alone.

    It does not follow from these points, though, that the total cost of developing and operating a model with a modelling system is necessarily greater. Savings on development and updating may far outweigh additional computer running costs during operation. Where a model is to be used infrequently, for *ad hoc* decisions, or for very few runs during an annual planning cycle, the economics of development and operation normally favour the modelling system. This is especially so where the relationships in the model need frequent revision. On the other hand, when a large number of runs are to be undertaken on a fairly routine basis, and the relationships in the model are stable over time (e.g. accounting conventions), use of a general-purpose language may be cheaper.

    Figure 7.8 shows a heavy emphasis, too, on the size restrictions imposed by most modelling systems. Time spans may be limited, ranging from five forecasting periods to any number specified by the user. The number of variables that can be handled by the system may also be limited, as may the maximum number of program statements. Even where no upper limit is set in the literature on the modelling system, one exists in practice, because the storage capacity of the computer is immense but not infinite.

These physical limits vary from computer to computer and apply equally to all programs and languages run. However, modelling systems use more of the computer's internal storage capacity (core store) than general-purpose languages, to store the programs that convert the programming statements of the model into the form that the computer executes. This leaves less core store for the model itself.

Further disadvantages mentioned by a number of companies stemmed from the fact that the modelling system may tie them to a particular bureau. To change bureaux usually means changing modelling systems and hence jettisoning the corporate model already developed. A number of users said that, once their models were well developed, the quality of service from the bureau to which they had then become tied declined.

This criticism was not levelled at a single bureau but seemed more general. The complaints might, of course, have imaginary causes but were strong enough to induce several companies to consider changing to another bureau. We were intrigued to find, on visiting two separate firms on two consecutive days, that each intended to switch to the bureau currently used by the other. Both gave poor service from the bureau as their reason. Such complaints were not frequent, though, and the majority of modelling system users were satisfied with the service they received from the bureaux.

7.4 *Choice of package*

The potential user of packages from bureaux will find himself confronted by a wide range of different packages. Relative advantages and disadvantages of each package can become increasingly obscure amidst the clamour of competing claims by bureaux salesmen.

Before so many modelling systems were available it was possible to test virtually all of them by running the same set of instructions with each. Such tests are called 'bench-mark tests'. The few systems which then seemed most promising could be subjected to more exhaustive testing. A more ambitious set of instructions, amounting to a simple, but typical, model were run. These 'test runs' allowed the potential user to gain quite a lot of information about the capabilities and limitations of the alternative systems. However, they are expensive. Few firms would now find it economic to subject many of the modelling systems available to such tests. Companies must normally be content with bench-mark testing only a short-list of systems before making a final decision.

How then should this short-list be selected? There is much to commend an approach whereby comprehensive, relevant information is collected and analysed systematically as a basis for comparison of the packages. As an aid to such an approach, a checklist is given in *Figure 7.10*. The questions in this checklist have been ordered with two principles in mind. First, they narrow from general aspects such as the range of applications, mode of operation, and so on, to much more detailed points about special facilities that are offered. Some of the later material, say on special facilities, may be of little interest to the non-computer specialist. Second, they move from issues so fundamental that they may lead to rejection of the package, to issues of secondary importance. However, costs are dealt with at the end of our sequence of questions because we think that it would be a mistake for the potential user to allow cost to bias him against a package before he knows what he would be getting for his money.

A considerable amount of effort is involved in collection and analysis of such information on packages. To help the reader in this respect, we have undertaken an analysis of most of the packages currently available in the UK, all of the major ones certainly being included. The results of this survey are given in Appendix 2. Because this is a rapidly developing field, those seriously interested in taking the matter further should contact the bureaux concerned, and find out whether the details have changed.

Use of the checklist, and the survey results appropriately updated, should provide a sound basis for selecting members of an initial short-list for more detailed investigation. Members of this short-list can be further checked by means of telephone calls and visits to other companies using them. Ideally, these visits should be arranged by disinterested contacts, to avoid the natural bias towards satisfied clients when bureaux make the arrangements. Even so, where the only way to get in touch with users is through the bureaux, it is certainly worth making visits arranged by them. Our own experience is that a lot is to be learnt from even satisfied clients nominated by bureaux about the limitations as well as the good features of the packages they are using.

Finally, once the short-list has been pared to a few packages, bench-mark tests can be undertaken on those remaining. Ultimately, the decision to adopt a package should be based on experience of its use, no matter how limited this may be.

We turn to a more general treatment of choice of corporate model in Chapter 11.

Figure 7.10 Checklist for selection of short-list of packages

Information category	Question	Purpose of question
1 Type of package	Is it a ready-made model or a modelling system?	To eliminate modelling systems if user wishes to avoid all model building effort or eliminate ready-made models if a tailored model is required.
2 Purpose of package	Is the package designed to facilitate: Financial planning (up to 1 year)? How? Financial planning (1 to 5 years)? How? Financial planning (over 5 years)? How? Project evaluation? How? Cash flow analysis? How? Production decisions? How? Marketing decisions? How?	To ensure that the package will be suitable for intended purpose (in a general way at least).
3 Hardware requirements	Can the system be used on an in-house computer or only on a bureau computer?	The firm may wish to use its own computer, for a variety of reasons, though in some companies this may not be an important factor.
	If on an in-house computer, which, and what peripherals are needed?	Most packages are designed for use with given makes of computer and other hardware. The potential user might as well find out whether he has the right computer equipment before going further!
	If a bureau computer, which bureau, and what equipment is used?	This will give some indication of the reliability of bureau service to which we turn below.

Information category	Question	Purpose of question
4 *Mode of operation*	Is the mode of operation of the package: Batch? Remote batch? Conversational?	Some packages give freedom for use in a number of different modes. Thus, for instance, conversational mode may be used for urgent, *ad hoc* planning (to reduce
	What would be the approximate cost of operating the model in the available modes?	turnaround time), whilst the cheaper batch mode may be used for longer, routine planning runs. It is worth finding out about these possibilities before committing oneself to a system.
5 *Reliability of bureau service*	How long has the bureau been established? Who are its external financial backers if it is new or small? What is its financial standing?	To check on continuity of service.
	How many customers has the bureau for its modelling system? How long has the modelling system been available?	New or little used computer systems (software) normally contain mistakes ('bugs') which are discovered by clients during use. After a system has been in use for some while, and by a reasonable number of customers, it is likely to be more reliable. It does not follow from this, of course, that all new and unused systems contain 'bugs', but the user should take this possibility into account.
	How reliable have other users of the modelling system, and bureau, found the service? Could we talk to them?	The proof of the pudding is in the eating. The prospective user might as well find out how well those who have eaten have been satisfied!
	How many computers has the bureau? What back-up facilities has the bureau in the event of a computer failure?	The company may want to run a model urgently at a time when there is a computer failure at the bureau.
	How many branches has the bureau and where are they located?	It is often useful to visit the bureau, or receive a visit from its staff, in the event of difficulties. Geographic proximity helps in this respect. Where there is a convenient network of offices it may help subsidiary companies, etc., to have access to the model. *(Continued)*

Information category	Question	Purpose of question
5 *Reliability of bureau service*	What provision for security of data has the bureau in terms of, first, avoiding accidental erasing of files and, second, preventing access to them by unauthorised persons? In the latter case, how frequently are code words or numbers changed, and how long would it take the brightest computer experts of a competitor to break the code?	Security of data is immensely important and provision for it needs to be checked. Most bureaux have adequate arrangements but it is worth making sure.
6 *General service available*	What after-sales support is available to users and for how long?	The extent of after sales service varies from zero to quite considerable help in getting a model set up and running. In some cases there is a time limit on free support but, where bureaux are used on a conversational basis, this is not normally so.
	Are training courses provided? If so, what are their lengths, what are they designed to do, will they meet the needs of the company, and what do they cost?	New users often find that manuals are an inadequate basis for use and benefit from training courses. But these vary widely in availability and quality. In many cases they are available to new users free of charge as an after-sales service.
	Are consulting services available from the bureau and at what cost?	Some companies find it useful to have outside help while they familiarise themselves with the package. Technical advice is given by most bureaux free of charge, but those that provide assistance in model building normally levy a consultancy fee.
7 *General capabilities of the package*	Does the system allow interlinking of models by use of disc files: In a given computer run? Between computer runs?	An interlinking facility permits a modular approach to developing the corporate suite, and each module is useful in itself as an independent model.
	Does the system give ability to transfer between models during a computer run?	This kind of flexibility can be useful when a suite of models is run in conversational mode.

Information category	Question	Purpose of question
	Does the system require interlinked models to be run in a fixed sequence or is there freedom for the user to change the sequence?	
	Can the user change the logic of the model? If so, how, and how easily?	Flexibility of model logic is normally imperative if the model is to truly reflect the unique operations and accounting conventions of the company. Moreover, the model usually needs to be updated if it is to remain valid.
	Does the system give the user ability to apply constant or parameter controlled growth rates to input data without having to code them into the model?	The ability to apply constants is useful where input data consists of foreign currencies which have to be standardised to a common currency unit, for example, £s. Use of growth rates is extremely useful in cutting down input data required, for example, to specify a rate of increase to cover inflationary factors.
	Does the package make unnecessary programming of input formats and instructions for reading input into the computer? Similarly, how much programming is required to provide the output reports required?	Where such facilities exist, as they normally do in the better systems, the costs of programming are greatly reduced.
	Has the user choice of: Output reports printed? Format of output reports? Sequence of output reports?	The sequence of output reports can be important where it is likely that urgent call may be made for different reports at certain times. It can be very frustrating to have to wait for profit and loss and balance sheet to be printed out if one just wants to check, say, key management ratios. Likewise, it is useful to have the facility to print out only the reports required. Formatting can be important if some non-detailed reports are required for presentation to management, but also detailed reports are required at other times.

(Continued)

Information category	Question	Purpose of question
7 General capabilities of the package	Does the package operate on a 'row' or 'column' updating basis or both? What problems would only row or only column operations present to the modellers?	'Row' operation means that the system calculates the values of each variable for all time periods up to the time horizon before passing on to the next variable. 'Column' operation means that the value of every variable is calculated for each time period before the computer passes to the next period. Where the logic is mainly consolidation, 'row' operations suffice and will invariably be more efficient, but they are less suitable for models where variable values in later time periods are highly interconnected with a number of other variable values in earlier periods. Column operation is then preferable. As mentioned in the text, some modelling systems have been unable to perform straightforward depreciation or tax calculations.
8 Size restrictions	What time periods are handled: months, quarters, years, any? What is the maximum number of time periods?	Where the company's activities tend to be seasonal management may desire quarterly reports. Hence a model handling years only will be of little practical use. On the other hand, when the time horizon exceeds five years it would seem ludicrous, in view of the uncertainties necessarily prevailing, to model in time periods of less than a year.
	What is the maximum number of: Input variables? Output variables? Program statements?	The package should permit the user to build a model of the requisite size. It should be borne in mind that where interlinking of models is facilitated the limits may be determined only by the power of the computer.

Information category	Question	Purpose of question
9 *Special facilities available*	Are the following facilities available: Backward iteration? Output of reports as graphs? Output of reports as histograms? Discounted cash flow calculation? Automatic sensitivity analysis? Significance testing routines? Consolidation routines? Others wanted by the company?	Facilities vary between systems. The user may not want those listed, some of which are widely found among modelling systems, but it is obviously worth finding out the capabilities of the systems.
	Does the package allow *probabilistic* models to be developed? If so, how does it operate? Is it relatively easy for the modeller to include any distributions he wishes to use?	Although probabilistic models may not be useful to the company immediately, it may have plans to use them at some future time.
	What *forecasting techniques* are available: Linear regression? Multiple regression? Curve fitting (least squares)? Power series? Arithmetic progression? Geometric progression? Moving averages? Exponential smoothing? Step functions? How appropriate are such techniques to the needs of the company?	Forecasting techniques are probably less important than the demonstrations of bureaux lead the potential user to believe. None the less, they can be useful aids, as long as they remain secondary to use of knowledge and judgement about changes in the business environment. However, some techniques are more appropriate to short-term than to long-term forecasting, for example, exponential smoothing.
	Is the company likely to want *optimising* facilities in the package? If so, are the following optimising techniques available in the package: Optimal search procedures? Other (e.g. linear, quadratic, integer or dynamic programming)? Would these be really useful to the company?	Some packages offer optimising techniques to their users which may be used in conjunction with simulation models. Optimal search procedures are the most frequently offered. These techniques may not be widely used at present, but there is a possibility that they will be useful in the future.

Information category	Question	Purpose of question
10 *Other facilities or aspects*	What other advantages or special facilities are claimed by the bureaux for their packages? How important are these?	Unusual features such as optimisation ready-made models, programs written in terms of numerals only, data scrambling facilities for additional safeguarding of confidential data, may appeal to some modellers.
11 *Costs*	What costs would be incurred: As outright purchase price? Initial fee to access? Annual support cost? Royalties payable? Costs of use of bureau computer?	Costs vary widely, as do the terms on which access to packages may be obtained, but what the packages offer also varies. Clearly, what each package can do must be balanced against its costs as a basis for short-listing. Where bureaux appear reluctant to publish appropriate rates, it could be because they would not compare favourably with others.

Chapter 8

Case studies

Introduction

Earlier chapters have tended, to a large extent, to be fairly general. We have discussed the nature of corporate models, their mode of operation and flexibility. However, Chapter 6 took readers through a tailor-made model of ATV in detail. We now present case studies, of five firms which have developed corporate models, narrated by the model builders themselves. Each writer has his own individual style and has been encouraged to write in the way he thinks the reader will find most interesting and stimulating.

The most interesting and useful case studies are often harrowing stories of failure. Unfortunately, only one of our 'reject' model builders could be persuaded to put pen to paper. So, we are restricted on the whole to models which the builders maintain are successful; the criterion being whether they consider that top management think the benefits of modelling exceed the costs. In each firm, though, practical difficulties were encountered and are reported frankly in the case studies. These have led to recommendations by the case-writers who place emphasis on the need to start with small, simple models that management can readily comprehend.

As we did not try to dictate to the companies which factors to cover in their contributions, inevitably many details have been excluded, indeed it would not have been possible to include them all in the space allowed. To get round this problem and to facilitate comparative analysis of the different approaches, we have produced *Figure 8.1*, which is a summary of the more important information gleaned from the very detailed questionnaires completed by each firm.

Three of the models should be of particular interest to accountants. They were built primarily by accountants and the case studies have been provided by very senior accountants. All of these models were developed using PROSPER, the ICL package which is provided free of charge as standard software to users of ICL computers. At Yorkshire Imperial Plastics the Finance Director did most of the modelling himself as he found this much quicker than trying to explain 'accounting and business logic' to systems analysts. Lansing Bagnall used a team approach to convert their cumbersome manual procedures into computer models, although again senior accountants were involved because of the confidential nature of much of the work. Anglia Building Society moved into the modelling field to relieve their accountants of dull, routine tasks and free them for more valuable, stimulating duties. They used the team approach but included an ICL modelling specialist in their set-up.

The other two models differ in that they have been developed by teams of operational researchers with general-purpose languages for the most part. The Rover company developed models which used deterministic simulation, probabilistic simulation (risk analysis) and optimisation techniques. However, because management did not understand the latter two techniques the company turned to deterministic simulation only. Subsequently, following organisational changes, even these models were shelved as 'too sophisticated'. At Fisons, however, they are continuing to use all three of the techniques mentioned. This does not make them unique among our total number of companies but they are in a very small minority.

Whilst considering these case studies the reader should bear in mind that they do not form a good cross-section of all modelling companies' activities. Only one of the companies, Lansing Bagnall, was using models in the conversational mode of operation and then only to a limited extent. The result is that the models are either relatively or totally inflexible. Users of the conversational mode have found that it leads to an increase in flexibility, especially where it is used allied with a modelling system. This caveat should be borne in mind, especially when looking at *Figure 8.1*.

Figure 8.1 Comparative analysis of case-study models

	Anglia Building Society	**Fisons**
Year in which modelling commenced	1972	1968
How acquired	Built by own staff with external assistance using a modelling system	Built by own staff with general-purpose language; some models built with a modelling system
How models are run	Own computer	Own and bureau computers
Mode of operation	Batch	Batch
Type of operation and level of aggregation	Financial modelling at the corporate level only	Financial and physical modelling extending down to divisions
Size	Under 1,000 input variables	Over 10,000 input variables
Class	Simulation	Simulation and optimisation. Approx. 10% of all runs are probabilistic simulation. Optimisation techniques in use; LP, integer programming and optimal search procedures
Facilities	Financial ratio analysis, compound interest	Backward iteration, financial ratio analysis, DCF, sensitivity analysis
Flexibility	Inflexible	Allows for major changes without reprogramming; choice of output reports
Cost	Approx £3,000	Approx £30,000

Lansing Bagnall	Rover	Yorkshire Imperial Plastics
1971	1967	1971
Built by own staff with a modelling system	Built by own staff with a general-purpose language	Built by own staff with a modelling system
Own and bureau computers	Own computer	Associate company computer
Batch and conversational	Batch and remote batch	Batch
Financial and physical modelling extending down to divisions	Financial and physical modelling at the corporate level only	Financial and physical modelling at all levels of business
Over 70,000 input variables	Under 1,000 input variables	Over 5,000 input variables
Simulation. Approx. 2% of all runs are probabilistic simulation	Simulation	Simulation
Financial ratio analysis, and histogram plotting	Backward iteration, financial ratio analysis, DCF	—
Allows for major changes without reprogramming; where conversational facilities used it is possible to stop run at any time to make changes	Allows for major changes without reprogramming; choice of output reports	Choice of output reports
Approx £12,000	Approx £6,000	Approx £7,000

Figure 8.1 cont.

	Anglia Building Society	**Fisons**
Model builders	Accountants assisted by ICL modelling specialist	Operational researchers with assistance of a programmer
Whose original idea	Assistant General Manager	Head of Central Planning
How used	In regular corporate planning	In regular corporate and divisional planning; also for *ad hoc* decision-taking
Who uses	Accountants	Divisional and head office planners
How well are models integrated into planning system	Fully integrated	Fully integrated
How much improvement in forecasts	Fairly significant	Significant
Success in terms of cost/ benefits	Yes	Yes
Management reaction	Agreeably surprised – there having been some initial scepticism	Enthusiastic – due to fact that they are consulted at each stage and feel that they have made a positive contribution
Problems encountered	Difficult to convey complex business knowledge to modelling specialist	Flexibility – overcome by modular approach
Would a different approach be taken if modelling were to start from scratch	In detail yes, in major principles no. May in fact do this	Always had philosophy of starting small and building up, but would follow it more rigidly

Lansing Bagnall	Rover	Yorkshire Imperial Plastics
Accountants and systems analyst	Operational researchers	Accountants assisted by a systems analyst
Financial Analysis dept	Operational Research Manager	Finance Director
In regular corporate and divisional planning; also for *ad hoc* decision-taking	In regular corporate planning; also for *ad hoc* decision-taking	In regular corporate and divisional planning
Financial analysts	Not now used	Accountants
They are the planning system	Were part of the total planning system	Integral part of the planning system
Significant	Significant	Significant
Yes	Yes	Yes
Favourable. Surprise that model could be so helpful for them	Enabled management to better quantify the effects of alternative decisions for discussions with British Leyland senior management (i.e. holding company)	Very favourably; they pay a great deal of attention to output
Tendency for each model builder to re-invent the wheel. Large run times initially due to inefficient programming	Tried probabilistic and optimisation models but neither successful. Problem because management found conceptual difficulties	First models were completely in one program and were thus too long – computer time was wasted to correct or modify only small matters
Smaller models. Avoid detail that is not significant	General approach more or less the same	Build smaller models which would interlink to form overall company model

8.2　A Corporate Model of the Anglia Building Society
(Article contributed by Arthur Brown, Assistant General Manager)

The business of a building society
In many ways a building society is a unique type of business organisation but it must none the less operate at a profit and marshall very carefully its liquid and other resources. The business is founded on the conventionally unstable principle of borrowing short and lending long. Well over a century of experience has shown, however, that such a situation can be extremely well-founded and can result in the provision of cheap loans for house purchase from funds raised by the accumulation of many small savings accounts.

Making a substantial profit is not one of the objectives of a building society. A main aim is to operate at as economical a cost as practicable. Inevitably the maintenance of tight margins between borrowing and lending rates can lead to problems in the event of adverse trading conditions. However, all building societies are aware of the dangers and most have built up substantial reserves over the years from modest profits which have not been distributed to shareholders. Furthermore, operating as the Society does as a bank, it must always ensure, day by day and indeed hour by hour, that enough cash resources are available in each of 100-plus branches to ensure that every demand from members for the withdrawal of savings can be met without delay.

Thus, there are two key issues which must be observed constantly: namely, profitability and availability of cash. For many years, the situation has been adequately controlled by the preparation of forward estimates, which in the main have been prepared manually by skilled accounting staff. These form the yardstick against which to measure actual results being achieved. By 11 a.m. every morning the Society's management has a total picture of the overall cash flow position up to the close of business on the immediately preceding business day. This enables suitable adjustments to be made in the Society's investment and banking resources to accommodate the rapidly changing needs of the organisation for cash and to indicate at an early stage, the emergence of any trend, adverse or otherwise, which may be affecting our total liquidity.

Reasons for modelling
The accounting skills and effort required to exercise the necessary degree of control were appreciable and, furthermore, tended by constant repetition of arithmetic formulae to become extremely tedious and routine. The computer provided the opportunity to eliminate the drudgery from this work and to carry out more detailed assessments which would be impracticable without its help. Although initially we were not confident about the real value of setting up a computerised corporate model, we had sufficient hope in the potential to consider it worth while devoting a limited amount of skilled effort to the study.

A small team (*Anglia* accountants plus an ICL modelling specialist) was set up. Initial scepticism was fairly quickly replaced by enthusiasm as the potential of this new facility came home to us and our understanding of the help which the accountants could obtain from the computer became apparent. The objective was to simulate the corporate financial behaviour of the Society. This involved us in:
 (i) Forecasting the cash flow situation in months for up to four years ahead.
 (ii) Forecasting the profitability in years for up to four years ahead.
 (iii) Forecasting the balance sheets for four years ahead.
All of the foregoing had to be compared with the previous year's actual figures. Forecasts had to be updated monthly. The current month's forecasts were replaced by actual figures when they were known. The information had to be supported by the necessary detailed schedules, and various control ratios computed.

Defining the method
We decided to work along the following guidelines:
 (i) We would utilise the PROSPER package supplied by ICL.
 (ii) With this we would build a simple framework of the financial models necessary using the basic principles of double-entry book-keeping.
 (iii) The initial framework would be capable of variation in the light of our
 knowledge as we progressed and of changing conditions in the future.
 (iv) Because at the outset the study was to be experimental only, we would at all
 times be prepared to come to the decision to scrap the exercise, if we found
 that the anticipated results would not justify the means.
Frequent steering committee meetings were held to:
 (i) Define the objectives in more detail.
 (ii) Plan the whole exercise and set out a reasonable time-table.
 (iii) Agree which parts of the model to elaborate and which to keep fairly simple.
 (iv) Note progress.
 (v) Produce a 'phase 1' working corporate model to be justifiably enlarged as
 experience and subsequent development indicated.
 Most of the detailed survey and ascertainment of formulae were left to a young
Anglia accountant and the ICL specialist.

Figure 8.2 Anglia Building Society – Corporate model flow chart

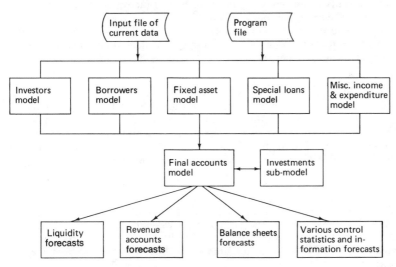

Structure of the corporate suite of models
Figure 8.2 shows the interrelationships of the models comprising the corporate suite.
Further details of the six models are given here:
(i) *Investors model*
 There are eight different types of investment possible in the Society some of
which carry different interest rate structures and tax rates. At present a decision is
made outside the model regarding the probable total net investment likely to be
received in each month ahead from all investors. The model then breaks this figure
down automatically on the basis of moving annual ratios into the eight categories of
investors funds and automatically applies the rules of administration to each class of
funds.

(ii) *Borrowers model*

This model deals with five classes of mortgage loan accounts. Each of these has its own rules of administration dealing with different interest rates, different calculation periods and taking into account such things as mortgages redeemed, lump sum partial repayments, insurance premiums chargeable to borrowers, survey fees, fines and costs on accounts in arrear, government subsidy on option mortgages, etc.

(iii) *Fixed asset model*

This model calculates, for different classes of fixed assets, the amount of depreciation to be written off each year, the written down values, the accumulated depreciation, capital allowances and also a computation of the tax equalisation reserve.

(iv) *Special loans model*

Loans received from special sources are dealt with at this stage and calculations are made of the interest due and repayments on specified dates, and balances carried forward.

(v) *Miscellaneous income and expenditure model*

The Society's operating costs and receivables such as insurance commissions, rents and sundry income are either input or generated for the period of time over which the model is to be applied.

(vi) *Final accounts and investments model*

This model, although a separate model in its own right which derives its own conclusions from given data, is also a consolidating model. It accepts data both input and generated from the other five models to produce:

(a) Control statistics which we consider to be key factors in the control of the business. These are set out in *Figure 8.3*.

(b) A liquidity forecast, a specimen of which is given in *Figure 8.4* (pages 118–9).

(c) A revenue account forecast which is in typical accounting format.

(d) Forecast balance sheets which are again conventional in layout.

Effort and cost

The flow charting and coding of these six models took the ICL specialist about 10 man-weeks. The external specialist was used to benefit from the wider experience of ICL and also to avoid involving our own hard pressed systems and programming staff. Approximately 20 hours of computer time was involved, although delivery of our new machine made available almost unlimited amounts of computer time. If we had to assess the cost of the whole exercise, this might total very roughly £3,000, although because the total work was spread over a period of about 12 months in all, the work was 'fitted in' by the accountants and there was no additional cost on their behalf. We were not obliged to meet any direct charges from ICL as their involvement was agreed to be part of the free service support negotiated at the time when the computer was ordered. In our eyes, therefore, it is reasonable to look on the whole exercise in terms of a marginal cost not exceeding £100, most of this having been spent in reimbursement of travelling expenses.

Conclusion and the future

It is clear that we have carried out a most helpful development which materially assists the Society's management. We will almost certainly, however, use our own programming staff from here onwards. Indeed, if we could in the early stages have spared effort from our programming team, they would have been involved from the beginning, but this was not practical at the time.

The work carried out has given the Society the benefit of:

(i) More accurate and frequent estimates than were practical before.

(ii) Much easier discovery of the results of various policy decisions and management controls.

(iii) Skilled accountants being involved in far less tedious work.
(iv) The accountants directly making use of the computer, instead of being somewhat remote from its operations.
(v) Recognising the feasibility of automatically updating models from a computerised general ledger which in turn would receive automatic postings from the daily computer runs on our two major updates, one covering the savings side of our business and the other the lending side.

We are now looking forward to the day when we hope that we can improve our ease of data input into the machine by substituting direct terminal operation rather than having cards punched in order to effect program and data changes as at present. Similarly there is a need to simplify further the demands made on the accountant carrying out the date entry operation. This still requires an amount of quasi-technical know-how which would be better avoided.

Figure 8.3

ICL 1900 PROSPER ON 04/03/77

	Management ratios(%)				
	1976	*1977*	*1978*	*1979*	*1980*
Growth	19.05	17.71	17.35	16.50	15.92
Reserves: year end assets	3.58	3.67	3.50	3.19	3.00
Liquidity: year end assets	13.55	13.76	15.07	16.70	16.14
Man. exp.: year end assets	0.68	0.67	0.67	0.66	0.65
Deposit av. interest rate	4.48	5.18	5.23	5.23	5.24
Share av. interest rate	4.91	5.60	5.63	5.63	5.63
Mortgage av. interest rate	8.15	8.64	8.64	8.63	8.63
Rev. surplus: year end assets	0.32	0.36	0.34	0.32	0.29
Total surplus: year end assets	0.46	0.42	0.34	0.32	0.29

Figure 8.4   Mortgage and liquidity Budget, 1977

Details of codes used
CT	Corporation tax
SL	Special loan
HS & SPEC	Housing Societies and specials
IT	Income tax
ORD	Ordinary
OS	Option mortgage subsidy
WT	Warrants

ICL 1900 PROSPER ON 19/07/77

	Investors		Mortgages repaid		Sundries	Total
January	3620		4384		68	3436
				IT:	4500	
February	1622		3985		83	5594
		OS:	282	IT:	212	
March	1311		4852		59	6104
April	4553		4179		264	8468
May	3693		4544		130	8409
		OS:	302			
June	4106		4410		287	5962
				WT:	2160	
				SL:	107	
	18905		26938		7870	37973
July	3500		4203		214	7489
August	3500		4347		175	8004
		OS:	332			
September	3500		4442		250	7692
October	3500		4514		170	7350
				CT:	494	
November	3500		4563		151	8267
		OS:	355			
December	3595		4606		140	5372
				WT:	2575	
				SL:	114	
	40000		54300		12153	82147

Mortgage loans (excl. ins. premiums)		+ or −	Liquidity		Mortgages granted (Outstanding)		Mortgage allocation	
ORD	HS & SPEC		Total short funds	Total long funds	ORD	HS & SPEC	ORD	HS & SPEC
			(9852	30065	14913	1650)		
5645	260	−3469	7173	29275	5546	414	5500	300
5811	236	−453	6526	29469	6066	278	6000	300
5757	281	−934	6678	28383	5793	161	5500	300
5942	182	2344	9575	27830	4264	109	4200	250
5503	199	2707	10074	30038	5339	187	5250	250
5157	175	630	10436	30306	5572	131	5500	2500
5815	1333	825			32580	1280	31950	3900
4672	287	2530	12966	30306	5750	250	5750	250
5103	281	2620	15636	30256	5750	250	5750	250
5362	275	2055	17993	29954	5750	250	5750	250
5517	271	1562	19655	29854	5750	250	5750	250
5610	267	2390	22245	29654	5750	250	5750	250
5666	264	−558	21699	29642	5750	470	5750	470
7745	2978	11424			67080	3000	66450	5620
			(Outstanding		14249	1672)		

119

8.3 *Modelling at Fisons*
(*Article contributed by Stephen Riley, Head of Operational Research*)

The development of models in Fisons

Fisons is an international research-based organisation which manufactures and markets pharmaceuticals, fertilisers and chemicals. Its involvement with computer models dates from 1964 when the Group's business was basically geared to the production and sale of agricultural fertiliser. The manufacturing process for fertiliser involves the production of several intermediates, many of which can be made by alternative formulations using existing plant. This type of structure seemed an ideal area for the introduction of LP (linear programming) techniques and a model comprising some 1,400 rows and 2,500 columns was constructed. Taking a sales forecast, raw material availability and costs, this model prepared an optimum production plan compatible with existing manufacturing capacity. A similar model is currently being used in the Fertiliser Division as an aid in planning production. In the Agrochemicals Division a rather simpler model was developed to schedule production and packaging of spray and powder chemicals in line with a given sales forecast.

The first true incursion into the field of financial modelling came with the construction of a new product model in 1968. This evaluated the effect of different world marketing strategies on overall Group profits and cash flow. It was apparent that many variations to a large volume of basic information needed to be studied in a short period of time to establish the optimal way of introducing Intal (a drug for the control of asthma). Accordingly the model detailed the costs and revenue of the product and simulated the organisational structure through which sale would take place. This type of model has continued to be useful in the planning of the introduction of other new products.

Following the successful implementation of the production planning models and the first new product model a plan was formulated for a hierarchy of models which is represented diagrammatically in *Figure 8.5*. The pharmaceutical budgeting/monitoring model, which was built next, was primarily conceived as a means of producing a budgeted plan of export sales contribution and of reporting actual results achieved against this plan. Within this simulation model, provision is made for every pack size of every product sold overseas by the Pharmaceutical Division, while sales can be routed through a chain of subsidiary companies into over 100 territories. All the models completed to date (including a number of financial models not included in the hierarchy), have had a good record of acceptance and use in decision-making by management. The corporate model appears to be the only one which is currently underutilised, largely because the finance/tax LP, the preceding link in the chain, is not yet operational. The aim of the finance/tax LP is to take expected pre-tax profits throughout the world and, subject to the major constraint that finance should be made available for overseas investment projects, to maximise net worth. Other future plans are more concerned with a consolidation of the present position than with any radical new departure. Thus it is hoped to harness the information already contained within the Fertiliser Division LP and Agrochemical Division production planning model so as to produce full budgets and an associated monitoring procedure.

Fisons

Figure 8.5 Hierarchy of models

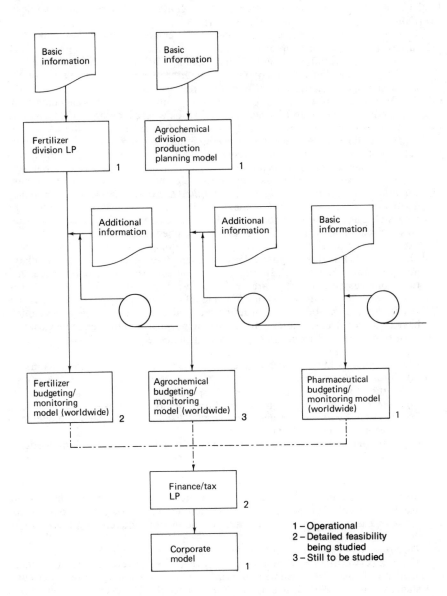

121

The modelling philosophy
In all its modelling activities the Group has been guided by four general principles:
(i)   *That efficient use is made of the computer*
     It is normally the case that a computer model can assist in decision-making if:
     (a) Optimisation is attempted or complex calculations frequently repeated. Such exercises are often beyond manual capability in any reasonable time. However, the value of the solution obtained depends on the validity of the assumptions made, and these require regular review.
 or (b) Minor amendments are frequently made to otherwise unchanging data. This facility is very useful for planning purposes where a number of alternatives need to be considered in a short space of time, although the use of the computer merely as a printing machine must be avoided.
 or (c) A complex structure can be easily simulated. This ensures the accuracy and timeliness of information produced at a reasonable cost, and often enforces a co-ordinated discipline on those providing data from a variety of sources.
(ii) *That the model structure is sufficiently detailed to assist efficient decision-taking*
     The model structure must have enough detail in order for meaningful results to be obtained, but must not be too detailed – otherwise unnecessary cost and time wastage would be incurred. For instance, it has been essential to avoid the use of excessive computer time in arriving at an 'optimal' solution for the Fertiliser Division LP. For this purpose relatively insensitive areas of the operation have not been modelled in detail. In order to get a model structure right it is necessary to establish those areas which are most sensitive. In a model which is to be used on a continuing basis – such as a budgeting model – it is normally possible to do some sensitivity analysis before constructing the model. However, very often models have to be constructed quickly for a specific purpose and the sensitive variables must be established from the experience of those requiring the model.
(iii) *That models must be as flexible as possible*
     Models must as far as possible be easy to change for the following reasons:
     (a) Situations change considerably from the time when the model is first conceived to the date when it is in full operation.
     (b) There are some communications difficulties between users and modellers. These in Fison's experience very largely disappear after the first model for a user has been constructed.
     (c) Experience with using a model indicates to both the user and the modeller new ways of obtaining more useful information. This is by far the most common reason for change in the Group's modelling experience.
     There is no doubt that the first models constructed between 1968–1970 suffered from being too inflexible, even though some account had been taken of the problems by splitting the editing, calculation and report stages of models. This problem has been partially overcome by the use of modelling systems, where these are applicable.
(iv) *That the way in which a model is built must be cost justified*
     This is a very difficult question. It can only really be answered after a preliminary estimate of cost of development and running of a model under different circumstances – and whether it is conversational or batch. The user must then assess what level of cost can be justified in the light of:
     (a) How much manual work it will save?
     (b) How many more alternative plans can be considered and how this will reduce the risk of undertaking the 'wrong' plan or investment?
     (c) Whether response time is of the essence, in which case a conversational model is indicated.

The modelling experience
Models which the Group has developed fall roughly into three main categories:

(i) *Optimisation models*

The production planning LP used in the Fertiliser Division and the finance/tax LP are the two main examples of optimisation models which have been developed or are being studied. However, there have been some other applications, mainly in the representation of production situations. Cost savings cannot be quantified accurately unless the performance of the 'optimal' plan is compared in detail with that produced by the existing method. Not only is this extremely difficult to do in practice but also one comparison can never be considered conclusive. It is therefore the Group's policy that such models are only used where expected savings can be demonstrated to be considerable.

(ii) *Simulation models for planning*

Where management wishes to examine alternative plans in some detail in order to take decisions, 'one-off' simulation has proved a very satisfactory technique. Areas in which it has been most utilised are the introduction of new products and the assessment of possible acquisitions. The time taken to develop this kind of model varies enormously. Some small models, using a modelling system, have been defined and written within a few days – others have taken up to three months to develop. For investment decisions, where the likely range of return is of prime importance, the techniques of probabilistic simulation have been much utilised. Again the development time varies with the complexity of the model to be defined. These types of model have proved particularly successful where they have been applied.

(iii) *Simulation models for planning and control*

These models take a great deal more time to develop than do the above models for two main reasons:

(a) They must be flexible enough to stand the test of time.

(b) The model must fit in with the existing (or revised) control systems.

Obviously the implementation time for a system depends on the complexity of the situation concerned, but as an example the budgeting/monitoring model used in the Pharmaceutical Division took approximately four man-years to develop to a useable state. However, the increased control over situations, together with the reduction in time spent on routine analysis, have more than justified the development costs involved.

Conclusion

Four main areas of benefit which financial and other modelling has given rise to in *Fisons* are:

(i) The complete problem is (normally for the first time) specified in formal terms.

(ii) The data required for effective decision-making is precisely defined.

(iii) Alternative plans can be examined speedily and therefore the risk of undertaking 'wrong' plans or missing 'better' strategies is reduced.

(iv) Clerical effort is reduced.

These benefits, unfortunately, can rarely be exactly quantified. However, *Fisons* are quite certain that the benefits arising from increased management control over situations have far outweighed the effort and cost incurred in the construction and use of models.

8.4 *Corporate financial models at Lansing Bagnall*
(Article contributed by Peter F. Hockley, Divisional Finance Director)

Introduction
This article describes the work carried out at *Lansing Bagnall Ltd* by a team of accountants in the development from clerical to computer-based budgeting, forecasting and financial planning methods. The work was carried out within the financial function and covered system design, programming, implementation and interpretation. Results were achieved by a blend of financial experience, package flexibility and hard work.

Background
Over a number of years the financial planning systems of the company have developed in two main streams:
(i) There has been a continuing need for operating staff to recognise that financial planning is a line responsibility in which all departments should make a contribution, and that it is not merely an academic exercise.
(ii) There has been a need to improve the analytical routines so that reliable and comparable data is available both for review of historical performance and current operating results.

Problems
The position was emerging that with growth, the operations of the company were becoming more complex, and the economic conditions under which business had to be carried on were becoming less and less certain. These factors produced a growing demand from management for stricter financial control and a faster evaluation of alternative courses of action.

It began to be a matter of concern, therefore, that the clerical systems required to produce the necessary detailed support were too cumbersome and therefore too slow for management purposes. Because of the confidential nature of the work senior accounting staff had to be used, although this did not make the most economic use of their time and ability.

Another danger stemming from the time constraint was that of becoming over-concerned with producing the financial plans to a deadline without properly analysing and criticising the planning assumptions or the results stemming from these assumptions.

Solution
Initially our attention was focused on the methods to be used to lighten the clerical load which showed every sign of growing, and our reaction was to identify those areas in the planning system which entailed a large content of arithmetic and analytical work. The evaluation of sales budgets and departmental expense budgets were isolated as significant in this respect, and we considered that programs could be written to handle this data, whilst preserving the current clerical system of linking the data together to provide profit statements, balance sheets, cash flow statements and other reports.

At this time we were preparing our planning forecasts on an annual basis, but considering certain base data in quarterly rests where this was necessary. After agreement by the Board the budgets and forecasts were then spread to accounting periods for control purposes.

We did not envisage any change in the basic way in which the financial data was co-ordinated and presented, nor did we believe that any significant improvement could be obtained in the validity and accuracy of the current methods. Our thinking therefore was towards partial mechanisation of the system, at a low level, which would leave the age-old problem of how to handle late changes in planning assumptions and ensure that such changes had been fully reflected in the financial plan. Cash flow forecasting was an area where we were continuously dissatisfied with our inability to reflect the results of changes in the operating plan.

At this time, however, we were introduced to the possibility of using a modelling system which would enable financial staff to program the financial planning methods, without calling upon management services staff, whose workload was sufficiently heavy to prevent them from being able to handle our problems in the time available to us. A short study of the potential uses and flexibility of the system indicated that we should probably benefit from its use, so much so, that very little effort was made to determine what alternative systems were then available. We have no cause to regret this however.

Our approach

As appraisal of the new methods proceeded it became clear that it would be not only possible to computerise that part of the planning procedures already identified as clerically cumbersome, but that it would also be possible to carry out the whole of the financial evaluation and consolidation of the business plan. Profit statements and balance sheets would be part of an integrated whole, and areas of earlier difficulty, for example cash forecasts, would now become part of the automatic information outputs.

So we were in the position of being able to visualise broadly the improved methods available, but were much less clear on how we should proceed with the implementation or indeed how long it would all take. The calendar showed that we had about eight months before we had to have the new system ready for use. We would, of course, run old and new in parallel, in order to prove the new arrangements and provide an alternative should we be unable to complete the work to our satisfaction.

With this uncertainty as to how long it would take to install the new methods for annual financial planning, consideration ranged over alternative courses available. The following three presented themselves as possibilities:

1   A short-term forecasting system (the top end of a fully detailed planning system, which would provide a rolling profit forecasting system, and also be a vehicle for training and experience); or
2   The full financial planning system including the necessary outputs to ensure control by cost centre; or
3   A corporate planning system.

We were prepared to defer alternative 2 in order to obtain experience and not to be continually fighting against a time limitation. Also it seemed more sensible to select a smaller task and be more certain of coming home with a working solution. Alternative 3 was fairly soon abandoned on the score that it would take too long to establish what information was required, and too many functions would be involved. Therefore, alternative 1 was selected as that most likely to achieve success; once this work was completed it was expected that it would be possible to expand it with little difficulty into the full annual planning system.

Development of the first model

The steps taken to launch the work were:

(i)   Broad definition of information output requirement.
(ii) Sub-division of the system between staff available.
(iii) Booking of training courses.

The break-down of the system between members of the financial analysis staff was based on individual accountants' knowledge of the clerical system, and broadly followed a split between:

(i) Sales volume and turnover.
(ii) Manufacturing volume and cost.
(iii) General and administration expense.
(iv) Profit statements and balance sheets.

This approach meant that the system would be constructed in four separate sections, the output from the first three sections having to be co-ordinated with the profit statements and balance sheet section. This required a high degree of co-operation between the accountants responsible for the various parts of the system. Each analyst had a sufficient knowledge of the whole manual operation to know the specific requirements from his aspect of the work which would be required by the others and proceeded to design, code and index his work separately, raising points as necessary at a weekly co-ordination meeting.

It was also soon realised that it was necessary to transfer a systems analyst to the project to guide the accountants through the more technical data processing problems which arise and to cover the administration of the processing. This proved invaluable to the success of the project.

As the work of programming and coding proceeded it became steadily more difficult to restrict the amount of detail being handled, and it became clear that the system was in too low a level of detail for profit forecasting, but lacked the necessary detail and flexibility for eventual conversion into the full annual planning requirement.

The danger then appearing was that we would not have the profit forecasting system finished by the time the annual plan had to be handled, and that we would still be operating the current manual system for another year. A detailed review of alternatives was made, and it was decided to opt for converting the forecasting system into the annual planning requirement. This entailed a certain amount of back-tracking on system design, but with the experience now gained work could proceed much faster than at the outset of the project.

In the event the system was completed and test run just in time to become operational for the preparation of the budget plan for the following year. Test running was based on the use of the previous year's data input into the clerical system, and we found that the new system produced a different financial out-turn. Now, more reliable cash flow data was emerging, and the effect of the timing of production and sales volumes was being reflected more accurately than with the manual procedures.

It was now fully appreciated that we had both a more reliable and more disciplined system, and that parallel running of computer and clerical systems was not on – they would not produce the same answers. It is also interesting to note that under the detailed scrutiny necessitated by the modelling, significant improvements in the basic accounting and reporting systems were brought to light and implemented.

Use in practice
The system worked and was used. Some modifications were made to the clerical methods of collecting input data, and with the knowledge of how the system would process the information, a greater degree of critical examination and questioning of basic planning assumptions was made.

We were also in the new position of being able to run out draft budgets much earlier than previously, each fully phased by accounting period and with full supporting detail. This facility enabled fuller appreciation of the effect of forecast production volumes, stock and despatch volumes, and early runs showed up unlikely or optimistic planning that the manual system would have failed to pin-point. Reviewing first results on a calendar basis enforced a critical appraisal of the logic of basic assumptions as regards time scale. The relationship between manpower and capacity was checked using the model and inconsistencies between planned production and manning were revealed and rectified.

In addition, the timing of events was reflected with greater financial accuracy. Pay and price changes and the effect on inventory of both price inflation and rate of throughput were reflected.

Overall it could be said that greater discipline was required in operating the system than had been required previously, but the capacity of the financial staff to handle the data and its evaluation increased considerably; where we thought we had a good grasp of how the company operated, we began to find areas where our knowledge had to be improved.

Lessons learned

It is now several years since the first system was put into use and experience has enabled improvements to be made. Certain structural changes have been made in the sub-divisions for the whole model, partly for convenience and partly for technical reasons. Interestingly, it proved relatively easy to simplify the full planning system to provide a rolling profit forecasting mechanism.

Acquired expertise in the use of the modelling system now gives more economic programs, and the trend has been to use smaller models, and to be more selective in the level of detail being used. It has also been necessary to develop efficient handling of data on discs, and the transfer of information between models.

It is imperative that sufficient time is given to defining output requirements at the outset if they are to be achieved effectively and economically, although the exercise of programming does prompt ideas for useful additions.

Design and coding must be well documented, particularly where changes are made to the system to reflect either organisational or operational changes by the company. Certainly care is needed at the outset to allow for expansion in the classification or analysis of data being processed; the system must be able to reflect the changing circumstances of the business, otherwise the initial investment will not mature.

Since the construction of the initial planning model was completed all planning requirements, major and minor, have been handled using the computer and it is unlikely that the financial staff would feel they were in a position to explore the alternatives adequately using manual methods.

Some advantages

Provided one is prepared to accept the discipline required, financial planning with a computer-operated corporate model will yield improved information, faster and better analysed and documented than under manual systems. It is possible to react to changes of plan, even of a fundamental nature, and produce both profit forecasts and balance sheets that reflect the changes, together with the required supporting analysis.

Our experience has been also that financial staff have improved their knowledge of the operations of the business and that the questions asked at the planning stage become more pertinent and demanding. In addition it has improved their awareness, not only of the variety of ways in which a computer can be used to advantage in their work, but also of the considerable attention to detail necessary to ensure the accurate and efficient handling of work on such a machine.

Perhaps as interesting as any reward from these methods is the fact that the accountants involved have had the opportunity to exploit more fully their financial training and experience in the management of the business.

8.5 The Development and Application of Financial Models at Rover
(Article contributed by A. W. McCurdy, Manager – Systems Research)

Introduction
The purpose of this paper is to give a practical account of the experience of a small OR (operational research) group in a medium-sized company in trying to develop and implement models as a management tool for the better evaluation of forward policy alternatives and the preparation of financial and operating plans.

The first section of the paper describes the development of a cash flow model of the company's operations. The second section attempts to identify the key factors which led to the success of this development. The third section describes how the cash flow model was further developed into a fully operational system, which was extensively used in the company for investment appraisals. The fourth section describes the way in which it was hoped the various models currently being developed would be applied, and how it was intended to provide a comprehensive company economic model which recognised all the main factors in the operation of the company. The final section details the reasons why these developments did not take place and why the use of the original model was terminated.

Section 1: Historical development
In 1967 the need for senior management to assess the economic desirability of galvanising pressed parts within the company, rather than at external galvanisers, led to the involvement of the OR Department in the financial evaluation of proposals made by the Facilities Planning Department. This in turn led to the development by the OR Department of a simple cash flow model to permit the evaluation of these proposals to be carried out successfully.

The decision to develop such a model was taken because it was felt that the use of DCF techniques provided a better basis for the appraisal of the capital investments associated with the various proposals, than the procedures then current in the Company. The necessarily tentative nature of forward sales estimates in the motor industry also meant that appraisals would have to be carried out for a variety of forward sales estimates to ascertain the sensitivity of the results to likely variations in sales, and to provide some measure of the riskiness of the project. This would not have been possible in the time available, other than on the computer. The characteristics of the model are shown in *Figure 8.6*.

The use of the model enabled a comprehensive economic analysis of the project to be carried out, and this successful application led to an extension of the use of the model, in particular the carrying out in 1968 of an extensive series of appraisals for Range Rover.

During this period it became obvious that the concept of attaching probabilities to forward estimates of sales volumes, costs and capital expenditure was not clearly understood by management, who were unwilling to provide such probabilities, and who were unable to attach significant meanings to the results. This facility was therefore dropped.

The model's ability to vary data speedily and to re-appraise projects enabled management to investigate the sensitivity of policies to changes in basic assumptions and provided quantifiable operational objectives on design costs, volumes, and launch dates. The results of such sensitivity analyses also showed the high variability of the profitability of projects to proportional changes in overheads compared with similar proportional changes in capital forecasts, reflecting the approximate 3:1 ratio between fixed overheads and capital depreciation charges in the company.

Figure 8.6 Characteristics of original cash flow model

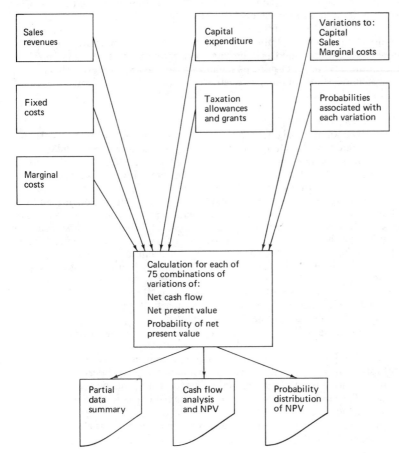

The use of the model increased significantly with the forward planning associated with two planned new cars, which shared many components, and where because of the consequent interdependency of the vehicles it was necessary to consider the phasing of their introduction. These appraisals were carried out on both a marginal and full company cash flow basis, and the provision by the model of a profit and loss forecast, at the request of management, enabled unacceptable forecast profit and loss figures to be highlighted, and the necessary re-phasing of vehicle introduction dates to be carried out.

Section 2: Environment for success
The main reasons why the initial model gained management acceptance, and was fairly rapidly developed over a period of two years, were felt to be:
    (i) It made use of existing information and procedures.
   (ii) It enabled variations in policy to be more easily explored at a time when future plans were being extensively called into question.
  (iii) The fact that management at *Rover* had considerable experience and

appreciation of and involvement with advanced computer applications pre-disposed them to accept the model, and allowed time for its usefulness and versatility to be demonstrated.

(iv) Finally the development and application of the model in small stages from simple applications, such as individual project appraisal, to the complexities of defining new product policies meant that management were able at each stage to understand and make constructive suggestions for further develop-ment of the model.

Section 3: Implementation on a fully operational basis
The model was programmed originally by OR staff, who were also responsible for supervising the collection, punching and processing of data, and the validation of output. This informal system which had contributed to the success of the initial development by providing a flexible approach was now proving an encumbrance, in terms of demands upon the time of the OR staff and in unnecessarily complicating the information flows from one department to another. It was therefore considered that the model should be put on a more routine, fully operational basis, which would allow management to use it directly via the new department which had been set up and given the responsibility for the proposal and evaluation of forward product policy. This implied that the new model, illustrated in *Figure 8.7*, should:

(i) Be to such a level of detail as matched the established needs of users and management.

(ii) Use basic data; there should be no need for manual pre-processing, with the associated extra clerical effort required and risk of error.

(iii) As far as possible be self checking and fail/safe.

(iv) Provide great flexibility of data manipulation without the need to re-input data.

(v) Present concise summary reports to management in as far as possible the final form required for the particular problem being considered.

(vi) Be linked with a formal system, defined in terms of procedures and respon-sibilities for supplying information, agreeing the basis of appraisals and validating the results.

Since completion the model was used frequently by management for new product policy appraisals and other economic studies.

Section 4: Development of the company model
The use of the model had highlighted the sensitivity of project profitability to variabil-ity in fixed overhead estimates, 75 per cent of which is represented by employment costs. In addition the complexity of some of the production capacity requirements led to product policy appraisals being carried out where, for example, planned production volumes were in excess of available or planned capacity. It was also considered that the procedures for estimating the operating costs of the company for different produc-tion levels and mixes were not satisfactory.

It was therefore decided to develop three further models for:

(i) Assessing the feasibility of projected sales volumes against the current and planned production capacity.

(ii) Forecasting the manpower requirements associated with future activity levels.

(iii) Estimating the variable operating costs associated with future activity levels.

The relationships of these proposed models to the cash flow model, which had already been developed, is shown in simplified form in *Figure 8.8*. It was hoped that the development and integration of these models with the cash flow model would produce a comprehensive company economic model.

Figure 8.7 Characteristics of the fully operational cash flow and profit and loss model

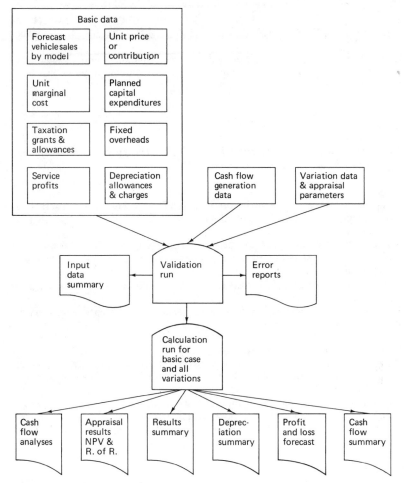

Figure 8.8 Integration of sub-models into company economic model

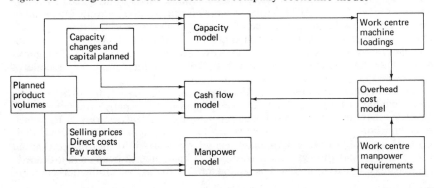

Section 5: Reasons for eventual failure

With the setting up at the instigation of *British Leyland* of departments responsible for Investment Analysis and Profit Planning priority was given by them to establishing basic systems and procedures in these areas in line with corporate standards. It was not considered appropriate to be developing sophisticated modelling based on shaky accounting foundations.

However, now that these procedures have been installed and are working satisfactorily further contact has taken place, and simple modelling work has been carried out, in the Profit Planning area.

8.6 Computer Modelling in Yorkshire Imperial Plastics
(Article contributed by A. E. Gardner, Finance Director)

Introduction

Within my company we have had a fairly sophisticated financial planning structure for several years, largely operated on a manual basis. Such a system (see *Figure 8.9*) is subject to limitations:

- (i) The amount of detail which can be processed in a given time is far less than with a computer system and there is a constant struggle against a deadline which is all too near.
- (ii) Too much time is absorbed in preparation of forecasts and not enough in consideration of the results.
- (iii) Plans tend to become inflexible due to the amount of work necessary to change them.
- (iv) Due to the work involved the time span is usually one year – to look further is usually a special 'one-off' exercise.
- (v) However desirable, there are some areas of the company's activities which cannot be forecast manually without an army of clerks because of the sheer volume of calculation.

Wishing to improve forecasting beyond the barriers of the manual system, *Yorkshire Imperial Plastics* turned to the computer and learned of the existence of modelling systems which permit the building of models by non-computer personnel. After a brief course of a week's duration had given us a good understanding of the selected modelling system, we were ready to try to apply it, but first we had to decide how we were going to do this.

Method of approach

At first sight, the attraction of building a model representing the whole company, the end product of which would be the total company profit, was very strong. On the other hand, we were also drawn to the idea of building models of parts of the company's operation to refine and enhance our existing financial planning methods. We eventually chose the second course, that is to write models of parts of the company's operations, but to write them so that they might be incorporated into a larger model of the company at some future time. Our reasons for this decision were:

- (i) Experience with our existing financial planning methods led us to believe that to build a truly representative model of the whole company's operations so as to reflect the interaction of one part on the other could be a very difficult task indeed.
- (ii) If we were to write a company model we would have to use fairly broad assumptions in many cases. Again our experience showed us that if one is using broad assumptions it is not too difficult to forecast profits fairly quickly

Figure 8.9 Financial planning structure

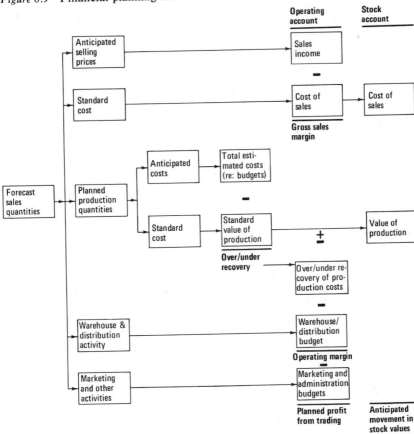

using just pen and ink. (Recent experience now leads us to believe we should develop this broad overall company model on top of our existing models, chiefly to quickly test alternatives before proceeding with the detailed models.)

(iii) As already stated, our financial planning system was fairly good but in one area we always had a great deal of trouble and it had never been satisfactory. This was the area covered by the balancing of sales forecasts with production capacities together with the estimation of stock investment to anticipate demand.

In order to gain experience we first wrote a fairly simple model to project our wages costs. This was an area which we knew well and we felt we would be able to validate the results which the model gave. A model was built fairly quickly which gave us the wages cost by normal hours and overtime hours for each class of worker, each cost centre, each department, for each period of the year (approximately monthly intervals), with facilities for projecting a further four years (see *Figure 8.10*). The validation tests proved very successful in highlighting errors in our model building.

Figure 8.10 Wages model

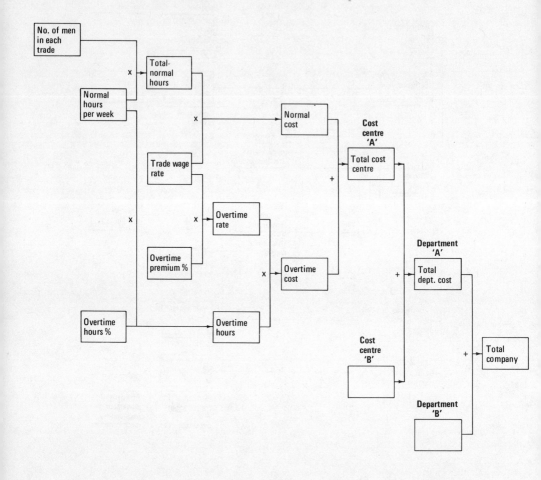

We next tackled the Sales Forecast in a more detailed way than we had previously attempted under our manual financial planning system. Again we started the model in a period for which we knew the answer; again, this proved most valuable in helping to locate errors, particularly in the logic, and in obtaining an accurate model. As with the wages model, the sales model covered each period of the first year with a view of the following four years (see *Figure 8.11*).

With this experience behind us we attacked our major problem area – sales balanced against production capacity. In this case we had only broad results against which to validate the model but our earlier modelling experience now proved extremely valuable. We had noted the type of error we were likely to make and the need to print-out intermediate stages of the model; this enabled us to trace what the computer was doing and helped in our efforts to quickly establish a reliable model. *Figure 8.12* gives an outline of the method of approach and indicates the model's potential for maximisation of production.

Figure 8.11 Sales model

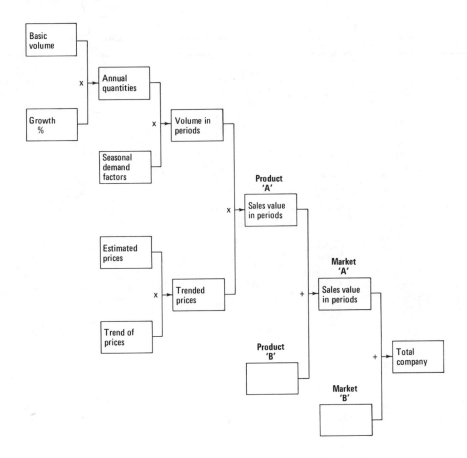

Lessons learned

All these models were written by non-computer personnel in a total time of three months and in doing so we learned that:

(i) It is critically important to have a thorough understanding of the relationships which determine a real life situation in order:
  (a) To program it and build the model.
  (b) To obtain valid results. (These can be critical and sometimes difficult, if not impossible, to check.)

(ii) It is best to write each model in a series of modules. Our first models were too big, a small change or minor error necessitated running the whole model again.

(iii) Initially it is valuable to gain experience writing models of well-known situations and where complicated programs are involved, print-outs of intermediate stages are useful. These intermediate print-outs can be eliminated once the model is working satisfactorily.

Figure 8.12 Sales/production model

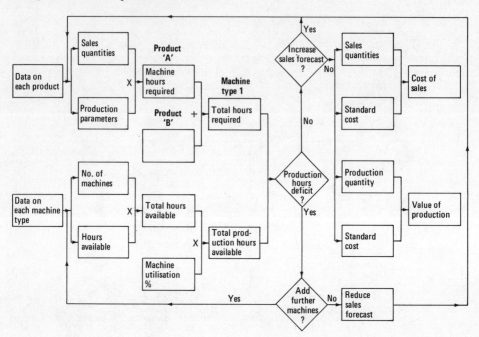

Results of modelling

As a result of our modelling activities we have definitely improved control of our business:

(i)   Before building models we were seriously contemplating buying a further large machine because of production capacity problems. However, the models enabled us to experiment with rearranging workloads on existing machines and as a result we were able to defer purchase of this large machine.

(ii) Finished stock values are projected for each month and our previous worries about the amount of goods produced for stock in seasonally slack periods has largely disappeared.

(iii) Our forward plans for machines, warehousing and distribution, and general space requirements are now on a firmer basis than ever before.

(iv) We have not yet introduced risk analysis into our models but this can be done in the future as we refine our planning.

(v)   Most important, we are now able to change our plans in an incredibly short space of time considering the amount of work and detail involved.

We have demonstrated to our satisfaction that it is certainly not necessary to have a model of the whole company before the computer can help in many areas of financial planning. None the less, the models were not written without cost, this cost being principally the very heavy demand upon the time of very senior accountants who were engaged in writing the models. Much effort and determination on their part was necessary to make the model succeed.

Appraisal of modelling activities
There is no doubt in my mind that financial modelling is a very powerful technique. Due to their involvement in budgeting and control systems, accountants are often better placed than most other disciplines to have a wide understanding and often unique knowledge of how their organisation functions. If accountants fail to master the new technique with the opportunity it offers to harness this knowledge and help management in overall control and direction of their organisations, then I fear much for the future status of the profession. There are many others, not so well qualified, who will be only too ready to present it as a new management science when, in fact, it is only the 'electrification' of the thinking and methods that good accountants have been doing and using for many years.

Chapter 9

Conditions for Success

The possibility of failure

In earlier chapters, the alternative approaches to corporate modelling have been explored. Examples quoted have been, on the whole, drawn from successful projects, because these are the ones companies are willing to have quoted. This could give the wrong impression as there have been failures, too. For reasons given in Chapter 3 the much-vaunted Sun Oil model was never used in practice.[1] The experience of Xerox in the USA was not favourable.[2] The Corporate Director of Planning of the Boeing Company in the USA has said that, whilst continuing to support modelling, he has found it a source of irritation.[3] An attempt to implement a model to assist investment analysts at Wells Fargo Bank in the USA failed.[4]

There are similar examples in the UK. A tobacco company developed a corporate model which was used once, to aid a diversification decision, and has not been used since. A paper-making company has a model which is well developed but has apparently been shelved because of a change in management. Problems have, indeed, been encountered with two of the early corporate models with which we were involved.

Success, though widely achieved, is not guaranteed. It is important, therefore, that both managers and corporate modellers should recognise conditions that contribute to success and those which may well lead to failure. Section 9.2 suggests conditions for success, then in Section 9.3 the results of the survey are used, as far as possible, to indicate the extent to which these conditions exist. In Section 9.4 we look at indications of success or failure of corporate models.

9.2 *Conditions for success*

Complete failure of corporate models can normally be recognised fairly easily. Development may have been abandoned before the model was ready for even initial implementation. The model may have been used a few times, or even not at all, and then conveniently forgotten. A new model may have been substituted in an attempt to get the approach right and with a strong faith that there must be something of value in modelling.

Conversely, a corporate model may be said to be successful if it is used for management decision-taking, top management think it is worth the cost, it is well received by management generally, and it is thought to have led to identifiable improvements in, say, forecasting. Unfortunately, degree of success is harder to define, but we return to this issue in Section 9.4.

Our own experience, comments of those interviewed during the survey of corporate modelling in the UK, and the published literature suggest six main, interrelated conditions for success. Failure tends to have followed where any three of these are absent. These are that:

(A) Sponsorship and continued support are given by top management.
(B) Top management understands the model, has confidence in it, and places at least some reliance on its results.
(C) The model meets specific management decision-making needs.
(D) Data required as input is readily available and not voluminous.
(E) The model is embedded in the planning process, i.e. it is used as a matter of course during normal planning.
(F) The model is properly documented throughout development.

A fuller account of each of these conditions is given below.

(A) *Top management support* is the most important single factor contributing to success. Ideally, this support should be stronger than mere approval, and should extend to application of pressure to promote development and use of the corporate model. At Lansing Bagnall, for instance, enthusiastic and active support by senior managers for corporate modelling has been one of the principal reasons for success. Generally, where top management interest is known, modellers have had few problems in obtaining necessary data, and in getting the model used as a practical aid to decision-making.

Where support comes from a single director, or other senior executive, successful development may be placed in jeopardy by changes in senior appointments. Loss of sponsor was a major problem in two of the companies with which we have been personally associated. In one, the corporate planning manager who was the main sponsor was promoted to other duties, and his successor had to be 'sold' on the model before development could proceed. In the other, the finance director who authorised the project and lent his support to it in a variety of ways, moved to another company. Whilst his successors did not cancel the project, they were not fully convinced of its value, and wanted the emphasis of the model to change. This slowed the rate of development and although the model is run spasmodically it is not yet used by management in decision-taking.

(B) Top management support is likely to be retained, once the model is developed, only if the corporate model is *seen to make an effective contribution to decision-taking*. Experience suggests that management will neither use nor have confidence in models unless it understands them. An understanding is more likely if management is involved in development of the model and if, on completion, it is properly presented to all potential users (see Chapter 6). More important, this understanding is more likely with simple models, for the non-specialist manager, beset by other pressures, cannot be expected to spend a great deal of time mastering complex models. This was one reason why, when asked what they would do differently if they were to start from scratch, many modellers said they would begin by building much simpler models. Again, we found a modular approach used widely (see Chapter 5) because of the flexibility that this affords and the opportunity it gives to build simple models initially which may be supplemented later.

(C) Management support is not likely to be sustained at any level of the organisation unless the model is appropriate to its *decision-making needs*. It must be possible to test the major alternatives open to management with the model and to do so easily. Since these alternatives vary with the level of management involved, a clear decision must be made as to the managers to be served by the model, which should be designed to meet the needs of this specific group rather than as a general aid to all (see Chapter 6). Further, separate but interlinked models may be added later to meet other needs as they arise.

In one respect it may be argued that virtually no corporate model is appropriate to management needs. Hall[1] has argued rightly that planning is a political process which involves qualitative, multiple objectives that have not been reflected in the models built to date. He then argues that they should be explicitly recognised in the models. However, we believe that this recommendation is wrong. Qualitative objectives change over time, with changing circumstances and membership of influential decision-making groups, and are best excluded from the model. Political considerations, and the kinds of business that management are willing to consider, should determine the alternatives tested by the model. By spelling out the financial implications of planning assumptions and alternatives tested, corporate models help to clarify issues and so make the political process more effective. By introducing a further discipline into the process, they permit the area of conflict between rival factions to be further reduced, and so contribute to final resolution of this conflict.

(D)   The importance of *availability of data* has already been stressed in Chapter 6. For the model to be used, it must be possible to obtain the information required by it within the time, effort and cost limits thought reasonable by management. These limits may be met much more quickly than many model builders fondly imagine. Perhaps because of professional pride, or a desire to produce a more powerful aid to management, model builders are tempted to build models that are large, complex, and have excessive appetites for input data.

Another point should not pass unmentioned. To produce mathematically correct non-accounting relationships, a considerable amount of data not normally collected by the company may be necessary. Sometimes this cannot be obtained. For instance, past records may have been destroyed or information from external bodies may not be forthcoming. Sometimes data may be collected only by experimental changes of important factors. Relationships between volume of demand and price changes, for instance, can be determined only from data collected immediately before and after price changes. Yet price variation can be highly disruptive and may not be permitted by management.

Consequently, there may be difficulty in obtaining data necessary to develop and update some of the more complex models, as well as in getting inputs necessary to operate them. It is instructive to note that one of the problems voiced most frequently by model builders was that of data availability.

(E)   A corporate model is more likely to be used and data required is more likely to be available if it is *embedded in the normal planning process*. In other words, the model should ideally use data produced as a matter of routine in the normal planning process and facilitate testing of the kinds of alternatives normally considered during such planning.

In one large company, a model was developed which required data to be input at divisional level. It was initially intended that this data, which was thought to be necessary for divisional planning, should be generated and input during divisional planning. In the event, the divisional managers found that some of the data was not normally collected by them and were not convinced that the output reports would make a major contribution to their existing planning work. Consequently, because it did not fit into the existing planning framework, and made excessive demands for data, the large model was shelved. Instead, a simple, corporate model was developed, which served the needs of corporate staff perfectly well.

By contrast at London Transport Executive the model stemmed directly from the needs of the existing planning system, and is in essence a computer version of procedures carried out previously by hand. It is fully integrated into the planning system, and is thought by all levels of management to be very successful, indeed the suite of models is now being extended.

(F)   *Documentation* of the model has already been considered in Chapter 6 and needs little further discussion here. For sake of completeness, we merely remind the reader of its importance, and of the difficulties of understanding or using a model which has not been adequately described when the model builder either leaves the company or moves to a new post within it. It is surprising that such a basic step is so often overlooked and that models fail for this reason alone. A realistic organisation should not allow a person, who has been promoted, to leave his old job until it is satisfied that model documentation is up-to-date.

These basic conditions for success suggest the following guidelines for corporate modelling:

1   Obtain sponsorship from the highest possible level of management.
2   Involve management likely to use the model at *all* stages of its development.

3 If possible, introduce members of departments that are potential users into the team that develops the model.
4 Allow for availability of data when designing the structure and inputs of the model.
5 Make the first model as simple as is reasonably possible and get it into use quickly.
6 Ensure that the model meets clearly specified needs of particular groups of managers and preferably aids solution of a difficult and pressing management problem.
7 Design the modules to facilitate interlinking with others in a corporate suite at a later date.
8 Ensure that documentation is adequate throughout model development.

9.3 Basis for success in the sample companies

To determine the extent to which the most important of the conditions for success existed within companies having corporate models we collected information on the initiation and general support from management for corporate modelling. Data was also collected on the functional background of the modellers, on those who were responsible for updating the models, and those using them. Modellers were asked, too, how far the model was integrated into the planning process of the firm, whether the model was used for *ad hoc* decisions or in regular routine planning, and also its range of uses. Complexity of the model was gauged from detailed answers about the type of model, number of input and output variables, number of program statements, and facilities offered by the model. The number of input variables also reflects directly the data requirements of the model. Some of the results of this analysis have already been presented in earlier chapters, but we now turn to those aspects bearing strongly on success.

Support for development
The positions of those who initiated proposals to develop corporate models and of the most senior managers fully supporting, or sponsoring, them are given in *Figure 9.1*. Proposals for development of models came mainly from three groups. In 35 per cent of companies, the demand for a model arose from a board member, in some cases from the managing director himself. Corporate planners, too, have been a major source of such proposals, having made them in 23 per cent of the companies. By contrast with these groups, both of which comprise potential users, a quarter of the proposals were initiated by potential model builders, whom we have grouped as 'management services'.

Motives
Views elicited during our interviews in the companies visited suggested mixed motivations for starting modelling. In many cases, models were constructed to meet a specific and clear decision-making need, as at Rover and at Yorkshire Imperial Plastics (see Chapter 8). In others they were regarded as desirable for general, unspecified, future decision-taking. A number of organisations, like Anglia Building Society (see Chapter 8), initiated modelling primarily to reduce the burden of manual calculations for long-term planning and budgeting. Others stressed the need to get the results of these calculations earlier. Where the management services group initiated the proposal there was a natural desire to extend its services into the area of strategic planning. Perhaps in some cases there was a desire to appear 'progressive', on the part of both managers and management service specialists, though we did not detect it. We were impressed by the genuine desire of modellers to make a practical contribution to improved

Figure 9.1 Initiation and support for corporate modelling

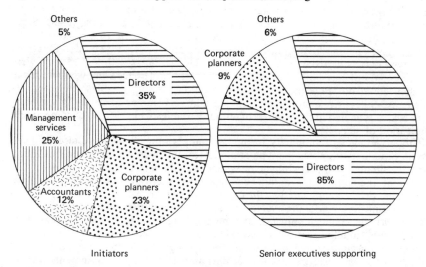

decision-taking. This, naturally, led to frustrations and irritations when management preferred to use personal intuition instead.

Although most models were initiated by managers and specialists below board level, they had succeeded in gaining support from at least one director in 85 per cent of the companies. We should qualify these general results, though, by mention of the degree of support. This ranged from the enthusiastic to the lukewarm. The Managing Director of CRC Information Services had even taken a hand in modelling as had Finance Directors at Lansing Bagnall, Patent Shaft Steelworks and Yorkshire Imperial Plastics. In a number of others, the director had approved the necessary expenditure on development, then adopted a cautious wait and see attitude, as at Anglia Building Society. In each organisation where support from directors had been enthusiastic there were clear indications of the success of the corporate models, except where those directors subsequently left the company.

Background of staff
The functional background of the builders (discussed more fully in Chapter 2) was related to the source of proposals to develop corporate models and the identity of the most senior supporter. Where the proposal was initiated by management services, there was a tendency for them to do the modelling, although in some cases they drew members of other functions into their team. In other companies accountants were often in the model building team. Indeed, in at least 9 per cent of the companies model development was done primarily by accountants. One of the largest models we encountered, that of the London Transport Executive, was built almost entirely by accountants as were the models at British Titan and Yorkshire Imperial Plastics. At ATV, Anglia Building Society and Patent Shaft Steelworks models were developed by accountants, but aided by generous free assistance from bureaux.

Data availability and size
Data availability was mentioned frequently as a problem by those we visited during the survey. We have already referred to this in Chapter 3 and in Section 9.2. Clearly, the greater the data requirements, the greater the problems in this respect. Consequently,

one of the features we explored was the number of input variables, (e.g. sales of product Y in each of 10 years to a planning horizon would count as one variable only, although 10 different figures might be required). *Figure 9.2* shows the result. Since many companies had suites of modules which could be linked or used separately, the figures are given per module. Almost half of the modules or separate models for which we received details had 100 or less input variables. Modules with less than 25 were quite common, but inevitably these were very simple, and hence somewhat limited in what they could do. Few modules had over 10,000 input variables. This reflects problems of collecting, handling and updating large volumes of data. This general picture is also reflected in the number of output variables which is also to some extent an indication of size.

The advantages of simplicity in the company's first model have already been stressed. Simplicity involves the type of model (for instance deterministic simulation models are simpler than probabilistic ones) and the number of relationships involved. At first sight, the number of program statements may seem an appropriate measure of the latter, but this is complicated by the fact that many more relationships are involved in a model built in a modelling system than in a model written in a general-purpose language with the same number of statements. The reason should be clear from Section 7.3 on modelling systems. None the less, the amount of work involved in developing, programming and updating the detailed logic is reflected to some extent by the number of program statements. Hence the numbers of program statements are also shown in *Figure 9.2*.

The overall picture to emerge is of a greater use of relatively small (in the range 1–1,000) than of large modules. Numbers of input and output variables are very closely associated, the latter showing the same declining frequency for categories above 1,000. Similarly, the number of program statements, which is usually in excess of the numbers of input and output variables, shows a very strong concentration in the 101 to 1,000 range, and thereafter the frequency of occurrence falls markedly.

Figure 9.3 gives details of the numbers of modules in the corporate suites of the survey companies. This shows that only 20 per cent of the companies had a single module constituting the corporate model. Over half of the companies had corporate models with two, three or four modules. Few companies had more than six modules in the corporate suites.

Figure 9.2 Number of input, output and program statements
in individual modules

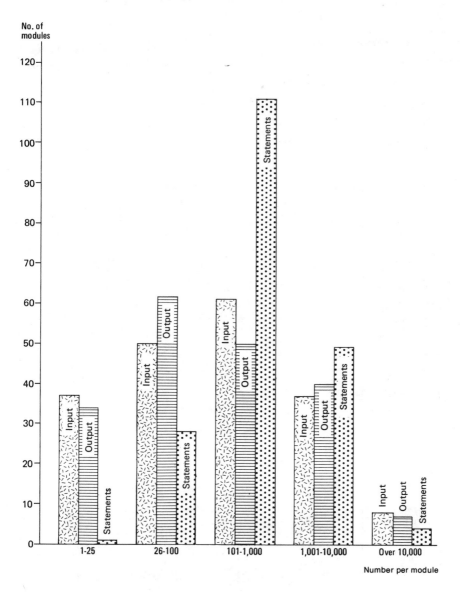

Figure 9.3 Number of modules per corporate suite

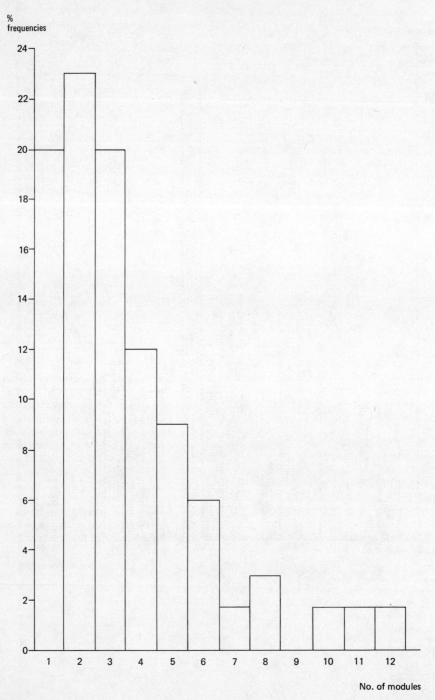

Figure 9.4 Type of planning in which models are used

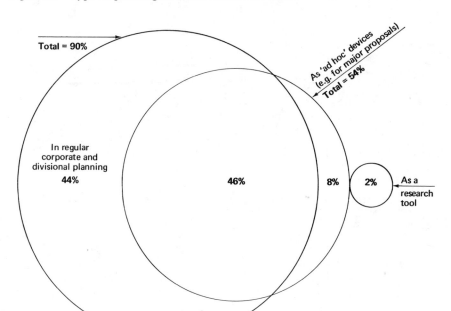

Use

Finally, we look at the extent to which models are used for *ad hoc* decisions and in regular planning, and also at the degree to which they have become integrated into the planning process. *Figure 9.4* indicates that the great majority of models are being used for routine planning. Half of these were also used to aid major, *ad hoc* decisions on issues like mergers. Less than one-tenth of the companies use their models solely for *ad hoc* decisions. This underlines the way use of models tends to be associated with regular long-range or corporate planning, a feature that Gershefski[5] noted in his survey in 1968, and that Boulden,[6] too, has stressed. It also emphasises the importance of full integration of such models into the planning process or procedures.

Figure 9.5 is consistent with the use of models in regular planning. It shows that the majority of models are used by those involved in regular planning (corporate planners and accountants). Only a fifth of all models are used by operational researchers or data processing personnel. This suggests that models may be integrated fairly fully into the planning process carried out by these users.

Figure 9.5 Model users

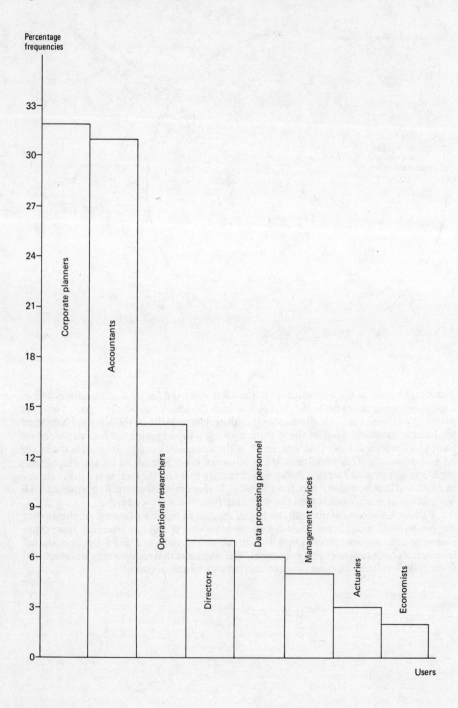

Figure 9.6 Integration of models into the planning system

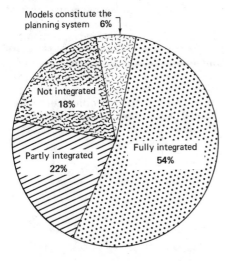

Models constitute the
planning system   6%

Not integrated
18%

Partly integrated
22%

Fully integrated
54%

Integration in planning
It is not surprising, therefore, that use of the models has become a routine part of the
total planning process or procedural system in most of the companies (see *Figure 9.6*).
In 60 per cent of the companies the models were said to either constitute or be fully
integrated into the planning process. In 22 per cent, they were said to be 'partly
integrated', which we interpret as meaning that they were used sometimes by those
taking decisions but not as a matter of course. The remaining 18 per cent of the
companies said that either some or all of their models were not integrated into the
planning process. This we interpret as meaning that they are not regularly used in
planning.

Such figures seem to confirm that a significant proportion of companies, but not
all, are using their corporate models fully.

4   *Success in the sample companies*

These results suggest that most but not all companies had conditions necessary for
success. It is instructive, then, to look at indications of the level of success among the
UK companies with corporate models. Unfortunately, no direct measure of success or
failure is possible, because few companies were able to place a monetary value on the
benefits derived from the model. Consequently, subjective measures were used, four
separate ones being employed to allow checks on consistency. In this way an attempt
was made to eliminate some of the more serious errors that often attend subjective
estimates. None the less, when interpreting the results it must be borne in mind that the
answers were supplied mainly by the model builders in each company, who may be
more inclined to report success than failure. Moreover, since many of the sample
approached us in the first instance, the sample itself may be somewhat biased towards
successful applications. In this respect, though, it is fair to note that we were
impressed during our visits to companies by a number of frank admissions of failure.
These related largely to failure to gain acceptance from top management. This seemed
to be a fairly general problem but was especially marked for probabilistic models.

Modellers were asked, first, what reliance top management place on reports from the models, on manual reports from line managers and specialist staff advisors and on their own intuitive judgement. They indicated the relative importance of each by distributing 100 points between them. The results, over all companies in the sample, are shown in *Figure 9.7*. On average, about as much reliance was placed on computer reports as on those still produced manually, but the factor which remained most important by far was the intuitive judgement of the decision-makers themselves. This is not surprising, and certainly should not be construed as implying failure, for strategic decisions are complex, involving multiple objectives and many imponderable factors of a qualitative nature, which cannot be readily represented within corporate models. In such circumstances, the corporate model may be expected to contribute to better decisions by a more thorough, faster evaluation of key financial aspects, but can never replace the judgement of experienced and able decision-takers.

Figure 9.7   Reliance top managers thought to place on reports

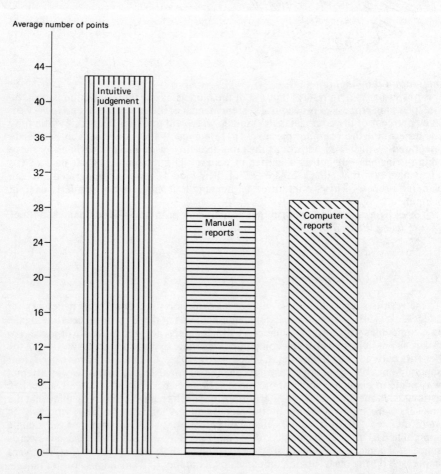

As a second means of assessing success, modellers were asked how much their corporate models had improved forecasts. The results given in *Figure 9.8* show that 62 per cent of respondents thought that the improvement was significant or very significant. Elimination of arithmetic errors and advantages of speed in giving more timely forecasts were frequently quoted.

Modellers were also asked whether top managers consider corporate models a success in terms of benefits derived given the cost. Their answers are shown in *Figure 9.9*. If we assume that the 14 per cent of companies which replied that it was too early to comment should have been classified as 'not successful', over half the sample would still have been regarded as successful and a further 18 per cent as at least partially successful. Consequently, even though we must qualify the results reported in *Figure 9.9*, it must still be true that most companies that have undertaken corporate modelling have not regretted it. There are clearly some, though, which have, and their number may be higher than the figure of 8 per cent suggests.

Finally, we asked how management, in general, have reacted to the use of corporate models. The responses of the model builders are recorded in *Figure 9.10*. From this it will be seen that in over half of the companies the reaction was thought to be good but was bad in 11 per cent. If we assume, again, lack of success among the 32 per cent of the companies which remained undecided then we find that reaction is poor in almost half the companies. Of course, such an assumption is likely to bias the results towards failure, and therefore gives an extreme position.

Figure 9.8   How much models improve forecasts

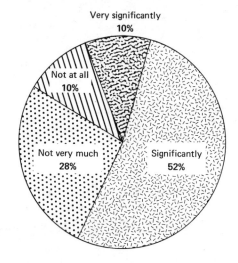

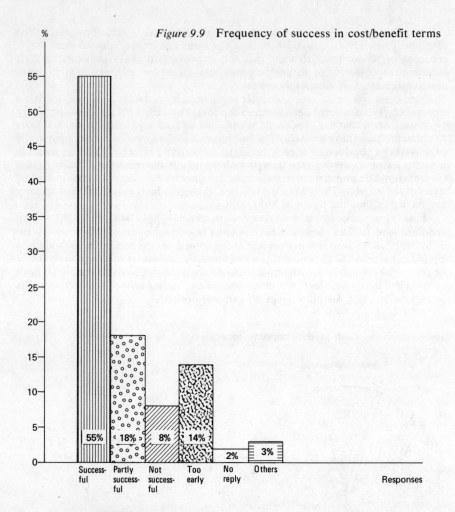

Figure 9.9 Frequency of success in cost/benefit terms

%

55% 18% 8% 14% 2% 3%

Success-ful Partly success-ful Not success-ful Too early No reply Others

Responses

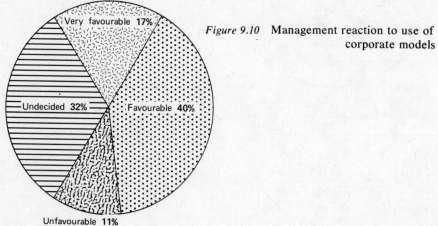

Figure 9.10 Management reaction to use of corporate models

Very favourable 17%

Undecided 32%

Favourable 40%

Unfavourable 11%

.5 *Summary*

The data collected during the survey was examined to see if the conditions for success advanced in Section 9.2 could be confirmed or rejected by statistical analysis. Unfortunately, statistical tests proved to be inconclusive, because the data was too crude. For instance, the fact that 85 per cent of the models were supported by a director prevents adequate analysis. Moreover, the survey data did not indicate the degree of support, whether it was enthusiastic or lukewarm, which is obviously important.

Further, an adequate measure of the complexity or simplicity of a model could not be derived for use with the survey data, and there was no way in which the data collected, even though it was extensive, could be used to establish how appropriate the model was to management decision-making needs. Throughout, one of the major problems was the fact that in many companies there were several modules, each of which was used in a different way, and in some cases by different groups of managers.

However, our four subjective *measures* of success suggest the same pattern of general success with a fairly high incidence of failure. The latter is related to the fact that the problem encountered most frequently by modellers was gaining management acceptance, because this meant breaking down old attitudes and in some cases vested interests. This confirms the importance of the three *conditions* for success that relate to gaining support of management (i.e. A, B and C of Section 9.2).

Similarly, almost a third of the companies reported problems in obtaining input data, which underlines the importance of the fourth condition. A number of companies had also had to abandon models, most of them starting again almost from scratch, because successors to modellers who had left the company or transferred to other jobs within it found poor documentation.

In general then, data collected tended to confirm the importance of the conditions for success suggested in Section 9.2, even though rigorous statistical analysis was not possible.

References

Hall, W. K.; Strategic planning models: are top managers really finding them useful? *Journal of Business Policy,* Winter 1972.

Brown, D. E.; Stages in the life cycle of a corporate planning model
Published in Schrieber, A. N.; *Corporate simulation models.* University of Washington Graduate School of Business Administration, 1970.

Goldie, G. H.; Simulation and irritation.
Published in Schrieber, A. N. *(op. cit.).*

Wagner, W. H., Akutagawa, L. T. and Cumpo, L. J.; Telecommunications earnings estimation model (TEEM).
Published in Schrieber, A. N. *(op. cit.).*

Gershefski, G. W.; Corporate models: the state of the art.
Management Science(Application), Feb. 1970.

Boulden, J. B.; Computerised corporate planning.
Long Range Planning, June 1971.

Chapter 10

The cost of corporate models

Costs and benefits

Ideally, a management decision to proceed with development of a corporate model should be based on an assessment of the costs and benefits. It is, therefore, most unfortunate that there is virtually no published data on either of these aspects.

Published cost estimates are virtually non-existent. The only one we found was made by Boulden[1] who estimated a typical cost as £20,000 for a 'sizeable' company and £10,000 for a company with an annual turnover of £10 million. These costs excluded detailed design of procedures for data collection, programming and operating costs. They were also based on information collected from his own clients, most of which were US companies. Our own data suggests that these figures are misleading. Apart from anything else, they are related solely to the size of the company, rather than to size of model. The type of model is completely ignored. The general validity of these figures was, in fact, in doubt before our survey was undertaken. As reported elsewhere,[2] our own experience in three companies gave us total costs figures, including programming, which were below those of Boulden.

Again, no adequate account of financial benefits resulting from corporate models is available. As pointed out in Chapter 6, because many of the benefits are intangible, the exercise of estimating their financial value is rarely performed. (Consequently, available sources of information on benefits is small.) But even in such cases there are benefits, such as the improved understanding of the company given to management, which have not been valued financially. It is difficult, for instance, to determine what financial value the London Transport Executive should put on more accurate and timely forecasts.

Boulden and Buffa[3] give examples which suggest that benefits exceed costs. Their account is given verbatim. 'After developing an on-line planning system, the finance department of a large foods company estimates that it is now the second largest profit centre in the firm due to the efficiency with which it is managing cash flow and generating interest income on surplus cash. A mining company has just re-evaluated its total corporate strategy concerning domestic versus foreign operations in the face of rising labour costs. A steel company estimates the first year of operation of their system saved sufficient managerial and clerical labour to pay for the entire installation. . . . A major plywood producer claims to have saved ten times the cost of their system in a lower purchase price negotiated on a single large timber tract. . . . A diversified firm believes that it has significantly improved the return on investment in major hotels through use of a management model.'

Our survey suggested that these instances of an excess of benefits over costs are fairly typical. It was shown in Section 9.4 that modellers in a majority of the companies thought their top management regarded the corporate model as a success in terms of costs/benefits. Although the benefits had been quantified in only a few firms, and then not fully, this rough subjective assessment is better than nothing. It is, moreover, the only evidence adduced to date in the UK on this subject.

Although it was not possible to place a financial value on benefits, we were able to estimate costs of developing models for many of the companies visited, and collected fairly detailed information. However, in many of the companies having their own computer no detailed account of computer and other costs of operation were kept, and many of the costs (e.g. of management time) were hidden in virtually all. It quickly became evident that operating costs were best excluded from the questionnaire which therefore concentrated on those of model development. Consequently, although our survey findings give details of the costs of developing corporate models, we are restricted to general observations on operating costs.

10.2 *Causes of cost variations*

In approaching measurement of costs of developing corporate models, it is necessary to recognise that models vary widely by size and type, and that costs may be expected to be related to these variations.

A first major difference is that of size. *Figure 9.2* showed that the number of inputs and outputs are roughly proportional. Each independently, or both jointly, therefore provide an index of the size of the model. For obvious reasons, as the size rises, the cost of developing the model tends to do so too. More data must be collected, more relationships established, more programming done, and so on.

Size alone is not sufficient as a means of differentiating between models for purposes of cost estimation. An obvious distinction is that between use of modelling systems and general-purpose languages. As seen in Chapter 7, the former permit the use of standard computer routines designed for planning applications, which reduce the time involved in both establishing and programming the logic of the model. On the other hand, computer costs of model development may be much greater with a modelling system. Many modelling systems are less efficient because of the extra operations necessary to convert the program into the instructions finally implemented by the computer. In addition, many modellers believe that the modelling systems used on bureaux computers have an added loading factor to allow the development costs to be recouped (see Chapter 7).

So, higher operating costs must be set against the lower costs of programming and reprogramming in the event of updating the logic, input format, or output reports. The relative economics of operating and maintaining a model with modelling systems and general-purpose languages turn, therefore, on the expected frequency of program changes, and the frequency of use expected.

Related to this difference between modelling systems and general-purpose language models is that between modes of operation. As seen in Chapters 3 and 7, use of most modelling systems is normally tied to bureaux computers, often in the conversational mode. This mode has the advantage of user interaction with the model and of fast response. But it is expensive; the time the user is connected with the computer costs £2 to over £12 per hour. Costs can be exorbitant if the modeller does his thinking at the terminal rather than at his desk, as in one insurance company, where development of the program alone cost £5,000 in computer charges.

A further factor that affects both costs of developing and operating a corporate model is its internal sophistication. An optimisation model is often more expensive to produce and operate than a deterministic simulation model receiving the same number of inputs. It is tempting for the advocates of simulation models to quote the BP linear programming model, which has cost in excess of £200,000 and has already taken six calendar years to develop. The operating costs of running this Goliath are also high. It is said to take six hours of computer time on each run. This example is, however, not typical. Although we obtained only a small sample of optimisation models, most of them were very much cheaper than this to develop and operate. Nevertheless, one may still expect optimisation models to be more expensive than deterministic simulation models of similar size, in other words with roughly the same number of input and output variables. This is discussed more fully in Section 10.5.

Similarly, because of their greater complexity and additional problems of testing and validation, probabilistic models are considerably more expensive to develop than deterministic simulation models with the same number of input and output variables. In addition, as mentioned in Chapter 3, their main routines must be repeated many times to test each alternative, sometimes several hundred times for each one of a deterministic model. The high cost of operating probabilistic models was, perhaps, one of the reasons why many of those we encountered during the survey had been little used.

Finally, models mapping physical operations of the company require a detailed analysis of these operations to establish appropriate relationships, and may therefore be expected to cost more to develop. Again, operating costs may be higher, because the data input to the model is normally more voluminous and more computer calculations are necessary before the results of an alternative are aggregated in financial terms to corporate level.

Although the effect of these differences between models on costs is intuitively clear, and should certainly influence the kind of corporate model built, no cost data has been available to date to aid management or the modellers in their choice. To remedy this situation, we have structured our analysis of the cost data to show the cost implications of these differences, and present the results in Sections 10.4 and 10.5. Before turning to these, though, it is important to indicate the difficulties of estimating the costs involved, and the basis on which our estimates were established.

10.3   Difficulties of estimating costs

Information was collected on the number of man-weeks taken by staff on each major stage of model building, namely feasibility study and development of logic, programming, and implementation. The reader may note that, for convenience, certain of the stages of model development dealt with in Chapter 6 have been combined for the purposes of this exercise. The cost per man-week was also requested of each company. Estimates of computer time taken and external consultancy costs were also obtained. This information was collected for both the initial and the present model.

Calculation of the costs of developing models raises problems, though, even given such data. Where the model is run on the company's own computer, which has spare capacity, how should use of the computer be costed? As suggested earlier, the marginal cost of the use of the computer is merely that of stationery and of staff employed to, say, punch cards, and the latter is zero if the operators would be idle otherwise. However, the in-house computer may have spare capacity on some occasions and have work queueing on others. How should the cost of running the model on the computer be calculated when it is depriving other jobs of access? The marginal cost, in this case, will certainly be in excess of that of the computer time and staff involved. But it is virtually impossible to obtain appropriate data. These problems were compounded by differences in the computer charges levied by computer departments on in-house users.

There are similar difficulties in calculating the cost of skilled manpower used in development. In most cases, modellers were not engaged in full-time work on corporate models, but combined this work with other duties. Hence no additional salaries had to be paid because of modelling work. If the modellers would otherwise have been idle, which we doubt, the marginal cost would have been zero. If they would otherwise have been doing other work, the marginal cost is the value of that foregone work, this being the economist's 'opportunity cost'. However, it is difficult enough to calculate the total amount of time they spent on the model, and we found no way of getting to such true costs.

Similarly, the time of top managers and other specialist staff is consumed in answering questions, collecting data, and in being educated in use of the system. What cost is so incurred? We found it impossible to get even rough estimates of the time and grades of staff involved. Even had we succeeded, it is most unlikely that we would have found the true costs involved, since the same problems would attend this exercise as that of determining the true cost of the modellers' time.

There were, too, inevitable problems in deciding the basis for charging overheads to the corporate model. This is, of course, closely associated with the cost of man-power involved. The major overhead cost was that of office accommodation. Supporting secretarial costs could also, in most cases, be regarded as an overhead. Estimation of these costs did not, on the whole, present too great a problem to those interviewed during the survey. A greater problem was to determine whether the overheads should be adjusted to allow for the very high costs of office accommodation and secretarial assistance in London. Such an adjustment would make the cost of individual firms more directly comparable. On the other hand, it might lead to a distortion in the average costs obtained, and would certainly mean that the ranges quoted would not be actual costs incurred by companies.

Consequently, we were forced to adopt a somewhat arbitrary approach to estimating costs, but one which we believe to have the virtue of internal consistency. Where external computers were employed, the full charges incurred by the corporate model were normally available, and these figures were used. Because there was no means of knowing whether the in-house computer had spare capacity at the time of model runs during development, and if not what the cost of displacement of other work was, the run times were charged at the rate levied internally for control purposes. Where no such charges were levied internally for use of the computer, we made notional charges, to ensure consistency.

As for the time of the modeller, we found no way of determining the true cost of his time, and so charged it at historical cost to the company including overheads. During the interviews the respondents were asked for the cost per man-week including overheads. We found wide differences in the bases for calculating overheads. These affected the costs per man-week quoted to us, which ranged from £60 to £280, with most estimates clustered closely around £100. Consequently, to obtain consistency between companies' costs, we calculated manpower costs on the basis of £100 per man-week including overheads. There was one exception. When calculating the range of model building costs the actual figures supplied by the companies were used (*Figure 10.6*).

No account could be taken of the time taken by management and other staff not specifically assigned to the project. This is, therefore, a hidden cost. In practice it is likely to vary in proportion to the size of the model and its complexity. Consequently, we may expect this hidden cost to widen any cost differentials found in this respect.

Thus the figures we present in the next section are as far as possible calculated on a consistent basis for each firm.

10.4   *Survey results on costs*

Using the approach outlined in Section 10.3, data collected from the survey companies was used to calculate costs of developing, first, the initial working model and, second, the present model. As the latter was an extended or refined version of the former its costs included those of the former. Where average costs were calculated we used what we have termed the 'inter-quartile mean' to avoid distortion by very high or very low extreme values. We calculated this 'inter-quartile mean' by excluding the top and bottom quarters of the range and taking the arithmetic average of the rest.

Man-weeks. As a first step, an analysis of man-weeks spent on model development was undertaken for the sample as a whole, the results being shown in *Figure 10.1*. This indicates that, for the first working model, the feasibility study (including design of the

Figure 10.1 Break-down of man-weeks spent developing models

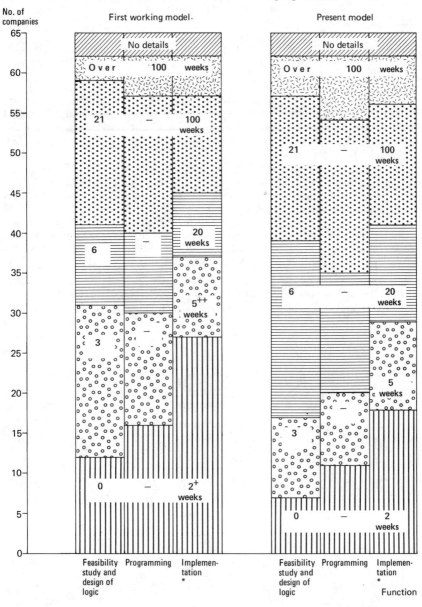

*Developing systems and data base to permit use as a planning tool; time spent by modellers in education of potential users.

+This shows the number of companies which spent 0 − 2 weeks on 'Feasibility study and design of logic' (12), 'Programming' (16), and 'Implementation' (27).

++Likewise this shows the number of companies which spent 3 − 5 weeks on 'Feasibility study and design of logic' (19), 'Programming' (14), and 'Implementation' (10).

N.B. The number of companies which spent *less than* 3, 6, 21, and 101 man-weeks may be read from the vertical scale for each of the three stages. For instance, 31 companies spent less than six man-weeks on the feasibility study.

model logic) and programming were roughly equally time consuming. Much less time, though, was taken on implementation – 27 companies spent no more than two man-weeks.

To get a better idea of representative times, extreme values were excluded, and average man-weeks for each stage determined. *Figure 10.2* resulted. This shows more clearly that programming was the most important single aspect, consuming 42 per cent of the total man-weeks required to develop both the first working model and the present model. The percentage for the feasibility study declined from 39 for the first working model to 32 for the present one.

Development of the present model from the initial working one involved, on average, an increase in total man-weeks from 26 to 43. It is evident that the modellers' task is far from finished when the first working model is completed. The 40 per cent increase in man-weeks for the feasibility study and logic development, the 64 per cent increase in the number for programming, and the 120 per cent for implementation underline the fact that many changes are required in the first working model. This is, of course, consistent with the view that many companies were starting with simple models and then making them more complex in easy stages.

Figure 10.2 Breakdown of man-weeks spent on average corporate models

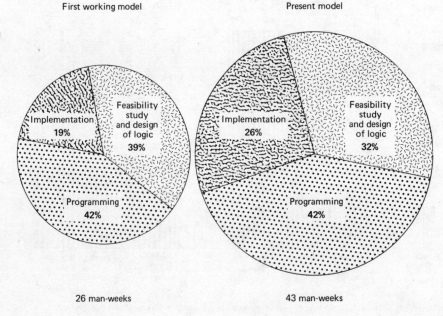

The cost of corporate models

Computer costs. Figure 10.3 gives the frequency with which different levels of computer costs were incurred during development in the sample as a whole, and the average after extremes had been eliminated to avoid distortion. It shows that almost half of the companies got both their first working model and present model for total computer costs of less than £1,000. On the other hand, over a quarter of the companies finally incurred computer costs of development in excess of £5,000. None the less, the average figures were still quite modest, £881 for the first and £1,669 for the present model.

Figure 10.3   Computer costs incurred in building corporate models

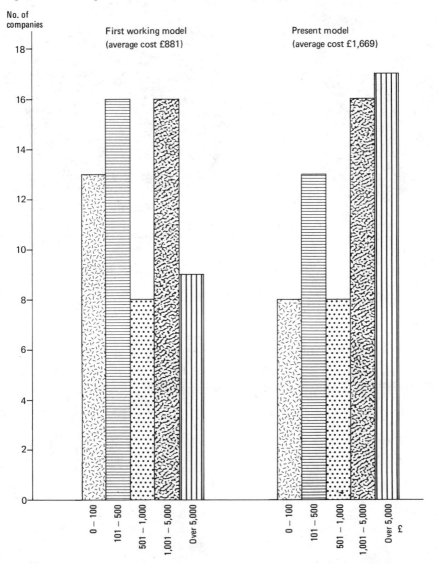

Consultancy costs. As was seen in Chapter 2, most firms did not use consultants, and hence had zero consultancy costs. Data for 15 of those which did are given in *Figure 10.4*. From these it will be noted that in the majority of companies using consultants, costs for both first working and present models fell between £501–£3,000. The mean cost for consultancy services for those who used them lay within the £1,501–£3,000 band for both the first working model and for the present model. This suggests that consultants were not used extensively once the first working model was completed.

Figure 10.4   Consultancy costs

Distribution of companies among cost brackets

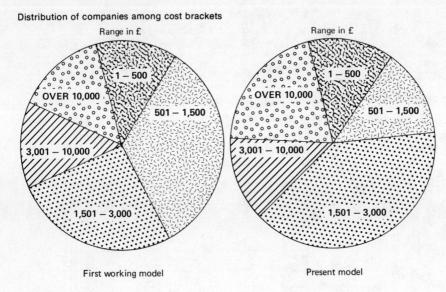

First working model   Present model

Average consultancy costs incurred

	Averaged over 15 companies £	Averaged over 62 companies £
First working model	1,950	471
Present model	2,571	622

The cost of corporate models

Average development costs. The average costs incurred on internal staff, consultants, and computing were summed to obtain fairly representative estimates of costs. These are shown in *Figure 10.5*. The average cost for the first working model was £3,952 and that of the present model was £6,591. One point we would make is that, if consultants were used, their cost would be considerably in excess of the figures shown, since these are the averages over all models including the majority for which consultancy costs were zero. Since averages over all the companies which returned cost data are shown, the low consultancy figures are to some extent balanced out by higher internal manpower costs than would be incurred by a firm using consultants.

Figure 10.5   Total development costs of the average corporate model

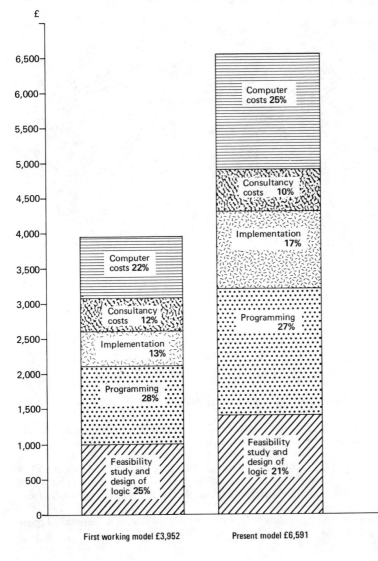

£

First working model £3,952   Present model £6,591

The average total costs of building first and present models given in *Figure 10.5* are consistent with the distribution of total costs given to us by the survey companies and shown in *Figure 10.6*. Over half the first working models cost less than £5,000 and the median cost for present models was within the £5,001–£10,000 band.

As indicated earlier, crude cost figures covering a variety of corporate models are a useful starting point but need to be qualified. Whether a particular company's model lies above or below the average may be expected to depend on the factors considered in Section 10.2. Since the range of costs was immense, from under £500 (for the ATV model used to illustrate modelling in Chapter 6) to £250,000, we obviously need to explore these issues further.

Figure 10.6   Cost of building corporate models: distribution of companies among cost brackets

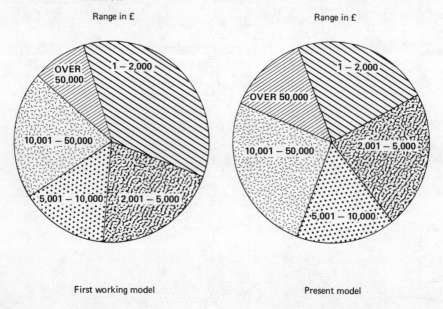

10.5   *Some factors influencing development costs*

Size is probably the most important single influence on costs. Since the number of program statements differs between modelling systems and general-purpose language models, for reasons given already, the number of input variables was used as the measure of size. Models for which cost data had been collected were categorised by size. There were obvious differences between costs of modelling systems and general-purpose language models which suggested that an analysis of the effect of size unrelated to the approach to programming would be misleading. Hence, for each size category, the average cost of models built with modelling systems or general-purpose languages was calculated. The results are given in *Figure 10.7*.

Figure 10.7   Average costs of models by size category

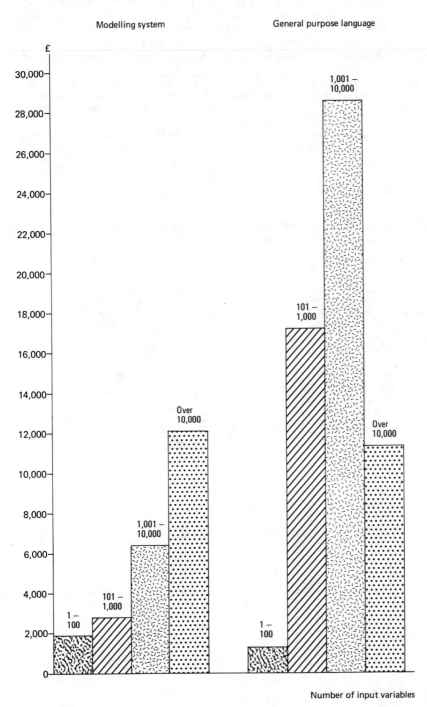

As a number of companies were using both modelling systems and general-purpose languages, and the costs of each could not be easily separated, our figures are necessarily based on smaller sample sizes, namely 20 models built with modelling systems and 24 with general-purpose languages. *Figure 10.8* shows how the models in these two subsamples were spread among the size categories. *Figure 10.9* gives the difference between the highest and lowest costs for both types of modelling, for each size category.

A number of interesting points emerge from a scrutiny of *Figures 10.7, 10.8* and *10.9*. First, the average cost of developing a model with a modelling system, although very much lower for models with between 101 and 10,000 input variables, is not consistently below that for doing so with a general-purpose language in all size categories. Second, the variability of costs tends to be higher with general-purpose languages. Hence the risk of a final cost much higher than the average, as well as the chance of one much lower, is greater. Third, there is a clear upward trend of development costs as size rises to 10,000 input variables.

Figure 10.8   Distribution of modelling system and general-purpose language models between size categories

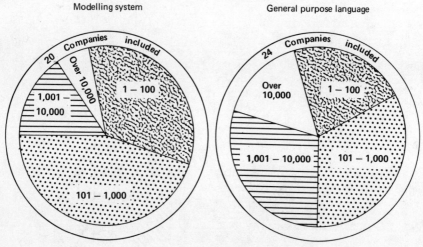

No. of input variables

Figure 10.9 Variation of costs

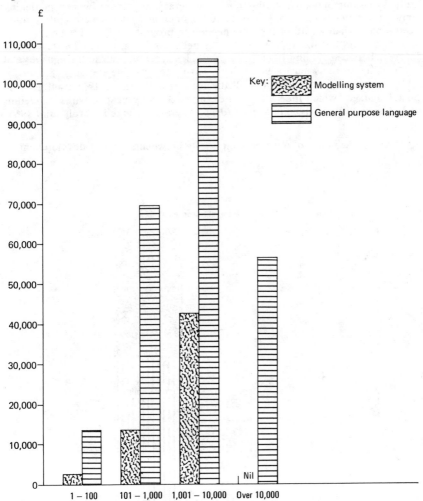

The differences in average costs are consistent with that between the average number of man-weeks for modelling systems and general-purpose languages (see *Figure 10.10*). It is strictly illegitimate to compare the average figures directly because of the tendency of models built with general-purpose languages to be bigger (see *Figure 10.8*). However, this objection does not apply to comparison of the proportions of man-weeks devoted to the feasibility study, programming and implementation. A far greater proportion of the time spent on general-purpose language models was devoted to programming, as expected, in view of the fact that modelling systems are basically programming aids. Reduction of programming times where modelling systems are used has already been mentioned; modelling systems were said by some to take no more than a fifth of the time needed to program in FORTRAN.

None the less the size of the differences between average costs for developing models with between 101 and 10,000 input variables in general-purpose languages and with modelling systems surprised us. This led us to examine the survey data for possible reasons. It was found that all the models built before 1968 used general-purpose languages which then led us to examine costs by year in which modelling started. The results are given in *Figure 10.11*. Average costs fell sharply after 1965.

Figure 10.10   Distribution of average man-weeks between stages of development

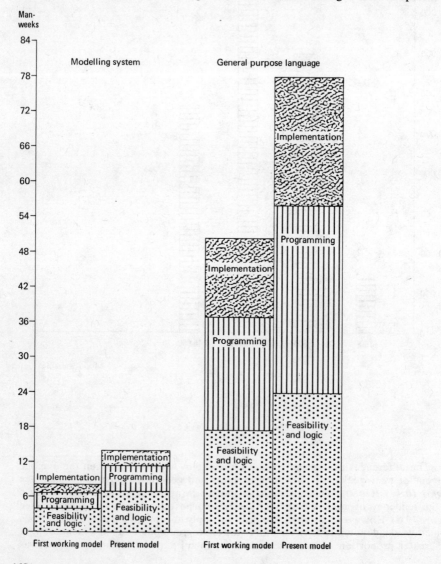

The cost of corporate models

Figure 10.11 Average cost of developing present model by year of start

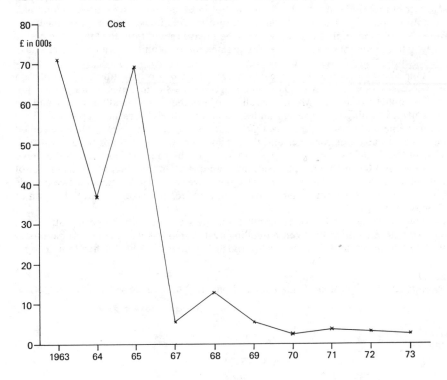

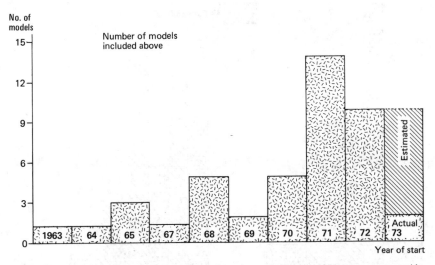

N.B. All but three of the models for which cost data were available up to 1971 were programmed in general purpose language.

This fall was no doubt due, in part, to a trend towards smaller models. However, it was also attributable, in part, to the dramatic fall in computer costs during this period. Computer costs for the early, large corporate models in general-purpose languages were considerably higher than they would be today. In addition, the longer the period for which a model has been in use, the greater the expenditure which tends to have been incurred on further development.

Our analysis of the difference between costs of optimisation and simulation models was less satisfactory. Data on costs of only 13 companies with optimisation models could be collected. Moreover, all but one of them used simulation, too, and the costs of developing optimisation and simulation models were not separated. Two features emerged strongly, though. Optimisation models were large. All but two had more than 1,000 input variables and three had over 10,000. Perhaps because of this, some of the models were very expensive, three of the four models we found to have cost over £100,000 included optimisation techniques. On the other hand, a number of these models cost less than the average for their size category, for instance two models with less than 1,000 input variables had a modest (for the size) cost in the region of £2,500.

Similarly, the number of probabilistic models was too low to permit statistical analysis, there being only seven modelling system models using some probabilities, five models programmed in general-purpose languages, and a further four using a

Figure 10.12　Distribution of financial and physical models between size categories

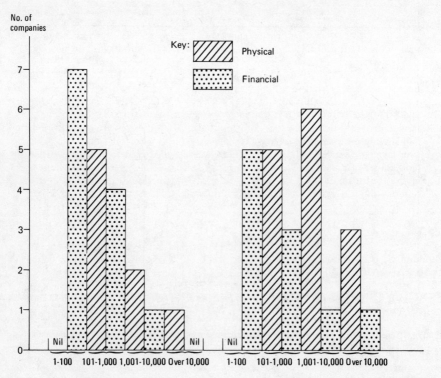

mixture of modelling systems, general-purpose languages or linear programming codes. Five of these models had costs below the average for corporate models of their size and approach to programming. Indeed, two of the five had costs well below their respective averages. Another five models had costs above the upper end of the cost range for the comparable category of deterministic models. Hence, it would seem that some use of probabilities need not be very expensive, but the costs of probabilistic models can be far greater than deterministic ones.

The study of the costs of corporate models incorporating physical as well as financial aspects of the company's business is more rewarding. There were more models which could be placed into each category but, unfortunately, there was a tendency for the larger models to embrace physical as well as financial aspects while the smaller models covered only the latter. This is shown in *Figure 10.12*. In the 101–1,000 input variables bracket there are enough models of both financial and physical varieties to allow at least a rough comparison of costs. In this category the average cost for models covering physical aspects and using modelling systems was £3,500, whilst that of purely financial models was much lower at £2,080. In addition, the spread of costs of physical models was much greater, ranging from £1,410 to £14,760 compared with £1,620 to £4,280 for purely financial ones. Similarly, means for physical and financial models using general-purpose languages, and in the 101–1,000 input variables category, were £41,688 and £4,850 respectively. The appropriate ranges were £5,300 to £71,450 and £1,475 to £8,500 respectively. These differences are substantial. Because of the small numbers of models involved, it was not possible to produce statistical results that demonstrated that these differences were not due to chance alone, but they are none the less strongly suggestive.

0.6 *Summary*

The most important points that have emerged from this chapter are:
- Costs are heavily dependent on the size of the model.
- Small corporate models can be developed for less than £1,000, and most models cost well under £10,000.
- The average cost of developing models has fallen from over £35,000 in the years up to 1965 to a figure in the region of £3,000 in years since 1970.
- Where physical flows are represented in corporate models the cost of development tends inevitably to be much higher.
- The largest element of costs is skilled manpower. This is reduced by use of modelling systems. Hence their use tends to reduce average development costs below that attendant on the use of general-purpose languages and also greatly reduces the range of such costs for all but the smallest models.

References

Boulden, J. B.; Computerised corporate planning.
Long Range Planning, June 1971.

Grinyer, P. H. & Batt, C. D.; Some tentative findings on corporate simulation models.
Operational Research Quarterly, March 1974.

Boulden, J. B. & Buffa, E. S.; Corporate models: on-line, real-time systems.
Harvard Business Review, July–Aug. 1970.

Chapter 11

Choice of Model

11.1 *Systematic approaches to choice*

Management considering development of a corporate model are confronted by a series of interrelated choices. In such circumstances, decision-taking can often be aided by a systematic approach, whereby the alternatives are explored in a logical sequence.

Broadly two approaches are open. Management may explore as wide a range as possible of ready-made models, modelling systems, general programming languages, types of model, modes of operation, etc., and then by successive selection of the best from competing alternatives may converge on a solution. As long as a complete range of alternatives is studied, this should yield the best solution, but at a very considerable cost in terms of time, effort and money.

A more practical approach is that of diverging from certain general decisions to detailed study of more limited ranges of options. This is shown in *Figure 11.1*. Because the amount of detailed study is greatly reduced, considerable savings of time, effort and money are effected, by comparison with the convergent approach. The attendant disadvantage is that the options studied may not include the one most suitable for the company. To reduce the risk of this, care must be taken to ensure that the sequence of decisions is logical, and that at every point decisions are based on sufficient information. Moreover, we may revert to an earlier decision when information uncovered later suggests that it may have been wrong. To show how information collected with regard to one decision may affect another we have shown the main interrelationships by broken lines in *Figure 11.2*.

11.2 *The major choices*

The first decision is whether to have a corporate model at all. As has been shown in Chapter 9 not all corporate models are successful, and it is ill-advised to launch out in hope without first checking that the conditions for success exist. Chapter 9 suggests some questions that should be put:

- Is sponsorship and continued support likely to be forthcoming from senior management and preferably a member of the board?
- What specific needs would the model meet?
- In particular, who would be helped by the model, to aid what decisions, how adequate are these decisions already without use of a model, and in what respects might improvement be effected by use of a model?
- Could use of a corporate model be integrated fairly easily into the existing decision-making process?
- Would the data requirements of a corporate model be met from information already collected and held?
- If not, how much additional information is likely to be involved, how disruptive would its collection be, and how much would it cost?
- How much is a corporate model, that would meet the needs identified effectively but in the simplest way possible, likely to cost?
- Are anticipated benefits worth this expenditure?

If there is an acceptable *prima facie* case for getting a corporate model, management may then proceed further to an investigation of the broad type of model likely to be appropriate, and the ways of developing it. The issues here tend to be closely related. Perhaps the key decision is whether the model should be ready-made or tailor-made. Where a model is adopted which requires no additional logic development

172

Choice of Model

Figure 11.1   Divergent approach

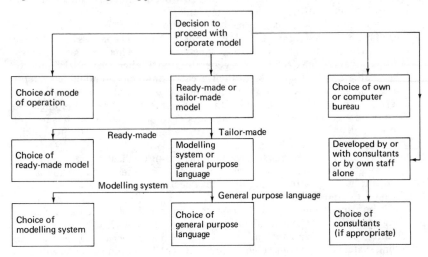

Figure 11.2   Divergent approach showing connections

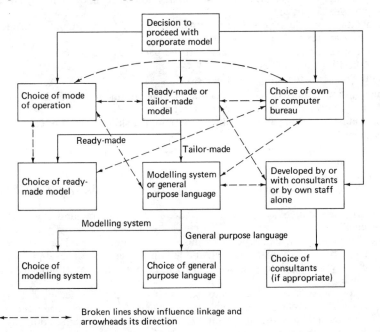

Broken lines show influence linkage and arrowheads its direction

or programming by the user, the choice between modelling system and general purpose language is clearly inappropriate, as is that on use of consultants as opposed to (or in addition to) internal staff to develop the model.

Similarly, mode of operation is closely related to whether or not a modelling system is used. Most modelling systems allow use of the model in conversational mode whereas few models built in a general-purpose language do so. This is because the cost of building the conversational facility into a general-purpose language model would not normally be justified. Again, because of their greater simplicity, modelling systems can be understood and used without great effort by those without prior knowledge of computer programming. Therefore, whilst the employment of consultants might be necessary to build a general-purpose language model when the company has not got appropriate specialists available internally, use of modelling systems can often make their employment unnecessary.

Because they are so closely related, the factors bearing on these choices tend to be common, although some affect one more strongly than another. Information about these can, again, be elicited by asking the right questions:

- How would the model be used?
- Would it be used frequently, and to process large volumes of data in routine planning operations, or less frequently on *ad hoc* decisions?
- Given the expected frequency and size of runs, is the greater cost of operating a modelling system likely to outweigh the lower cost of developing a model with it?
- If so, is the greater cost likely to be justified by other benefits accruing from a modelling system?
- Would the proposed applications require much modelling to develop an acceptable model with the available packages?
- How would this compare with the cost of developing a model entirely in a general-purpose language?
- What advantages would the users gain from use of the batch, conversational, and remote batch modes respectively?
- What are the strong and weak points about the packages available?
- What are the time and cost constraints?
- How do these affect the company's decision?
- How adequate would provisions for maintaining the confidentiality of data be in each of batch, conversational, and remote batch modes?
- What specialist modelling and computer programming skills do staff of the company possess?
- Could those with appropriate skill, if any, be released to work on development of a corporate model?
- If not, who could be released, and would they be capable of quickly learning to model build either in a general-purpose language or (more likely) a modelling system?
- What external assistance is available, how adequate would it be, and how much would it cost?

Other decisions are clearly dependent on those already mentioned. For instance, a decision on the best ready-made model, modelling system, or general-purpose language is scarcely appropriate if a decision to pursue a different approach has already been made.

The use of a detailed checklist, visits to existing users, simple bench-mark tests and test runs of slightly larger but still small models have already been discussed in Chapter 7 as aids to selecting the most suitable package for the specific company. Rather than duplicate this material here, we emphasise their importance and refer the reader to Chapter 7 for an account of the factors involved. *Figure 7.10* should be particularly valuable within the framework of a wider selection process.

Where it has been decided that a general-purpose language should be used its choice is not difficult normally. An investment of time and effort is involved in gaining mastery of any general-purpose language and the company is well advised, therefore, to use a language with which its programmers are already familiar, provided this is suitable. In general, ALGOL, FORTRAN, and PL/1 are each suitable for financial models. These languages are among the most flexible, as may be seen from Appendix 3, and can do anything required of them by financial corporate models. They are widely used, especially FORTRAN, and it is consequently much easier to obtain the services of programmers experienced in them. BASIC, JEAN and other languages for conversational use on bureaux time-sharing computers often have size of program limitations. Most of the other languages were designed specifically for other types of application, which makes them less suitable for financial corporate models.

If the company does not have specialist programmers, which probably means that it does not have its own computer, we would advise it against embarking on a general-purpose language model at all. Programmers can, of course, be employed on a temporary or full-time basis. There may be problems, though, if they leave during construction of the model. The problem of updating, too, should not be overlooked. There may not be enough work to justify continued employment of a programmer, but his services may be required from time to time to update the model. Under these circumstances, the attractions of modelling systems that can be learnt by most intelligent accountants and managers in under a week, and which do not demand a high level of programming proficiency to produce a reasonably efficient model, are obvious.

1.3 *A detailed approach to selection*

The major choices considered in Section 11.2 may be placed into three categories. In descending order of both generality and importance these are:

First-order:	Whether to proceed with detailed study of corporate models or not.
Second-order:	Whether to use ready-made or tailor-made models.
	Whether to use modelling system or general-purpose language.
	Whether to use batch, conversational, or remote batch mode of operation.
	Whether to use consultants to help develop the model.
	Whether to use own or bureau computer.
Third-order:	Choice of ready-made model (if appropriate).
	Choice of modelling system (if appropriate).
	Choice of general-purpose language (if appropriate).

To these could be added a whole series of related, but more detailed, decisions that we could designate fourth order. These include selection of particular members of the company's staff who are to be responsible for modelling; the extent to which relationships based on non-accounting logic will be used; what physical operations, if any, will be modelled; the level of aggregation of detail of input data; and so on. Factors that bear on these decisions have been discussed in earlier chapters. Readers of these chapters will be struck immediately by the fact that they affect, indirectly but strongly, first-, second- and third-order decisions, too. Consequently, they cannot be ignored during the selection process, and an outline of the possible solution in each case must be held in the mind of the decision-taker when dealing with more general issues. These decisions relate to detail of the model, though, and to avoid writing the entire book into its last chapter we restrict ourselves here to first-, second- and third-order decisions.

Figure 11.3 Flow chart of divergent selection procedure

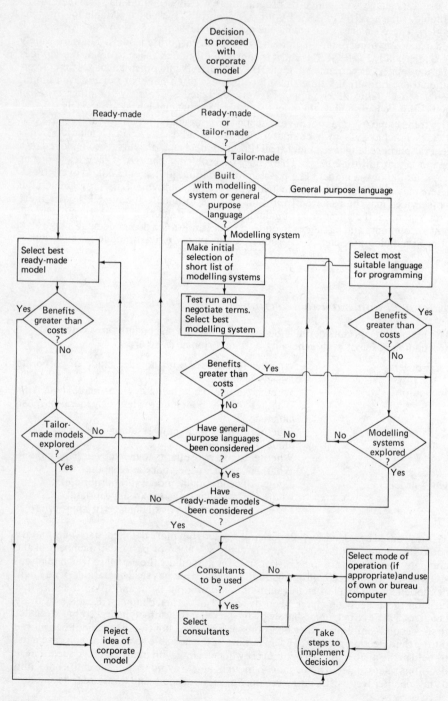

First-, second- and third-order decisions are included in the approach to selection illustrated in *Figures 11.1* and *11.2*. These figures need to be expanded, though, to allow for the possibility that the path taken may lead to a dead end. This occurs when further information shows that the type of option selected at an earlier, more general stage of the process is not appropriate. The earlier decision is then reversed. This is recognised explicitly in *Figure 11.3* which also gives more detail for some of the activities, such as selection of the most suitable modelling system for the company.

By following the steps of *Figure 11.3*, a company should be able to reach a satisfactory decision on corporate modelling, but not necessarily the best one. To be sure of getting the best method of modelling for the company, all the possibilities would have to be investigated, that is a convergent approach would have to be taken. But this is palpably impractical in most circumstances. It is therefore important that the divergent approach be made to work. The quality of the ultimate decisions depends, in this approach, on that of first- and second-order decisions especially. Consequently, these decisions must be based on the right information, which should be a sufficient basis for an initial decision without being as detailed as that used for third- or fourth-order decisions.

To give some indication of the level of detail appropriate, and as an *aide-mémoire* on some of the more important questions to be asked, checklists for the first- and second-order decisions are given in *Figures 11.4* to *11.9*. A detailed checklist for selection of bureaux packages is already available (*Figure 7.10*).

Figure 11.4   Checklist: Decision on whether to proceed with feasibility study

1.   (a)   What decisions would be assisted?
     (b)   Who makes them?
     (c)   How successfully are they made now?
     (d)   How would a corporate model help?
     Hence is there a need for a corporate model?

2.   Would decision-takers involved accept, understand and use a corporate model?

3.   (a)   Would at least one member of senior management, and preferably the board, give support to corporate modelling?
     (b)   Who would oppose development of a corporate model?

4.   (a)   What sort of data is at present available for strategic planning?
     (b)   Is this likely to be sufficient as input to a corporate model?
     (c)   How easily and at what cost could it be supplemented?

5.   (a)   What is the present planning process?
     (b)   At what points would the corporate model be used?
     (c)   Could it be integrated on a routine basis into the planning process?
     (d)   Would it be used in regular planning or on an *ad hoc* basis?

6.   (a)   What broad type of model, and level of aggregation of detail of input, would seem at first sight to be appropriate?
     (b)   What is the probable size?
     (c)   What is the range of costs and average cost for such a model (see Chapter 10 for data which needs to be adjusted for cost changes)?

     Would expected benefits justify this expenditure?

In general, is a corporate model likely to be successfully developed and used, what benefits might be expected from it, and would these justify anticipated expenditure?

Figure 11.5 Checklist on ready-made versus tailor-made models

1. What ready-made models are currently available?

2. Are the inputs required by them already available in the company or could they be obtained easily?

3. Do they claim to facilitate the decisions on which the company is most likely to want aid?

4. Are outputs in a form readily understandable to management involved with these decisions?

5. (i)   What is the internal logic of the models that look most suitable?
    (ii)   Is it likely to represent the accounting conventions and other relationships within the company fairly faithfully?
    (iii) If not, how easily and at what cost could it be changed to make it adequate?
    (iv)   How easy would it be to update the logic of the model to allow for possible future changes in tax regulations, accounting conventions, or in the business?

6. How well would the better ready-made models compare in these respects with modelling systems or models built in general-purpose languages?

7. How soon could a ready-made model to meet foreseeable decision needs be used by the company? How soon could a comparable tailor-made model be available? Is the time difference important?

8. Are internal staff available for corporate modelling? If not, would the company be prepared to use consultants, and how much would it cost?

9. Are ready-made models likely to be better in cost/benefit terms than tailor-made models?

Figure 11.6 Checklist on choice between modelling systems and
general-purpose languages

1. What modelling systems are available?
    What do their proprietors claim for them?
    Are these claims supported by any information already available to the company?

2. Does the company have specialist programmers already familiar with general-purpose languages? If so, would these languages be suitable for corporate models?

3. Is it intended to run the model in batch, conversational, or remote batch mode (if in conversational mode a modelling system is likely to be preferable)?

4. How often is the model likely to be used? How many runs are likely on each occasion on which it will be used? Consequently, are higher operating costs of modelling systems really an important factor?

5. How frequently is the model likely to require change and updating? What would be the difference in cost between updating a modelling system and a general-purpose language model?

6. Are the special routines offered by modelling systems likely to be of much value to the company?

7. How much longer would it take to build a model in a general-purpose programming language? Is this likely to be important?

8. How much extra is it likely to cost to develop a general-purpose language model? Is this extra cost justified by savings in computer costs?

Figure 11.7 Checklist on mode of operation

1. (i) How much data would be involved in each run of the model?
   (ii) How many runs are likely per year?
   (iii) Hence how great are the annual cost advantages of batch against other modes, and of remote batch against conversational mode?

2. Are managers really likely to use the conversational facility to interact with the model? If not, who will use the model, and would they gain from the conversational mode?

3. (i) What is the turnaround time likely to be for each of batch, remote batch, and conversational modes?
   (ii) Is the model likely to be used in routine planning or for urgent, *ad hoc* decisions, or both?
   (iii) How important are turnaround time differences between the modes of operation?

4. (i) Is time on the company's own computer likely to be available?
   (ii) In what modes could the model be operated on the company's own computer?
   (iii) How much extra would it cost to run in conversational mode on a bureau computer?

5. How much extra would it cost to build a model for running in conversational mode?

6. Are security safeguards adequate in each of batch, conversational and remote batch modes?

Figure 11.8 Checklist on use of own or bureau computer

1. (i) Can own computer be run in the preferred mode of operation?
   (ii) If not, is this important?

2. (i) Can the preferred modelling system be operated on the company's own computer?
   (ii) If so, would the proprietor of the system allow this, and on what terms?
   (iii) How would the costs and benefits of such arrangements compare with those of use of the modelling system on the bureau computer?

3. Are security safeguards of a bureau computer adequate? How do they compare with those for the company's own computer?

4. What kinds and levels of service is company likely to receive from bureau?

5. (i) Has the company's own computer enough spare capacity to run the corporate model as often as is likely to be necessary without displacing other work?
   (ii) If so, is this likely to continue, and for how long?
   (iii) If not, will the effects of such displacement be serious?

6. What turnaround time could be given by the company's own computer and by a bureau? Are the differences important?

7. Do back-up facilities of bureaux computers make their service more reliable than that of the company's own computer in times when rapid use of the model is necessary? Is this likely to be important?

Figure 11.9 Checklist on use of consultants or own staff

1. What skills are required to construct the kind of corporate model required by the company?

2. (i)   Are these available within the company?
    (ii)   If so, could they be released for development of the corporate model?
    (iii) If not, could they be developed among existing staff relatively easily, or brought in by recruitment of appropriately qualified persons?

3. Have consultants special expertise that would enable them to make a special contribution?

4. What steps could be taken, if consultants were employed, to ensure that internal staff of the company could gain sufficient command of the model to maintain and update it once the consultants leave? Would these suffice?

5. How would internal staff view use of consultants? Would their co-operation in development and subsequent use of the model be more or less likely than if only internal staff were used?

6. How much quicker would it be to develop a model with the help of consultants? Is this important?

7. How much more would it cost to use consultants? Would benefits derived justify this extra cost?

The value of such checklists is largely as reminders of the kind of information that should be collected for each decision. Management normally prefers to weigh this in a largely intuitive way when reaching decisions. Sometimes, though, it helps to make the relative importance of the different factors explicit, that is, to estimate the relative importance of each factor and record it. Ratings, or weights, can be useful in this respect. By distributing, say, 100 points between the different factors in such a way that the number of points allocated to each reflects its relative importance, we can get a set of figures that can be used in calculating the relative attractiveness of the different alternatives. This is illustrated, with a purely hypothetical example, in *Figure 11.10*. Clearly, the same approach could be applied to each of the checklists.

Such a way of making subjective judgement explicit has advantages. It highlights differences in judgement of different parties to the decision as a basis for further discussion. It also provides a means of narrowing consideration to a very small number of alternatives. However, its apparent objectivity should not mislead those using it, for the alternatives with the highest final scores may not always be the best. Quite apart from the fact that the subjective estimates on which the results are based may be wrong, there is a danger that a crucial factor may not sway the decision because its importance is submerged in the process of calculation. This is related to the fact that, whilst within reasonably expected bounds a factor may not have a very great weight attached to it, beyond them it may become of critical importance. Let us look at an example to make this point clear.

Suppose a company needs a corporate model especially to evaluate, in the first instance, the possible implications of a potential merger under a range of possible assumptions as to future performance and terms of sale. Management thinks that the right point to move in with a bid would be in about five to six months' time. A range of corporate modelling options are considered and assessed by the rating method. The option which achieves the highest score does so by virtue of a very high rating for all the factors but one, that of elapsed time to full operation of the model. Only options that would give a fully operating model in six months, according to 'best estimates',

(Continued on page 182)

Figure 11.10   Example of use of a weighting procedure for selection of programming language

(i) Factor	(ii) Distribution of 100 points between factors	(iii) Distribution of factor points between alternatives				
		A L G O L	F O R T R A N	B A S I C	D Y N A M O	G P S S
1 Experienced programmers available	40	10	20	5	3	2
2 Appropriate for operation in batch mode	20	6	6	2	3	3
3 Appropriate for primarily financial model	20	6	6	6	1	1
4 Language has good compiler supplied by the computer manufacturer	20	8	8	1	1	2
Total	100	2,880	5,760	60	9	12

Procedural steps

1. List the factors thought significant to decision-making in Column (i).
2. Allocate 100 points between these factors to determine relative weightings and record in Column (ii).
3. Determine the alternatives to be judged and place in Column (iii).
4. For each factor in Column (i) distribute the points awarded in Column (ii) to the alternatives in Column (iii). In the example above the 40 points for 'Experienced programmers available' are distributed between the alternatives as follows:

ALGOL	10
FORTRAN	20
BASIC	5
DYNAMO	3
GPSS	2
Total	40

This indicates that great stress is placed on the availability of programmers experienced in FORTRAN.

5. Multiply the points awarded to the alternatives in Column (iii). So, the score for ALGOL will be $10 \times 6 \times 6 \times 8 = 2,880$. This multiplication of factors highlights differences between alternatives and can be shown to be more acceptable than a system where factors are added only.
6. The alternative with the highest total score (in this instance FORTRAN) is assumed to be the preferred option.

have been considered. The option with the highest total score is given a low score on the time factor because it would not be available for five months. Should management adopt the option with the highest total score? In these circumstances, a wise management might well prefer an alternative that has a lower total score, but would be ready for full operation in three months. This would not only give adequate time for management to find out the capabilities and limitations of the model before entering the takeover battle, it would also mean that the risk of the model not being available within the critical period would be reduced to an acceptable level.

None the less, as long as it is not permitted to obscure the importance of individual factors, the subjective rating approach can be a valuable aid to selection. Whether or not it is useful for the individual firm depends largely on its approach to decision-taking.

Clearly, the checklists given in this section can be used with or without subjective rating, and similarly the detailed approach set out in *Figure 11.3* may be used without the checklists. Equally, the checklists could be used without the steps of *Figure 11.3* being followed, and the rating method could be applied to any list of factors of the company's own choosing. It would be presumptuous to assume that the full approach given is desirable for even the majority of companies. However, it is likely to be suitable for some, and most companies should find some aspects of it, such as the checklists, useful. The alternative to some form of systematic search is, after all, a sequential examination of the options as they present themselves, and selection of the first that appears to be satisfactory. This is unlikely to lead to selection of the type of corporate model best suited to the company.

11.4 *Some concluding points*

There is evidence that corporate models are becoming more widely adopted and, under the pressure of selling by computer bureaux, may become one of the latest bandwagons of 'modern', 'progressive' management.

In many respects this is good. Certainly, corporate models should improve major decisions in many companies, because of the way they allow rapid testing of a wide range of alternatives. Decisions on mergers, new products, new productive capacity, and raising new finance, for instance, can all be facilitated. Consequently, corporate models should help management to avoid some of the major errors that have been made all too often in the past.

No company should assume, though, that benefits will necessarily follow possession of a corporate model. The extent of benefits will depend partly on selection of the right kind of corporate model. Factors influencing the various aspects of choice of model have been discussed during the book and some of them have been reiterated in this chapter. However, a good choice from among the options open is not the decisive factor. Our visits to companies with corporate models showed us again and again that the crucial factor is enthusiasm for the corporate model among top management (and especially senior financial management). Other conditions for success exist, see Chapter 9, but this is the one of overriding importance.

Enthusiasm for, or antipathy towards, a corporate model in any specific company is related to the way those with vested interests think their rôles and influence will be affected by it. Those in the financial function, in particular, can feel threatened. Accountants in industry seem to be split in this respect. Many accountants we met regarded corporate models as a natural extension of existing financial planning exercises and spoke about them enthusiastically. Others seemed to fear them. In one company which we know well, the chief accountant has obstructed corporate modelling because he seems to fear that the board will no longer rely on his particular mix of skills and knowledge, and he may well be right!

Certainly, modelling systems have brought corporate modelling within the scope of most intelligent accountants, and in many of the companies we visited modelling had been done by the financial function. Indeed, examples have been given earlier of companies in which the finance director himself had been deeply involved in developing the corporate model. This promises a new role for the accountant, and particularly the young one, as a financial modeller. Moreover, it offers an opportunity for the more mature accountant to develop more strongly as a planner with a fuller, more extensive grasp of the financial implications of a whole variety of major decisions within the company. Corporate models may, after all, give both senior financial management and other top management a fuller grasp of production and marketing aspects of the company, for instance, than they had formerly. Moreover, corporate models can release time for thinking, by relieving the financial function of many routine, tedious calculations, whilst giving it more muscle power.

The problem is, of course, that the muscle power can also be used by other managers, who can arrive at financial results without intervention of financial management. It is perhaps for this reason that Boulden[1] found that in many companies using his modelling system the finance function sought to keep control over use of the corporate model. It would be foolish to deny that corporate models make top management less dependent on the routine, calculating skills of the accountant, and that in some companies the accountant will therefore lose influence. This will happen, though, where the accountant is a routine, human calculating machine, rather than a mature member of the top management team. The able, mature financial manager has indispensable skills to apply in generating financial dimensions of alternatives in a wide range of decisions, and in interpreting the true significance of what corporate models produce.

Corporate models need, then, to be recognised for what they are. They are not automatic financial experts or decision-takers, which operate with alarming speed and accuracy, and make their human predecessors redundant. They are aids to analysis of alternatives created by human imagination. They are limited to processing data that they have been designed to accept, to produce reports that they have been programmed to print out. Because they can do this very fast, and accurately, they are very useful. However, their results are no better than the alternatives they are given to test, and the related forecasts of demand, costs, and so on used as input.

Corporate models should, then, provide a new and enriched role for the accountant in industry, and a valuable aid to decision-taking by top management in general. By removing the drudgery of routine calculation, and permitting rapid testing of more alternatives, they should help to remove the emphasis from analysis of a few alternative extensions to existing business to the perception of opportunities and creative generation of alternative strategies.

Consequently, we urge you to take a hard, close look at what corporate models have to offer your company, bearing in mind their limitations and conditions necessary for success, too. If they look promising, why not undertake a deeper study, following the lines suggested earlier in this chapter if they seem to be helpful? Should you decide to start to build your own corporate model, we suggest that you should take a modular approach, committing yourself initially to nothing more than a simple, relatively cheap, and possibly purely financial model receiving highly aggregated, corporate data.

Alternatively, the first model may be more detailed, and related to a pressing, more immediate problem such as that of production capacity at Yorkshire Imperial Plastics. A financial model can then be added to the suite to process data from this earlier model as well as aggregated data input directly. The important thing is that the first model should help solution of real problems without itself being too ambitious. In this way, your company can learn about modelling, and top management can find out whether the exercise is worth while, without committing the company to major expenditure first. It can still proceed to develop other interlinked models.

Hardy,[2] writing in *A Mathematician's Apology*, argued that both power and elegance in mathematics lie in generality and simplicity. There is a parallel with corporate models. It is a greater achievement to build a model which is relatively simple yet meets the decision-making needs than one which is sophisticated but complex and unwieldy.

References

1   Boulden, J. B.: Computerised corporate planning
    Long Range Planning, June, 1971

2   Hardy, G. H.: *A mathematician's apology, Cambridge University Press, 1970.*

Appendix 1

Corporate financial modelling in the UK

Results of a survey conducted by
Professor Peter H. Grinyer
and
Jeff Wooller

This appendix is written as a self-contained section to permit experienced modellers interested in the results of the survey to use it without reference to the main text.

Contents

Acknowledgements

During the course of this survey we have accumulated a considerable debt of gratitude. Certainly the greatest is to the Institute of Chartered Accountants in England and Wales. Its Research Committee has financed the work. Ernest Barnes and John Flower, members of the Committee, have provided encouragement and support throughout the research.

Paul Neild of Phillips and Drew and our colleagues Andrew Chambers and Richard Taffler have been sources of that most precious of contributions to research – informed and constructive criticism.

The editors of *Accountancy, Accountancy Age, Accountants Weekly, The Accountant, Computer Weekly, Dataweek, Long Range Planning Society Newsletter, Operational Research Society Newsletter*, and *Professional Administration*, who published an account of our work and an invitation for modellers to contact us, also deserve our thanks.

Others who have helped have been too many to mention. All of the modellers who completed our lengthy, and to them no doubt tedious, questionnaire deserve a special award for tolerance. Throughout the survey we have encountered help and encouragement from almost every quarter.

Introduction

This report presents the results of data collected during our survey between January and October 1973. It presents an account of the extent and nature of corporate modelling in the UK. Well over 100 modellers in a total of 82 companies completed questionnaires. For a variety of reasons explored below, 17 of these 82 companies were excluded from our final sample of 65 companies. A copy of the questionnaire can be seen in Section F of this report.

Subjects covered in the survey, and analysed in this report, range from those of general interest to management to those of a more technical nature. More general topics include the year in which corporate modelling started, staff who built and use the models, the costs of developing corporate models, and management reactions to them. Technical aspects include, for instance, numbers of inputs, program statements and outputs, types of forecasting routines used, languages in which models were written and so on. To permit the reader with little interest in technical aspects to escape the tedium of reading the whole report, we have organised it into virtually separate compartments, so that any one section may be read without the others. The one exception to this general rule is that the early section in which a number of general terms are defined should be read first.

As far as we know, there has been no comparable study, to date, though an excellent piece of work was done by Neild using questionnaires completed by 28 UK companies.[1] Wagle and Jenkins,[2] too, have provided a somewhat more impressionistic, but none the less useful, view of the subject. The information collected in our survey has been more extensive and also, where it overlaps with the earlier work, sometimes more detailed. Most of the firms in our sample were visited, a number of interviewees being seen in many of them, whilst Neild[1] and Gershefski[3] used postal methods. Our survey relates to the UK whilst Gershefski's study (the most thorough previously undertaken) covered only US firms.

References

1 Neild, P. G.; Mathematical models as a tool for financial management; Financial modelling in UK industry
   In: European Federation of Financial Analysts Societies VIIth Congress, Torremolinos, 1972 Proceedings.
   (A shortened version of the second paper appears in *Journal of Business Policy*, Spring 1973.)

2 Wagle, B. V., and Jenkins, P. M.; The development of a general computer system to aid the corporate planning process.
   UK Scientific Centre, IBM UK Ltd, Peterlee, County Durham, 1971.

3 Gershefski, G. W.; Corporate models – the state of the art.
   Management Science (Application), Feb. 1970.

Survey methodology

Active participation in the corporate modelling of three companies had already led, at The City University Business School, to a number of hypotheses that it was our intention to test by a wider survey. As with any survey, it was necessary to establish, first, the population from which the sample should be drawn; second, the manner in which the sample should be selected; third, the way in which information should be collected from the selected members of the sample.

In this wider survey, our interest was exclusively in management, cost and technical aspects of corporate modelling. Further, we restricted ourselves to modelling in the UK, and in business firms. Business, under our definition, included nationalised industries, public services, and financial institutions offering services to the public, as well as private manufacturing industry.

Ideally, the sample should have been drawn along classical lines, by determining a sample frame in the light of the points made above, then sampling from members of the set so defined. In this instance, we found this approach to be infeasible, because the percentage of the total population of business firms involved in corporate modelling is low (see results of the telephone survey). By purely random sampling, an enormous effort would have been necessary before a sample as large as 65 modellers was located, and moreover some companies with long and interesting experience of corporate modelling, like *BP*, *ICI* or *Unilever*, may possibly have been excluded.

Consequently, we have taken a less respectable, but none the less, hopefully, valid approach. Three surveys were undertaken. One on 'financial modelling packages', i.e. computer software available from computer bureaux, consultants, and hardware manufacturers, is covered in a separate report. In this we sought to cover all the important packages. The second, main survey, the results of which are given in this report, was unrepresentative and most probably biased towards the more successful modellers. For the reasons already advanced, we did not select members of the sample randomly, but gained contact with them in three separate ways. Invitations to contact us were published in the financial and computer press as well as in newsletters to members of appropriate professional societies. Twenty-seven completed questionnaires, not all usable, were finally obtained from those who contacted us and were, therefore, self-selecting.

Others were approached because of knowledge we already had of the existence of corporate modelling within those companies. Contacts we already had, and others we developed during the survey, gave us further leads to follow. Again, this process was recognised to involve dangers of collecting a highly unrepresentative sample, a risk we tried to reduce by using as many independent networks of contacts as possible to reach our final total sample. In this way, we have been able to include in our sample many of the firms in the UK which have extensive experience, both favourable and unfavourable, of corporate modelling. Similarly, there is a wide range of start dates for modelling among the companies in the sample, from as early as 1963 to 1973. A wide range of specific technical characteristics was also encountered during the survey. None the less, for the reasons already given, the sample could well be biased.

Size of sample is, of course, an important factor. Our objective in this respect has been to obtain a large enough sample to cover most types of corporate model, modelling experience, and business context. Given the restraints imposed by the time and resources available, we initially set ourselves a target of 50 usable replies. However, in the event we were able to exceed this number. Questionnaires were completed by modellers in 82 organisations. However, 17 of these organisations were excluded from the sample, for four reasons. First, some of the organisations could not be classed as 'business'. Second, some of those which could did not have models which satisfied our definition of corporate models. Third, one company from which we received a completed questionnaire was located in Texas, and was excluded by our decision to confine the survey to the UK. Fourth, one company replied so late that it could not be incorporated into the analysis. Consequently, our final sample comprised 65 companies. This is, as far as we know, the largest sample used in any survey to date, in the UK or elsewhere, on the subject of corporate models. It is also more extensive in terms of information collected.

In view of the information required, lack of general agreement on definitions of terms currently used in relation to corporate models, and the somewhat sensitive nature of some of the information sought, we chose to use structured interviews rather than mailed questionnaires. Details on 44 of the models included in the final 65 were gained during visits to the companies involved. The remaining 21 were covered by mailed questionnaires, supplemented where necessary by telephone calls, due to the distance involved in a visit.

The information collected, and the networks of contacts used, suggested that there might be biases in certain respects. For instance, there is a users' club for one well-known package, and those using it are consequently in a well-developed network of contacts. Though we assiduously tried to avoid too great a use of this network we suspected our sample might be biased towards users of this package. To check for biases of this kind, a purely random survey was undertaken, where companies were selected, by use of random numbers, from 'The Times 1,000'. In all, 100 firms were approached, and basic information to test for bias was elicited from each of them. The results, which are covered at the end of this report, suggest that our main sample is, on the whole, unbiased.

Firms participating in survey

Figure 1 Classification of modellers included in the survey

	No. of companies		No. of companies
Banking and finance	3	Engineering and metal	9
Beers, spirits and tobacco	2	Food, catering, etc.	6
Building and construction	5	Insurance	3
Chemicals	8	Motor	4
Cinemas, theatres and TV	2	Newspapers, publishers	2
Coal, nuclear energy and steel	3	Oils	4
Computer bureaux	2	Paper and printing	3
Electrical and radio	4	Transport	5

Total = 65

Figure 1 gives a classification by industry of the 65 companies whose completed questionnaires form the basis of this report. Their number included a building society and nationalised industries which fell within our definition of 'business'. Thus throughout the survey we use the word 'company' very loosely to include organisations such as *Anglia Building Society, British Airports Authority, British Rail* and *British Steel Corporation*.

Definition of key terms

During the survey, we have encountered a certain amount of confusion about terms applied to corporate models and modelling and consequently define some of the key terms below. This is, apparently, at present a prerequisite to clear communication! We have sought, as far as possible, to use definitions which accord well with common usage of the terms.

Term	Definition
Bureaux	A term used by us, for convenience, to embrace computer bureaux, consultants, and computer hardware manufacturers who offer special computer software, i.e. programming languages or suites of programs, for corporate modelling purposes.

Models

Model	A representation, or mapping, of the subject modelled. In the cases with which we are interested here, the representation is by means of logical and mathematical expressions, which are usually converted into a form suitable for computer operation.
Corporate model	A model which represents key operations of the entire corporate body. This is taken to mean that all items entering the company's profit and loss account and balance sheet are taken into account. It need not, though, print out all these items to be corporate. For instance a model producing only statements of corporate cash flows would be classed by us as corporate. In addition, the model must either give the user the facility to find the results of varying key aspects of the corporate business, or alternatively be an optimising model which suggests a 'best' solution to important aspects of the company's total business.
Module	A module is part of a corporate model. In effect it is a sub-model. A corporate model may comprise a number of such sub-models or, alternatively, may not be broken down into sub-models at all. In the latter case we have, for convenience, called it a single module model.

Modes of operation

Batch	The batch mode of operation applies where the user inserts his data, normally in the form of cards or tape, and there is none of the prompting associated with the conversational approach. Another distinguishing feature is the way in which batch jobs are queued until such time as the computer is free to accept them. However, once the job is accepted it normally stays on the computer until completed.
Conversational	The conversational mode of operation applies where the user is connected to the computer by keyboard printer or VDU (video display unit), and receives prompts from the computer in a question and answer manner which gives the impression that the user is engaged in a dialogue with the computer. The conversational mode is usually associated with time-sharing where many users are able to use the computer apparently simultaneously. In fact, each user is given a quantum of time during which the computer is working on his program; if it does not complete the operation in that particular quantum of time, then the user must wait until his next quantum comes round. When there are many users of time-sharing at the same time, the user is conscious of the computer working in 'fits and starts', whereas at less crowded times the lags are hardly perceptible.

| Remote batch (including remote job entry) | Remote batch is associated with use of a terminal at a distance from the computer installation. This terminal may operate by cards or tape, alternatively the user may key-in via a keyboard printer. Where input is conversational the mode is termed CRJE (conversational remote job entry). However, whatever the method of input a characteristic is that programs are always run in the batch mode. Output may be in the form of computer reports from fast line-printer or via keyboard printer terminal. The latter is more time-consuming as the user is usually restricted to print-out speeds of no more than 30 characters per second; in fact most keyboard printer terminals seen were capable of only 10 characters per second. |

Packages and languages

| General-purpose language | The code by which the logic of the model is converted into a form acceptable to the computer is called a programming language. A general-purpose programming language is one that is capable of a wide range of mathematical, scientific or business applications. FORTRAN, ALGOL, BASIC, COBOL and PL/I are the most widely used general-purpose languages. |

| Modelling system | Modelling systems are designed to reduce programming effort by providing routines to perform operations frequently required for corporate models, which would otherwise have to be programmed in detail in a general-purpose language. One of the features of use of a modelling system is the ease with which it handles the time dimension. The user merely specifies the time periods he requires and the modelling system handles the number of columns, width of columns, etc. In so far as it leaves freedom to the user to build his own logic into the model, and to link together the routines in a way most appropriate to his needs, the modelling system is more flexible than a ready-made model. It can be regarded as a tool to assist construction of tailor-made models. |

| Package | Modelling systems or ready-made models. In each case the package comprises a program or suite of programs (software). |

| Ready-made model | A model not designed specifically for one company. For instance, general routines on balance sheet calculations, discounted cash flows, and so on may be incorporated without reference to the unique accounting conventions of the company. A ready-made model is bought-in from a bureau and does not require the user to do any programming whatsoever. |

| Tailor-made model | A model which incorporates logic unique to the company. This may be developed either in a general-purpose language or a modelling system. |

Section A

General aspects

1.

When companies began modelling

Figure 2 shows the year in which the 65 companies started to develop corporate models. They suggest more rapid growth of modelling since 1970 which appears to be associated with increased availability of modelling systems. The figure for 1973 should not be taken as suggesting a fall in the rate of development, since this is the year in which the survey was conducted. Although many modellers have informed us that they have started to build models in 1973, we found only two which were sufficiently developed to be included.

Figure 2 UK modelling starts

Year started	No. of companies	Year started	No. of companies
1963	2	1969	4
1964	2	1970	8
1965	6	1971	18
1966	1	1972	13
1967	2	1973	2
1968	7	Total 65	

2.

Category of model

The terms 'modelling system', 'ready-made', and 'tailor-made' model are treated in the section on definitions. From the definitions, it is clear that a corporate model may be either acquired from a bureau without additional programming being required, i.e. ready-made, or be to some extent at least designed specifically for the company, i.e. tailor-made. Corporate models may be simulation or optimisation. Where the model is optimisation (defined on page 203) a special linear programming code or other appropriate language may be used to write the program, to minimise programming required and permit use of powerful software (such as matrix generators). However, in some cases optimisation models may be written in general-purpose programming languages like FORTRAN. Simulation models (discussed more fully on page 203) may be written in a general-purpose language like FORTRAN or special simulation languages. Many special simulation languages, like CSL, GPSS, SIMSCRIPT, are not suitable for corporate models, being devised specifically to map physical operations. However, this is not true of modelling systems, which may be regarded as special high-level simulation languages, that have been designed primarily for corporate modelling.

A tailor-made model may be built by external consultants only, by the firm's own staff with no external assistance, or by the firm's own staff with aid from consultants.

The data collected from the sample companies was analysed to show the relationships between these aspects. It should be noted that a firm was classified as using consultants only where they were from outside the organisation and the work was of a type that normally has to be paid for. Where bureau after-sales assistance was received, free of charge, this was not treated as consultancy work.

Figure 3 Category of corporate model

Category of model →	No. of companies with ready-made model	No. of companies with different types of tailor-made models			
Approach to acquisition		General-purpose language	Modelling system	Optimisation code	Total
Bought-in	2	—	—	—	2
Built by own staff only	—	37	24	4	65
Built by consultants only	—	6	2	3	11
Built by own staff and consultants	—	6	9	2	17
Total	2	49	35	9	95

The number of models shown in *Figure 3* exceeds that of companies in the sample because some companies had models in more than one category. The extent to which companies had used more than one approach to corporate modelling is illustrated in *Figure 4*.

Figure 4 Category of corporate models

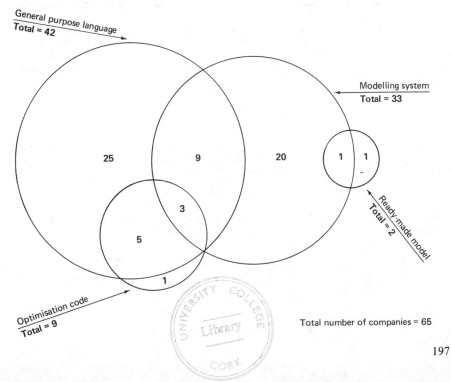

General purpose language
Total = 42

Modelling system
Total = 33

Ready-made model
Total = 2

Optimisation code
Total = 9

25   9   20   1   1

3

5

1

Total number of companies = 65

197

The Venn diagram illustrates that 25 companies used a general-purpose language only, 20 a modelling system only, 12 both a general-purpose language and a modelling system, eight both general-purpose language and optimisation code models. Three of these latter companies also used a modelling system. One of the two companies with a ready-made model also used a modelling system, the second relied solely on its ready-made model.

The prevalence of models built in general-purpose programming languages is apparent. However, we noticed a marked trend towards use of modelling systems from 1970, and anticipate that in the near future at least as many, if not more, corporate models will use these. By comparison, there is little use of either ready-made models or optimisation models, indeed we noticed a trend away from optimisation models.

Although it might be thought that, because of the greater ease with which they can be learnt and used, modelling systems would involve less use of consultants than general-purpose language models, no significant difference may be observed in this respect. What was apparent, though, was a wider use of modelling systems by non-computer, non-operational research specialists. Few accountants, corporate planners, or actuaries had built corporate models in general-purpose languages, but a growing number were found to be doing so using modelling systems.

3. How models are run

3.1 Use of company or bureaux computers

Figure 5 Extent of use of company or bureaux computers

	No. of companies
Own computer only	20
Bureau computer only	25
Both	20
Total	65

Figure 5 shows that more companies were using bureaux computers than in-house computers for their corporate models. There appeared to have been a trend towards use of bureaux computers from about 1970 which seemed to be associated with the growing use of modelling systems. Many of these systems are tied to use of a bureau computer. This is not alone an adequate explanation of the number of companies using bureaux computers. Indeed, detailed examination of the completed questionnaires reveals that quite a lot of models programmed in general-purpose languages are run on bureaux computers. Difference in turnaround time is one of the other factors that explain the number.

3.2 Turnaround times

Turnaround time of batch-run models in this survey is taken as the lag between the data leaving the user and the printed output reaching his desk. The maximum of the 'average turnaround' times stated by respondents was 72 hours and the minimum less than one hour. The most commonly quoted times were 12 and 24 hours, with the overall average being 18 hours. Several companies arrange for their batch models to be run overnight so that the output reports are available first thing next morning. Special concessions are given by most bureaux for models run in this fashion.

The modes of operation

Models may be operated in three modes, namely batch, conversational or remote batch (including remote job entry) – see page 195 for definitions of these terms. The ways in which the corporate models of the sample companies were operated is illustrated in *Figure 6*. A number of observations may assist interpretation of these results.

Figure 6   Classification of the modes of operation

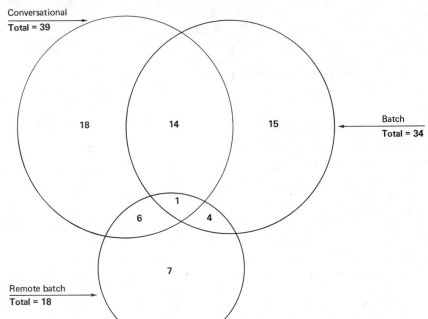

Models built in general-purpose languages tended, as we anticipated, to be run in batch or remote batch mode. Modelling systems were associated with a fuller use of the conversational mode. The overlap between modes of operation shown in the Venn diagram is due largely to the fact that where a company had several models, these were often run in different modes. However, we also found that there was an increasing flexibility in mode of operation of models developed with modelling systems, due to the more attractive terms offered by bureaux for batch running. A fairly typical example is given in *Figure 7* for use of a modelling system on a bureau computer.

Figure 7   Typical costs of a modelling system used on a bureau computer

Cost of run	£8	£5	£3
Computing	Conversational	Conversational	Batch
Printing	Conversational	Batch	Batch

5.   *What the models are designed to do*

As may be seen from *Figure 8*, which shows the number of the 65 companies in the survey which identified the use as one to which their model was put, the most widespread uses of corporate models were for financial planning. Five years was the most popular planning horizon, but the models were widely used for planning up to 10-year horizons too. Where the model was used for planning up to a period of one year, it was found to be basically a budgeting model, which used considerably more detailed data than those for longer term planning. Use of models for cash flow analysis was also found to be widespread, and in a few companies like the *Butterfield-Harvey Group* the model was orientated especially towards this aspect. Most companies, though, seemed to regard income statements as more important.

Figure 8 also shows that, although the most important use was financial planning, corporate models were also widely used to aid marketing, distribution and production decisions.

Some of the uses which have little emphasis are interesting by virtue of this fact. Financing decisions have been stressed as a possible use of corporate models since their inception but only nine companies used their models for this purpose.

Figure 8   Major uses of models

Application	No. of companies
Financial planning (up to 1 year)	25
Financial planning (1 to 5 years)	51
Financial planning (over 5 years)	29
Cash flow analysis	49
Aid marketing decisions	42
Aid production decisions	39
Project evaluation	29
Aid distribution decisions	25
Financing	9
New venture evalution	9
Acquisition studies	8
Manpower	8
Aid purchasing decisions	7
Market share forecasting	5
Computer evaluation (purchase or rent)	3

Section B

Tailor-made models

5. *Whether companies have suites of models*

6.1 *Numbers of modules in corporate suites*
Many of the early corporate models were large and complex. However, there are clearly advantages, such as earlier date at which the model may be used and ease of updating, in adopting a modular approach whereby a series of sub-models are produced that may be used either separately or jointly. For instance, a marketing model may be used by itself or with the rest of a corporate suite, which in total amounts to an old-style corporate model.

To gauge current practice in the UK on this score data was collected, where applicable, on the number of modules in the corporate suite of each of the 65 companies in the sample. Results are given in *Figure 9*. This shows that only 13 companies had a single module corporate model. Details of a total of 224 modules were given in all and the trend is definitely towards a modular approach to model building.

Figure 9 Frequency distribution of modules per corporate suite

No. of modules	1	2	3	4	5	6	7	8	10	11	12	Total
No. of times occurring	13	15	13	8	6	4	1	2	1	1	1	65

6.2 *Model interlinking and integration facilities*
For a modular approach to be efficient an effective means of interlinking modules is necessary. Information collected on the extent and nature of such interlinking is tabulated in *Figure 10*.

Figure 10 Linking between models

	No. of companies	No. of companies
Integration and interlinking	5	
Interlinking only	19	
Models not linked or linked manually	28	
Total no. of companies with suite of models		52
Companies without suites of models		13
Total		65

This shows that only five companies had suites in which models could be integrated within the computer run. This facility allows models to be merged together in the same computer run as well as allowing them to be run independently. With this facility the user is able to transfer between models and call up information from any model. Many modellers could not see any need for this facility. A more widely used approach is for the models to be interlinked outside the computer run with the models run independently of each other and results placed on to disc. Other models can then call for these results as and when required; 24 companies had models which were linked in this fashion. All of the companies having integration facilities also had linking facilities.

6.3   *'Chaining' of models*
Only two suites of models were 'chained' so that they had to be run in a certain sequence, whereas all the remaining 50 companies with suites gave the users an option to choose the order in which the models could be run.

7.   *Level of aggregation of detail*

An important feature of any corporate model is the detail in which the company is mapped. Some models are restricted to financial aspects and to the corporate level only, whilst others cover both physical logistics and their financial implications at operating unit level, too.

To permit the results to be analysed, the structure illustrated in *Figure 11* was used, because it was found convenient and more typical than alternatives. *Figure 12* gives the levels, in terms of this structure, to which corporate models extended in the 65 companies.

Figure 11   Assumed company hierarchy

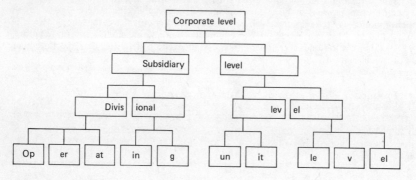

All the models included financial operations at the corporate level, indeed, it would be difficult to visualise a corporate model which did not do so. However, only 54 models went deeper into the organisation to produce more detailed information for management than is possible with a model which remains purely at the corporate level.

Figure 12   Levels to which corporate models extend in the 65 survey companies

| | No. of companies | |
Level	Physical flows represented	Financial flows represented
Corporate level	37	65
Subsidiary level	33	54
Divisional level	29	46
Operating unit level	19	28

Where the company is modelling physical operations at the operating unit level, the models tend to be larger and more complex. Here the models may be of use to lower level management for tactical day-to-day decision-taking. Conversely, where the models do not extend below the corporate level of the organisation the decisions are almost inevitably restricted to major strategic decisions at the board level.

8. Size of models

From Section 6 it may be seen that the total number of modules in the 65 participating companies was 224. Details of the size of 193 of these modules are given in *Figure 13* below in terms of input and output variables and program statements. Two companies gave no details at all and 12 others did not give details of all their modules.

Figure 13   Numbers of variables and statements in individual modules

Range	1–25	26–100	101–1,000	1,001–10,000	Over 10,000	No details	Total
Input variables	37	50	61	37	8	31	224
Output variables	34	62	50	40	7	31	224
Program Statements	1	28	111	49	4	31	224
Total	72	140	222	126	19	93	672

It would be extremely difficult to produce a definition for input variables which would be suitable for all models in the survey. For many of the systems in use, an input variable would be required for each type of goods purchased/sold, etc., although on some models sales would be aggregated and would thus become just one variable. Where different figures were fed in for, say, the same type of goods in different years, this has been treated as one variable only. Thus, in most models the number of input variables will be independent of the number of time periods.

More or less the same considerations apply to output variables as to input variables. In many instances the number of output variables generated was not very different from the number of input variables. Thus, *Figure 13* does not reveal any clearly apparent differences. Problems arose where the output of one module was fed onto disc and used as input to another model. In this case the modules were dealt with as separate entities, and the input was treated just as if it had been fed in on cards.

Program statements are a little easier to define. They are the number of lines of instruction and comment included in the module programs. Most of the programs for which details were received fell in the 200–500 range. In the largest suite of models an input of over 70,000 variables was manipulated to produce over 500,000 output variables by means of a program consisting of over 38,000 modelling system statements. This was the model of *Lansing Bagnall* which has been built by and used extensively by the accountants of the company. One of the reasons for the success of this model has been the interest shown by the management (particularly the Divisional Director of Finance, who has played a large part in its implementation) in results of modelling, when compared with existing methods. Another large suite was found at *Wates* where program statements totalled 14,000 statements using APL, a general-purpose language. Other large models were found at BP and *National Westminster Bank*.

9. Class of models

Optimisation models are defined as those incorporating 'mathematical programming' techniques such as linear and integer programming. These models produce an 'optimal' or 'best' answer to a problem.

Simulation models are either deterministic or probabilistic in nature. Deterministic models produce the answer to a given set of inputs, but do not search for one best answer. The decision-taking manager will usually work on a trial and error basis to test the sensitivity of the answers to various input changes. Probabilistic models produce a range as an answer to input distributions. The answer will generally differ each time the model is run. With both types of

Figure 14 Nature of models

	No. of companies
Optimisation only	1
Simulation only	51
Both	13
Total	65

simulation model the actual taking of the decision is left to the manager, as opposed to optimisation models which produce the 'best' answer.

Figure 14 shows that 64 companies were using simulation models, only one firm was relying exclusively on optimisation models, and 13 companies were using both. With the notable exception of the oil companies the users were not generally happy with their optimisation models. *Black and Decker* the one exclusive user of optimisation techniques is currently testing simulation modelling systems.

Figure 15 Types of optimisation models in use

	No. of companies
Linear programming	10
Quadratic programming	1
Integer programming	2
Dynamic programming	3
Optimal search procedures	4

Figure 15 shows the dominance of linear programming over other optimisation techniques. Ten of the 14 companies using optimisation techniques used linear programming. Other optimising techniques were used, too, in some of these companies. Two companies had integer programming, one dynamic programming and one optimal search procedures as well as linear programming in their models. Optimisation techniques were used in conjunction with simulation models in some companies, for instance, the *Van den Berghs* model used quadratic programming, dynamic programming, and optimal search procedures within a corporate suite.

10. *Facilities available*

Many of the models, particularly those using modelling systems, provided special facilities to aid the decision-taker. The number of companies in which the main facilities were built into the models is shown in *Figure 16*. It will be noted that financial ratio analysis and calculation of discounted cash flows are the most widely used.

Backward iteration, which enables the decision-makers to find what combinations of variables will yield a given result, and sensitivity analysis are both extremely valuable aids. We were surprised that no more than 23 companies had routines for backward iteration in their models, though it must be admitted that it may sometimes involve complex logic which inflates the cost of model construction. The fact that only 26 companies had routines for sensitivity analysis in their corporate models was even more surprising.

Again, we expected greater use to be made of histogram and graph plotting facilities, for graphical displays are often more intelligible than tabulated data. A possible explanation for the low number of users is the tendency we observed in many companies for analysts to digest the output and represent it in a more easily understood form before it was presented to management.

Figure 16 Facilities included in the model

	No. of companies
Financial ratio analysis	42
Discounted cash flows	40
Sensitivity analysis (without input changes being necessary)	26
Backward iteration	23
Graph plotting	14
Histogram plotting	11
Significance testing	5

I. *Risk analysis*

Figure 17 Types of simulation models available

	No. of companies
Probabilistic only	1
Deterministic only	48
Both	15
Total	64

Although *Figure 17* shows that 16 companies have models which incorporate probability distributions, only two companies use probabilities for more than half of their total of model runs. (With a probabilistic model a model run may constitute, say, 500 or more program runs; a deterministic model needs only one program run for each model run.) With one exception only, the other modellers use these risk analysis models for 10 per cent or less of their total model runs. Only one company which used risk analysis for over 10 per cent of all runs was happy with the technique and this was, inevitably, an oil company, whose management is familiar with such techniques. Three of the 16 models are not currently in use, although they are available at any time.

Quite a large number of modellers spoke of earlier attempts to implement probabilistic models. These had almost invariably failed to get management support. Thus, although many modellers realise the potential of risk analysis they have also learned that management are not yet ready to accept it. In addition, many have found it difficult to obtain information in the form of probability distributions. *Selection Trust* decided to abandon its risk analysis model because of difficulties encountered in trying to ascertain the inter-dependencies of the input variables; others too have emphasised this problem.

As management gradually become more numerate there should be a tendency for greater acceptance of risk analysis models, as few deny the validity of the concept. However, experience of companies in our sample of 65 suggests that modellers would be unwise to build such models until management has become more familiar with simpler deterministic models.

The probability distributions shown in *Figure 18* are those available for use with Monte Carlo techniques in 15 companies. At *BOCM Silcock* a different approach has been taken in which pessimistic, most likely, and optimistic estimates are made. These are then used to produce distributions of results.

Figure 18 Types of probability distributions in use

	No. of companies
Normal	7
Uniform	5
Exponential	3
Binomial	2
Log normal	1
User specified (i.e. non-standard)	6

12. *Forecasting techniques*

Figure 19 Number of models incorporating forecasting techniques

	No. of companies
Models with forecasting techniques	30
Models without forecasting techniques	35
Total 65	

Figure 19 shows that 30 of the 65 companies used mathematical forecasting techniques in their corporate model, whilst the remainder preferred to produce required forecasts outside the model.

The fact that half of the companies chose to make no use of forecasting techniques in their corporate models is worthy of note. There was widespread acceptance among modellers that, whilst extrapolation of past trends can be useful, the assumption that they either should or will continue must be questioned seriously. Conditions which led to past patterns of sales, costs, and so on may change. Thus statistically derived forecasts should not be accepted without critical scrutiny. This is succinctly expressed by the Finance Director of *Yorkshire Imperial Plastics*, who advocates trend analysis modified by commercial assessment and judgement.

Those companies incorporating forecasting techniques in their models used a variety of specific approaches. Details are given in *Figure 20*.

Figure 20 Forecasting techniques used by modellers

Geometric progression	13
Linear regression	13
Moving averages	13
Arithmetic progression	12
Exponential smoothing	12
Curve fitting	11
Linear trend analysis	10
Multiple regression	10
Step functions	5
Power series	1

Other techniques mentioned were weighted regression, time series analysis using Shishkin's Method, and harmonic analysis (i.e. curve fitting with special assumptions used for seasonal analysis). One company used the method of estimating forecasts for one and five years and then interpolating to obtain values for intermediate years.

Flexibility of logic

Forty of the companies had models which allowed for major changes in their business (e.g. acquiring a new division) without additional programming being required. In many cases an additional division meant only that another set of inputs would be required, causing no problem so long as the division was compatible in nature with other divisions. In a smaller number of companies flexibility was provided by means of redundant items. These may be thought of as spaces in the model deliberately left blank for use at some time in the future. For instance, a firm with three existing subsidiaries might program for four, leaving one module without information, so that, if another subsidiary should later be acquired the information could be slotted in and the model run without undue delay. Such devices add, of course, to the cost of constructing models, although not greatly, while later saving of time by this method may be vital in a takeover situation where time is of the essence.

Figure 21 Flexibility of model logic

	No. of companies
Models without inbuilt flexibility	22
Models with inbuilt flexibility	40
Question not applicable	3
Total 65	

Companies not having this kind of flexibility of logic were asked to specify approximately how many man-hours they thought would be required to make the necessary changes. Only three companies would require more than 50 man-hours to make the necessary changes; naturally, elapsed time may be far greater than this. One company modeller said that for one of the models the question was not applicable, but explained that if their Dutch factory was integrated with the British factory an additional two man-years would be required.

Figure 22 Man-hours required to allow for major changes in business

Range	No. of companies
0– 10	8
11– 50	4
51–100	1
Over 100	2
No reply	7
Total 22	

Three companies replied that the question was not applicable to them. For example, *Anglia Building Society* stated that it would be difficult, under the restrictions imposed on building societies by present legislation, to envisage any allowable major changes in the nature of their business.

14 Flexibility of input

14.1 Details of companies with flexibility of input units

Figure 23 Flexibility of input units

Characteristic	No. of companies
Ability to input in terms of any of a range of convenient units	3
Ability to change unit of input by choice of control parameters	13
Not flexible: inputs in units prescribed by model documentation	49
Total	65

Figure 23 shows that there was very little flexibility as far as input was concerned; only three companies could input at will, say, absolute figures, annual absolute changes, or rates of change. In these companies the models themselves were programmed to ascertain which particular methods were being used and were able to standardise inputs. Thirteen others were able to do this on different model runs by use of control parameters. Most companies felt no real need for this kind of flexibility on input and had therefore not included it in the model.

14.2 Characteristics of changes to data base

A further aspect of flexibility is the ability of the user to change values of input variables during a computer run. Figure 24 shows that 38 (i.e. all except one) of the conversational models in use allowed the user to change particular items of data within the computer run. It also shows that in seven systems the changes became automatically permanent, in 13 they remained temporary until made permanent, three suites contained modules which were not consistent in this respect, and the remaining 15 had the option of having changes permanent or temporary. Where a change is made in the data the calculations can be re-worked incorporating the changed items. This may be a major advantage over batch systems, where changes can be made only at the beginning of each run, which may be wasteful of computer time.

Figure 24 Characteristics of changes to data base during computer runs

	No. of companies	No. of companies
Data base change is permanent	7	
Data base change is temporary	13	
Data base change is temporary in some models but permanent in others	3	
User has option of permanent/temporary change	15	
	—	38
No changes allowed during computer run		27
Total		65

Not all conversational systems are equally flexible. Those which are fully flexible allow the user to stop the computer run at any time to change information, then the run will continue using the amended information. Some other, less flexible, systems allow interruption of a model run to change data but require the run to start again from the beginning in such an event.

Flexibility of output

Choice of output reports

Figure 25   Choice of output reports

Characteristic	No. of companies	No. of companies
(a) Choice achieved by use of control parameters	25	
(b) Choice by being on call in conversational mode	14	
(c) Both (a) and (b)	12	
(d) Other	1	
	—	52
(e) No choice		13
Total		65

Users in 52 of the 65 companies had a choice with respect to the output reports they could call. This flexibility was achieved by means of control parameters input at the outset of the run in 37 companies, 26 had models where flexibility was achieved by reports being on call in the conversational mode. These figures include 12 companies which had models in both of these categories. Section (d) of Figure 25 'Other', covers the Butterfield-Harvey Group model which is run in remote batch mode. At the end of each phase of its model an option is given to the operator to continue or to terminate the job.

Choice of format of output reports

Choice of format of output reports was possible in 22 companies. This was achieved in almost all instances by having sets of alternative reports available which could be called by use of control parameters or report control files. By these means it is possible on one occasion to have information which is suitable for presentation to management, and on others to produce detailed working reports.

Fixed or flexible sequence of reports

Figure 26   Choice of sequence of output reports

	No. of companies
(a) Fixed sequence only	32
(b) Choice of sequence	27
(c) Both (a) and (b)	6
Total	65

Figure 26 shows that there was a fixed sequence for reports in 38 companies, in 33 companies the sequence of reports could be changed, six companies had modules which had both fixed and optional sequences. The optional facility can be useful if one particular document is required urgently.

209

15.4 *Printing of output reports*

Where the company uses a keyboard printer terminal it should be possible to run small reports on it and call for lengthy reports to be run on a fast line printer. Thus, sensitivity tests can be done in the conversational mode and then the reports can be run on the line printer. In this way the use of the executive's time can be reduced and computer costs kept lower, too. This can lead to problems as one company discovered. It was found quicker to have their reports run on fast line printers in the USA and have the print-out flown to the UK, rather than to have it printed. by their bureau in this country. Unfortunately, on one occasion the output was delayed, missed the usual Friday plane, subsequently got caught up in a Heathrow Airport go-slow, and never arrived.

16. *Output reports by models*

All of the companies with the exception of the *Butterfield-Harvey Group* (mentioned earlier in this respect) produced profit and loss accounts at the corporate level and most also produced balance sheets, cash flow statements and financial ratio analyses. Where a cash flow statement was not produced a source and use of funds statement was often produced instead, although half of the models produced both types of report. The source and use of funds statement can normally be provided from the data required to produce a balance sheet. A cash flow statement is more detailed and tends to require additional information especially on the timing of cash flows.

Figure 27   Output reports produced by models

Report	Total company	Subsidiaries	Divisions	Operating units
Profit and loss	64	28	26	14
Balance sheet	51	24	16	8
Cash flow	50	24	18	10
Financial ratio analysis	44	20	15	12
Source and use of funds statement	36	18	13	7
Marketing operations	22	16	20	15
Project evaluation	22	16	8	10
Production	22	14	18	14
Distribution	19	11	13	11
Purchasing	7	5	5	4
Manpower	6	4	6	4
Financing	5	1	1	1
New venture	2	1	2	1

From *Figure 27* it can be seen that in many companies the models produced reports on production, distribution and marketing, too. Large complex models incorporating physical features are often used for these purposes, especially where they extend down to the operating unit level of the companies. These reports should be useful for lower level as well as top managers.

Only 10 companies stated that they can produce manpower reports. However, *British Rail* in particular place great importance on manpower studies, as it is a critical aspect of their long-term planning. Modelling for manpower planning may well become a growth area.

The frequencies with which reports are produced at corporate, subsidiary, divisional and operating unit level are consistent with *Figure 12*, which showed how all 65 companies modelled at the corporate level but only 28 of them extended their corporate models downward to the operating unit level. Similarly, both *Figures 12* and *27* show how financial aspects are dominant at all organisational levels, but at lower levels reports on physical aspects of the business are relatively more important than at higher ones.

7. *Handling of time periods*

7.1 *Numbers of time periods*

Figure 28 Maximum number of time periods which can be handled

Range of time periods	No. of companies
1– 10	19
11–260	37
No limit	7
Not applicable	2
Total 65	

Figure 28 shows the maximum number of time periods which can be handled. This is important to many modellers especially when the model has been constructed to study time periods of less than a year. Some modellers needed 60 time periods as they wished to consider monthly periods over five years. At least one ready-made model on the market restricts its users to quarterly reports over five years. As the model is intended for long-term planning, the bureau concerned considers that monthly reports are unnecessary. Detailed reports, extending down to the operational level of the company, are clearly inappropriate as a basis for new ventures in an uncertain future.

7.2 *Time periods specified in models*

The question of time unit was not applicable to two organisations. The first *Black and Decker* has in the past relied exclusively on its optimisation model, which works in terms of multi-time periods. The second model is that of *British Rail* which does not work in time periods, as such, but is modelling a steady-state position (where stability is reached following a period of fluctuations).

As may be seen from *Figure 29* one year was the period used most frequently in model runs; 81 per cent of the 59 companies that specified a time period used it. This no doubt reflects the fact that data on a month-to-month basis are not normally appropriate for strategic decision taking. It was consequently surprising to find that the second most widely used period was one month. As many as 39 per cent of the 59 companies stating time periods used one month. An explanation is implicit in *Figures 12* and *27*, which indicate that 28 models extended downward from the corporate to the operating unit level, and were obviously used by management at the latter level, too. A month is an appropriate period, normally, for evaluating operating alternatives open to functional line managers.

This fact explains, in part, why 29 per cent of the 59 companies chose to use more than one basic time unit in their model runs. Eleven used years and months, one years and quarters, two quarters and months, and three years, quarters and months. In some of these companies, data was received and manipulated by some parts of the corporate suite on a monthly basis and aggregated to annual figures for use by other models in the suite. Some other companies used the same model, on different model runs, with monthly, quarterly or annual data as appropriate, this being possible where the accounting logic was unchanged by the basic time period used.

Design of a corporate model for use by different levels of management, and hence input of detailed data at operating unit level which is aggregated successively to divisional, subsidiary, and then corporate level is intuitively appealing. It is, though, inefficient because data needed at the corporate level could often be input directly and repeated aggregation could have been avoided. In *Unilever*, for instance, it has been found preferable to use separate models for operating level and corporate decisions, for this reason, amongst others.

Figure 29 Time periods specified in models

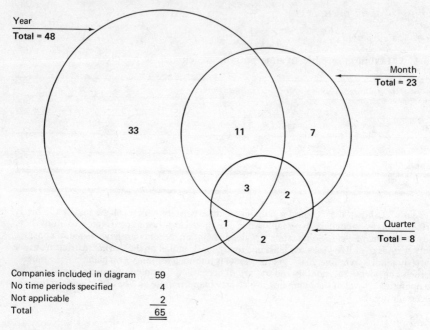

Companies included in diagram	59
No time periods specified	4
Not applicable	2
Total	65

18. *Languages in use*

In *Figure 4* we showed that 42 companies are using general-purpose languages. Ten of these companies have FORTRAN modules as well as modules built in another general-purpose language, and one other company has FORTRAN modules plus modules in two other languages.

Figure 30 Use of general-purpose languages

Name of language	No. of companies	Percentages
FORTRAN	34	63
BASIC	6	11
PL/1	6	11
COBOL	3	5
ALGOL	2	4
APL	1	2
JEAN	1	2
TELCOMP	1	2
Total 54		100%

FORTRAN is easily the most widely used language for corporate modelling, although it is far from ideal in many respects. Probably its popularity owes much to its greater availability. One major disadvantage of FORTRAN is the time which is required in most modelling applications to format output. A further disadvantage is the lack of good diagnostics.

Of the languages listed in *Figure 30* many computer professionals consider that (COBOL excepted) FORTRAN is the least suited to company modelling. The advocates of ALGOL maintain that it is superior in almost all respects and is certainly easier to learn and more flexible. PL/1 is the most general of all these languages. It has been designed so that new programmers can soon write PL/1 programs, whilst it remains suitable for professional programmers, who wish to use the full range of the computer's capabilities. BASIC is very useful for modelling in the conversational mode and is relatively easy for the non-computer professional to use. APL, JEAN and TELCOMP are excellent for many aspects of conversational modelling but are, as yet not widely used.

In spite of its relative disadvantages, no other general-purpose language is making any headway against FORTRAN, which if anything seems to be gaining in strength. This may be due, in part, to problems that may arise if a modeller leaves before the model is properly implemented. This may involve the company in trying to find another programmer experienced in the language, which can be quite a difficult task unless it is already used widely.

Time taken to build models

Figure 31   Calendar months taken to build modules

| | No. of modules | |
Range in months	First working model	Present model
0– 1	79	52
2– 3	57	49
4– 6	30	47
7–12	18	24
Over 12	10	22
No details	30	30
Total 224		224

By our definition, a model becomes a 'first working model' the first time it is run with actual data and can be used to aid decision-taking. Where the companies were using the modular (building block) approach, many of the modules were relatively simple, and were finished easily within one calendar month. Naturally, where the firms were working on one large complex module more time was required. *Figure 31* shows quite clearly that much time was spent on further development of modules after the first working model state. Many modellers found it extremely difficult to estimate the elapsed time spent developing the present model. Where a model has been in use for several years and is updated (amended) each year, the present model may have taken many months to reach its present level of sophistication.

Great care should be exercised in interpreting the figures shown in the table above. Very few people work full-time on a model for much longer than one month, and there are wide fluctuations between calendar-months and man-months. Again, calendar elapsed time is heavily dependent on the level of resources donated to the model, and the degree of urgency communicated to the modellers. To produce an average elapsed time to complete a first working corporate model would perhaps be misleading in these circumstances. ICL for instance started work on corporate modelling in 1963. The first version of the present model was developed initially in 1964. Over the years it has been updated to such an extent that it differs considerably from the first working model. To give accurate elapsed times in this case would be difficult.

Thirteen companies gave no details of elapsed time for some or all of their modules or gave us one blanket figure for the whole of their corporate suite of models. These figures have not been included as they would tend to exaggerate the time spent on developing individual modules. These 13 companies account for the 30 modules shown as 'No details' in *Figure 31*.

20. *Cost aspects*

20.1 *Calculation of cost*

Calculation of the costs involved in developing corporate models is fraught with difficulties, because of the problems of finding satisfactory answers to the following questions:

(i) Where there is spare capacity on the company's computer, how should use of the computer for corporate modelling be costed?

(ii) Where a model is run on a company's own computer and is depriving other jobs of computer access, how should this be costed?

(iii) In most cases modellers were not engaged in full-time work on corporate models and no additional salaries had to be paid because of the corporate modelling activities. How should this be accounted for?

(iv) Personnel other than those directly involved in modelling were involved in answering questions, collecting data and being educated in the use of the system; what cost does this incur?

If a marginal costing approach had been taken many of the models would have cost nothing, where they were run on the company's own computer and the modellers were salaried, not employed specifically to work on the model. As some companies make an internal charge for use of their own computer even when it has spare capacity, on the grounds of consistency, a notional charge has been made in respect of those not levying internal charges. As far as the question of modellers' time is concerned, an arbitrary decision has been made to charge it out at cost to the company including overheads, but not to take account of the time of the other personnel mentioned in question (iv) above.

20.2 *Range of costs of corporate models*

Figure 32   Cost of building corporate models

Range in £	No. of companies First working model	Present model
1– 2,000	22	14
2,001– 5,000	13	14
5,001–10,000	9	10
10,001–50,000	13	16
Over 50,000	5	8
No details	3	3
Total 65		65

Figure 32 shows that the range of development costs was very wide. If individual values had been shown it would have been seen to be from a few hundred to £250,000. However, 53 per cent and 43 per cent of companies had acquired their first working and present models respectively for less than £5,000.

10.3   *Details of man-weeks spent developing corporate models*

Figure 33   Break-down of man-weeks spent developing corporate models

First working model	*Feasibility study	Programming	**Implementation
Range in weeks	No. of companies	No. of companies	No. of companies
0– 2	12	16	27
3– 5	19	14	10
6– 20	10	10	8
21–100	18	17	12
Over 100	3	5	5
No details	3	3	3
Total 65	65	65	
Present model			
0– 2	7	11	18
3– 5	10	9	11
6– 20	22	15	12
21–100	18	19	15
Over 100	5	8	6
No details	3	3	3
Total 65	65	65	

*Feasibility study and determination of model inputs, outputs and logical structure.
**Developing systems and data base to permit use as a planning tool; time spent by modellers in education of potential users.

Figure 34 shows the man-weeks calculated by taking the arithmetic average of the inter-quartiles of the items appearing in *Figure 33*.

Figure 34   Man-weeks spent on average corporate models

	First working model		Present model	
	Man-weeks	Percentage	Man-weeks	Percentage
Feasibility study	10	39	14	32
Programming	11	42	18	42
Implementation	5	19	11	26
Total 26		100%	43	100%

Figure 34 indicates that the modellers' task is not finished when the first working model is completed. Often this may be just a springboard from which future ideas can be generated and modelled. The 65 per cent increase in man-weeks required to take the first working model through to the present model indicates that many changes are required to the first working model. This is

215

further evidence that companies are starting with simple models and then making them more complex in easy stages.

20.4   *Consultancy costs*

Figure 35   Break-down of consultancy costs incurred building corporate models

Range in £	First working model No. of companies	Present model No. of companies
1– 500	2	2
501– 1,500	5	2
1,501– 3,000	4	6
3,001–10,000	2	2
Over 10,000	2	3
Total 15		15

Average costs of consultancy services, where they were used, may be calculated from the data shown in Figure 35. These are given in *Figure 36*.

Figure 36   Average consultancy costs incurred

	Averaged over 15 companies £	Averaged over 62 companies £
First working model	1,950	471
Present model	2,571	622

The first column shows the average costs incurred by the 15 companies using consultants. The second column shows the average over all the 62 companies replying to this question. *Figure 36* also shows that most of the costs were involved on development of the first working models. On five out of the 15 models where consultants were involved no costs were incurred after implementation of the first working model.

Figure 37   Break-down of computer costs incurred in building corporate models

Range in £	First working model No. of companies	Present model No. of companies
0– 100	13	8
101– 500	16	13
501–1,000	8	8
1,001–5,000	16	16
Over 5,000	9	17
No details	3	3
Total 65		65

Figure 38   Average computer costs involved

	£
First working model	881
Present model	1,669

0.5   *Average costs for model development*
The average costs shown above can be summarised to reveal (*Figure 39*) the total cost involved on what may be termed an average model. The inter-quartile average has been chosen to ascertain the cost of the average model rather than the simple arithmetic mean, which can be seriously affected by the inclusion of extreme items. The largest suite of models cost £250,000 which is considerably more expensive than any other corporate model, although three other models cost more than £100,000. Use of the arithmetic mean would have meant that each model would be apportioned with over £13,000 as its share of the four giant models.

Figure 39   Total development costs of the average corporate model

	First working model		*Present model*	
	£	%	£	%
Feasibility study	1,000	25	1,400	21
Programming	1,100	28	1,800	27
Implementation	500	13	1,100	17
Manpower costs	2,600	66	4,300	65
Consultancy costs	471	12	622	10
Computer costs	881	22	1,669	25
Total	3,952	100%	6,591	100%

An arbitrary figure of £100 per man-week (including overheads) has been used in these calculations. In Central London the figure may be higher whilst in the Provinces it would tend to be lower. The actual cost per man-week stated by the modellers varied between £60–280, but £100 was the figure quoted most and many other figures were in this region.

The treatment of consultancy costs is very arbitrary and should be interpreted with care. The figures shown for consultancy costs in the table are the averages over all models, rather than just the 15 models using consultants. Firms using consultants should expect to pay more for consultancy than in this table. However, savings should be effected on other aspects of the modelling and there is no reason why the overall figure should be significantly changed by the use of consultants. Naturally, the charge per man-week of a consultant will be high, but modelling expertise should lead to time savings.

Model builders

1.1   *Backgrounds*

Figure 40 shows the functional backgrounds of those who developed the models in the 65 companies. The last category, 'Others', included degree holders in engineering, physics, chemistry, medicine, and business studies, and some others with functional backgrounds in marketing, and personnel management too.

Although operational researchers remain the most important single category of model builders, accountants have forced the data processing specialists into third place. Indeed, only 50

217

per cent of all models were developed by operational researchers, data processing specialists or mathematicians/statisticians, who together have been the model building specialists in the past.

Examination of the detailed figures revealed that the early models (in the 1960s) were largely built by operational researchers, whilst there has been a trend since 1970 towards development of models by accountants, planners, and other potential users. This has been associated with the spread of modelling systems and wider use of the conversational mode on bureau computers which facilitate model building by the non-specialist.

Figure 40 Functional backgrounds of model builders

Type	Frequency
Operational researchers	78
Accountants	44
Data processors	42
Analysts	23
Planners	19
Actuaries (insurance companies)	11
Mathematicians/statisticians	10
Economists	8
Others	27
Total	262

21.2 *Team approach*

There were five companies where one man had built the corporate model. Although a team approach is often advocated, the results of these five models did not differ significantly from the others. Two were very successful, two reasonably successful and only one struck serious implementation problems. The reason given for the failure was changes in top management, in particular three finance directors in four years, which had meant a lack of continuity and loss of earlier enthusiasm. It is a moot point whether a team approach would have fared any better under these circumstances.

A further 11 companies had models built by one particular department only, mainly operational research sections. The team approach generally advocated is not to have all the personnel from one sector of the business, but to take personnel from the different departments which are likely to be involved in the modelling. However, an advantage of having more than one modeller from one department may be that the continuity is assured if one of the modellers leaves.

21.3 *Size of team*

The average number of modellers engaged on modelling was four, the numbers ranging from one to 23. The firm with 23 modellers said that this was the number who could be working on the model at any one time. The backgrounds of three of the 23 were indicated, the remaining 20 included in 'Others' in *Figure 40* were 'from wide-ranging backgrounds'.

22. *Reasons for rejection of bureaux packages*

Modellers who had not used packages were asked to distribute 100 points between reasons for rejection. Mean scores, rounded to the nearest integer, are shown in *Figure 41*.

Figure 41 Aspects deterring modellers from use of bureaux packages

	Ready-made model	Modelling system
Inflexibility of		
(i) Logic	21	9
(ii) Inputs	12	3
(iii) Outputs	14	4
	47	16
Costs	10	21
No knowledge of suitable model	8	9
Size restriction	7	8
Not available when job started	5	4
Appropriate models not on market	4	4
Not considered	3	9
Model intended as research tool	3	7
Insecurity of data	3	4
Contrary to company policy	2	4
Discontinuity of service	2	3
Difficulties of data transfer	2	2
Extra time learning system	2	2
Advantages not so great as to outweigh time spent on package evaluation	2	0
Presence of own programmers experienced in a general-purpose language	0	7
Total 100%		100%

Quite clearly the greatest deterrent to use of ready-made models is the lack of flexibility. The next most important consideration is the cost factor, which may appear paradoxical as the idea of ready-made models is to share the development costs amongst the users. However, cost may be a deterrent where the ready-made model does not exactly fulfil management requirements: even a relatively cheap model may be poor value for money if its usefulness is very limited and it is very expensive to make changes that will improve it.

The difference between scores for modelling systems and ready-made models is instructive. Modelling systems are more flexible, and fewer modellers said that they were deterred by their inflexibility, though this was still a major deterrent to use. More important was recognition of the greater costs of operating modelling systems. Size restrictions were also thought to be an important limitation by some. If the answers against 'No knowledge of suitable model' and 'Not considered' are summed, a total of score of 18 is obtained, which is second in importance only to costs. This is largely explained by the fact that many of the models built in general-purpose languages were developed before modelling systems became widely available (about 1970). Given the heavy investment in past modelling effort there was little incentive to seriously consider switching to modelling systems which were known to involve greater costs of operation. A further, but no doubt less important, factor was the cost of evaluating the increasing variety of modelling systems which have been marketed in the last three or four years.

23. *Technical problems encountered*

23.1 *Core store too small*
The most commonly quoted difficulty was that of building a model which could be accepted by the computer on which it was expected to run. Many modellers failed to solve this problem and had to transfer to larger computers. Others disciplined themselves by writing more efficient models or by reducing the level of complexity of the models. One company overcame the problem by running their models overnight as the bureau system then allowed use of double the core store.

23.2 *Restriction on program statements*
Several modellers had problems with the use of bureaux packages. One modelling system allowed only a relatively small number of lines in the program. There were difficulties in that the modellers were obliged to split modules into smaller programs. This led to further difficulties in transferring results from one module to another. The system designed to facilitate transfer of data also made it easy to pick up figures unintentionally unless great care was exercised.

23.3 *Carry-forward difficulties*
Some modellers had encountered difficulties when using modelling systems for carry-forward operations. An accountant in preparing accounts for a number of years will work out 'year 1' before proceeding to 'year 2' as the closing balance of 'year 1' will constitute the opening balances of 'year 2'. With many modelling systems it is difficult to carry balances from one year to another, because the computer is programmed to make a calculation for all years before proceeding to the next calculation. One consultant almost gave up using modelling systems because he was having difficulty in finding one which would satisfactorily deal with carry-forwards from period to period. Many bureaux have now remedied this situation and their systems permit either row (all years for each calculation before proceeding to the next calculation) or column (all calculations for each year before proceeding to the next year) operations or a mixture of both. Details will be found in the analysis of packages (Appendix 2).

23.4 *Deficiencies in manuals*
Some manuals were found to be ambiguous and even incorrect, and did not indicate all restrictions in the model. Others could not be classed as 'user manuals' and were therefore not specific enough for most modellers. One neglected area was file handling and many modellers had problems in the initial stages in this respect. In some cases these early problems were eased by help from the bureaux but not all found the bureaux staff particularly helpful.

23.5 *Communications 'hang-ups'*
Modellers on-line to bureaux reported communications problems. Often when things went wrong the bureaux blamed the GPO or the terminal. However, when these were checked and found to be in order the users became frustrated with the whole set-up. *Wates* experienced problems of this nature. The nearest bureau computer which it found suitable for APL, the language it used, was in Paris. Unfortunately, it found that only one telephone call in 20 actually led to connection with the computer. As each call involved dialling 13 digits, each connection was, on the average, the result of dialling 260 digits. *Wates* now uses a computer in the USA accessed by a call to the London terminal of the bureau concerned. Still, although it is seen as an improvement, the position is far from ideal. Because of clock differences between UK and the USA, the computer cannot usually be accessed until after lunch-time in this country.

23.6 *System changes*
Another grumble against bureaux was that they changed their systems without informing the users. This naturally led to irritation in the cases where modellers had spent a lot of time trying to ascertain why their models would not work properly. Users complained also because they were expected to change their systems to fit in with those of the bureaux.

3.7 *Modelling system failure*
Most of the models of *Mullard*, as a member of the *Philips Group*, are based on packages developed by them. They previously tried to use a bureau modelling system and state:

'With regard to the package mentioned in our discussion the decision not to proceed with this model was primarily based on the efficiency of the package. Preliminary work on the application of the model to our concern took several hundred man-hours, in spite of some assistance on modifying the package from the supplier. The package was marketed as a facility that could be taken over by accountants with a minimum of technical support, but our experience was that at each stage of implementation a considerable reliance had to be placed on internal computer expertise not only in operation but also in testing.'

3.8 *Minor nature of technical problems*
However, on the whole, most modellers managed to overcome the technical difficulties without too much effort and 19 said thay had had no problems of this nature. It was generally considered that technical problems were minor compared with the problems of getting the models introduced, understood and used.

Section C

Bureaux packages

24. *Types in use*

Figure 42 Packages used by modellers for corporate modelling

Name of package	No. of companies
PROSPER	14
SIMSTRAT	4
AS	3
FORESIGHT	3
FEP	2
GPOS	2
ORACLE	2
PLANMASTER	2
BUDGET 6	1
COLYPLAN	1
DELPHI XX	1
PAUS	1
PLANCODE	1
REPORT	1
Total 38	

All the packages listed in *Figure 42* were being used for simulation models. One mentioned specifically for use with optimisation models was UMPIRE, although bureaux software was in use in other companies for this type of model. We would reiterate here that our sample selection probably led to biased results as some bureaux assisted more than others in arranging visits to users (However, we tended not to approach all contacts given, preferring to try to see as many systems as possible.) The proportion of companies using each of the packages listed in *Figure 42* should not be used, therefore, as a reliable index of its popularity.

Five modellers found it necessary to use two packages for their models. One or two bureaux have highly sophisticated statistical routines which modellers have found very helpful for special areas of their models. However, for their general requirements they have found other bureaux better, perhaps, because of cost considerations. One of these five modellers, *Knowles Electronics,* was using a modelling system as well as a ready-made model. However, another company, *Helena Rubinstein,* was relying solely on its ready-made model. As can be seen from *Figure 3*, though, few of the companies were using ready-made models, whereas about half of the companies in the survey used modelling systems.

Another survey undertaken at the same time as this one was designed to provide details of the packages currently available. Most of the bureaux visited were helpful in arranging meetings with at least one user, which may explain why so many packages appear in *Figure 42*. Some of the packages have few users, whilst others have a considerable number in spite of low frequencies of occurrence in *Figure 42*.

5. *Bureau charges*

In nearly all the 65 companies the charges quoted coincided with the published rates of the bureaux. One bureau juggled with connect time and CPU time when assessing charges, but the users accepted that this was reasonable in the circumstances. The fact that few users quoted rates which showed a discount on those published may indicate that such discounts were not being received. Alternatively, it is possible that firms receiving discounts did not wish to publicise the fact.

Many users were not able to provide details of initial fees to access packages, annual support fees or outright purchase prices, probably because in many instances these were not applicable. However, most modellers were able to give details of connect time, CPU, file storage and transmission charges. These are not published, though, because they could be misleading. Factors like the quality of the packages, the amount of CPU time required, and the amount of use affect relative costs of using the different bureaux, too. CPU time varies with the power of the computer and the efficiency of the package. In addition, it was widely thought that several bureaux deliberately load CPU time for use of their systems in order to recoup the costs of developing the modelling system.

6. *Average annual fees*

Nineteen companies using packages gave us estimates of what they expect to pay in average annual fees to bureaux. These ranged from £100 to £13,500 with an average of £2,400. We would expect annual costs to vary with the size of the model, its complexity, the mode of operation, and frequency of use as well as with the bureau used.

7. *Training courses*

Fourteen companies had sent staff on training courses provided by bureaux. Thirteen of the companies sent only prospective modellers but the fourteenth sent general management, too. It did this to broaden their knowledge and give them an insight into the capabilities and possible applications of corporate models. All 14 companies thought that the courses were good value for money. The longer courses developed a basic competence at modelling and an enthusiasm for modelling. Many of those who attended courses went on to model within their respective organisations on their return. The duration of the courses varied between one day and one week. One enterprising bureau runs free courses for its users, demonstrating a variety of techniques from programming languages to file-handling. Not all of the courses were run on a regular basis. Several bureaux will put on a training course, on request, if they consider that it is warranted in terms of expected future use of the system.

8. *After-sales support*

Twenty-eight companies were happy with the after-sales support provided by the bureaux. In no case was a charge levied for casual assistance with the installation of the modelling system or for advice over the telephone. Charges were made only where a consultant was engaged for completion of a specific task or for a period of time. One bureau provides a team of technical assistants who are scattered around the country and are available at any time to give general advice. They also make routine calls on their clients to ensure that all systems are working adequately.

In one case only was a modeller not satisfied with the after-sales service. He required the services of a consultant until such time as he was able to familiarise himself with the system. This was inevitable as the manual provided was a guide to the system rather than a user manual. In addition he found that the bureau concerned had no intention of amending/updating the system unless they were paid to do so. This particular user now intends to build his own modelling system using FORTRAN.

29.   *Consulting service*

Twenty-eight companies thought that the bureau they were using provided a consulting service, but very few had any idea of the service given or the fees charged. One or two were able to hazard guesses at between £40 – £100 per day. There was a feeling amongst some modellers that consultants' fees were extortionate which may explain why so few modellers had made enquiries as to the consulting services available.

At least two out of the 15 firms using consultants had done so because it was the only way to learn how to use the bureau systems. One was reasonably happy with the service given but the other was disillusioned. The latter company was charged £12,000 for the use of one consultant to help install its corporate model. The consultant was with it not more than 12 weeks and he was also looking after other clients at the same time. The company had signed a fixed/variable contract in which it was agreed that the consulting charges be between £10,000 – £20,000 depending upon the extent of assistance received from the company's own staff.

Two other companies had every reason to be happy with fixed price contracts with consultants. One of these paid £6,000 for a very sophisticated model, which the consultants reckon cost them £30,000 in normal charging out fees. The other company had a similar experience. Fortunately, both companies were dealing with well-known consultants, who honoured their agreements, and there is no evidence that the models suffered in any way.

In general, companies were happy with the services rendered by consultants. Often the consultants actually fed in the data themselves on their own terminal and produced reports for their clients which could be sent to them by mail if desired. From the point of view of the companies this was an ideal set-up because they incurred no capital expenses on equipment, nor had they to visit a bureau. Companies adopting this approach rated the services of their bureaux as 'very good' or 'excellent'. The charges for this kind of service are high but not unreasonably so considering the service received.

30.   *General comments on service*

Comments on the services rendered by the bureaux ranged from poor to excellent, with users more or less evenly distributed along the range. Only one computer bureau was considered to be consistently good, which may be because it is only just getting 'off the ground', and thus has to give a better service to attract new clients.

One modeller visited was not happy with bureau A and was changing to bureau B with whom he had had a little experience. On the following day we met another modeller who was changing from bureau B to A for the very same reasons. It is possible that some bureaux make a big effort to attract new clients and then become complacent once the client has been 'hooked'.

One bureau was thought to allocate 25 per cent of its budget to providing free after-sales service, free consulting for limited periods, and free training courses. However, as this bureau was not in London, this was perhaps the only way in which it could attract and retain its clients. Many modellers expressed a preference for a locally sited bureau which they could visit when they had problems. Modellers found difficulties in explaining their problems over the telephone.

Eleven companies passed unfavourable comments on the services provided by the bureaux. Typical comments were:
  (i)   'Problems in getting some of the exotic features of the modelling system to work. Sometimes found that the supplier has not implemented them.'
  (ii) 'Hardware not too reliable and so had to arrange special back-up facilities for emergencies.'
  (iii) 'Often problems in getting into system.'
  (iv) 'Technical assistance has on several occasions left room for improvement; response time from the computer has often been poor.'

31.   *Factors leading to adoption of packages*

Often the package was adopted because it was readily available as part of the software provided by the computer manufacturer. Where there is spare capacity on the computer, and an available package, modellers who use their own spare time for their modelling work see the whole exercise as costing nothing.

In a few cases bureaux salesmen were able to sell a package to top management, who then passed it down the line to the intended modeller. The latter naturally did not think that this was the ideal method of selection, and it has led to dissatisfaction. If modellers themselves choose the package used it puts the onus on them to make it work.

Many companies had spent considerable amounts on testing the alternative packages available. When there were only three or four available this was sensible, but now with the proliferation of packages available it is less likely that companies will be able to afford to test each, though bench-mark tests on a short-list are no doubt still worthwhile. It may be reassuring to potential users to know that most of the modelling systems currently available are capable of being manipulated to perform all that is required of them. Many operations may not be done in the most efficient manner, but they can at least be done.

Some modelling systems have been adopted because they are easily understood by the intended users, who may be management without any previous experience of modelling or programming. A number of users have commented that it is easier for them to spend time learning a system than it is trying to communicate effectively with computer specialists. Other systems on the market require a knowledge of FORTRAN, or some other general-purpose language, and will thus be more suitable for modellers experienced in these languages.

One modeller gave his reason for using one package as the existence of a users' club. Here modellers from various organisations can meet and discuss modelling problems. This can lead to mutual benefits. The tendency for each modeller to re-invent the wheel can be overcome to a great extent by these regular meetings.

Recommendation by other users was a further, important factor. One of the bureaux visited in connection with our bureaux 'packages' survey said that several pharmaceutical manufacturers were using its system. Apparently, the company that had first introduced the system recommended it to other firms in the industry. This implies considerable faith in the integrity of the computer bureau, and in the effectiveness of its systems for maintaining the security of data, as the long-range plans of companies that were in competition were held on its disc packs. It is also representative of the attitude of some modellers to those in competing companies who are starting modelling. Many modellers are willing to give, and receive, advice from their counterparts in competing firms. For instance, during our survey we heard that the potential modellers of one giant construction company were visiting construction firms with corporate models and were receiving valuable advice on the lessons that the latter had learnt. It is a moot point whether such free communication of technical information to competitors is good or bad from the point of view of the companies which had gained it at a cost.

Other reasons for adoption advanced were:
(i) 'System allowed for sensitivity analysis and backward iteration with no extra programming.'
(ii) 'Lack of entrance fee and met requirements.'
(iii) 'Intention was that senior managers especially accountants would be involved, therefore supposedly simple system selected.'

Section D

Management aspects

32. *Initiation of proposals to develop corporate models*

Figure 43 Initiators of proposals to develop or use corporate models

	No. of companies
Directors	23
Planners	15
Accountants	8
Operational researchers	7
Management services	5
Computer specialists	4
Others	3
Total	65

    Figure 43 shows that well over half of all proposals to develop corporate models were initiated by members of the board or by corporate planners, and only seven by operational researchers. It is natural that planners should wish to use corporate models as many see them as useful tools to assist in routine planning. The frequency with which directors were involved was particularly gratifying because support by top management is likely to be stronger and more enduring where the proposal to develop the model has come from directors (see Section 39 too).

33. *Use of models*

Figure 44 Type of planning in which models are used

	No. of companies
(a) As *ad hoc* devices (e.g. for merger proposals) only	5
(b) In regular corporate and divisional planning only	29
(c) Both (a) and (b)	30
(d) As a research tool	1
Total	65

    From *Figure 44* it may be seen that 59 of the 65 companies used their corporate model in regular corporate and divisional planning. Of these, 30 also used models in *ad hoc* planning, for instance to evaluate proposals for mergers, new products, or new factories. A further five used their models for such *ad hoc* planning but not for regular planning. One company built a series of corporate models, on an *ad hoc* basis, as research tools. Once completed and used for the intended purpose, the models were shelved. Some had, though, been used as an internal teaching aid (as the basis for a business game). The model builders in this company, who were operational researchers, believed it more efficient to build a series of models tailor-made for the major problems than to develop a more general corporate model that could not map the specific problems in such detail or so faithfully. This view was not shared by modellers in other companies in the sample of 65.

34.   Personnel using the models

Figure 45   Model users

	No. of companies
Planners	21
Accountants	20
Operational researchers	9
Directors	5
Computer specialists	4
Management services	3
Actuaries	2
Economists	1
Total	**65**

The high proportion of models used directly by planners and accountants emerges strongly from the survey findings. *Figure 45* shows that in only 13 of the companies were models used by operational researchers and computer specialists as opposed to ultimate users. The models involved in these cases tended to be optimising and called for special skills in interpretation of the output. For instance, the significance of 'dual' or 'shadow' prices frequently required such interpretation where linear programming was involved.

35.   Use of computer reports

The company modellers were asked how much reliance they perceive top managers place on computer reports, manual reports, and their own intuitive judgement. The modellers were required to distribute 100 points between the three categories. *Figure 46* shows the mean points per category and the extremes encountered. Most modellers had difficulty in answering this question and two said they could not.

Figure 46   Reliance modellers perceive top management place on reports

	Computer reports %	Manual reports %	Intuitive judgement %	Total %
Average	29	28	43	100
Extreme 1	50	50	0	100
Extreme 2	0	50	50	100
Extreme 3	50	0	50	100
Extreme 4	100	0	0	100
Extreme 5	0	0	100	100

Over the sample as a whole, therefore, we found that modellers thought the board placed about as much reliance on reports generated by the corporate models as those produced by more conventional, manual processes. Individual companies varied widely as can be seen from the extreme values given. However, care must be taken in interpreting these, for instance in the case of 'Extreme 2' the computer reports were converted into typed reports before presentation to management. Hence a score of '0' was inevitably returned against 'Computer reports'.

Intuitive judgement was clearly seen by most modellers as the dominant influence over strategic decisions. It was given almost half more weight than either of the other two categories, accounting for 43 of the 100 points on average. Indeed, in one company the board were seen to rely exclusively on their intuitive judgement, and in a further three it was given 90 of the 100 points. Whilst no modellers accepted this level of reliance on intuitive judgement as desirable, many recognised that strategic decisions involved imponderables, and that consequently corporate models (though valuable in exploring quantitative aspects of corporate problems) cannot be more than one basis for strategic decisions.

Because the answers given by the modellers were subjective ratings, there is a distinct possibility that they might be biased towards a greater weight for computer reports, because of a desire to appear more successful either to the interviewer or themselves. However, if such a bias exists, it does not seem to be strong. The weight given, on average, to computer reports does not appear to be unreasonably high. Moreover, quite a few modellers reported that very little reliance was placed on computer reports. The possibility of bias should not, though, be disregarded.

36.   *Integration of models into total planning system*

Earlier involvement in development of corporate models in three companies had suggested to us that successful implementation depends, among other factors, upon the extent to which the use of the model becomes integrated into the routine planning procedures. As may be seen from *Figure 47*, in four companies the corporate models were said to constitute the planning system, i.e. without them there would have been no planning system. Formal planning had been relatively unsophisticated in all these companies before introduction of the corporate model and hence development of the model and the planning system tended to coincide. The problems of integrating a corporate model into a planning system which is already well developed and complex may be much more considerable.

Figure 47   How well the models were integrated into the planning system

	No. of companies
Models constituted planning system	4
Fully integrated	35
Partly integrated	14
Not integrated	12
Total	65

It is encouraging, therefore, that in 35 companies, use of the corporate model was thought to be fully integrated into the planning system. In another 14 companies it was said to be partly integrated, but was not used as a matter of course in planning, though efforts were being made to achieve this condition. The main problem perceived was that of overcoming resistance by many of the managers involved in planning.

A further 12 models had not been integrated into the corporate planning process at all. In two of the companies there was never any intention that they should be. One company in the construction industry regarded its models as research tools and developed a separate model for each new problem (see Section 33). The other thought its corporate model appropriate for *ad hoc* decisions but not regular planning. Modellers and their management sponsors in a further five companies intended that the model should be integrated into the planning system as a routine tool but found the management involved unwilling to accept its use. Modellers in the remaining five companies intended that ultimately use of the model should be a normal part of corporate planning, but because the model was still at an experimental stage, had not taken steps to realise their intentions at the time of the survey.

Again, although the possibility of bias towards full integration (i.e. towards success) should not be disregarded, for the reasons advanced in Section 35, we do not believe that the answers given by those interviewed were heavily biased. Most modellers frankly admitted difficulties they had met and mistakes they had made, which is inconsistent with a general desire to convince either us or themselves that they had been a marked success. Moreover, further information was produced to explain the answer that, for instance, the corporate model constituted the modelling system.

37.   Degree of improvement in forecasts

Bureaux selling modelling systems have placed heavy emphasis on the improvement to forecasts that may be expected to stem from corporate models. Consequently, although it was impossible to obtain other than subjective judgements in a survey of the kind undertaken, modellers were asked for their views on the extent of such improvement. Because the answers were subjective there could well be a bias towards reporting success, because of possible motivations mentioned already in Section 35. However, for the reasons advanced there and in Section 36, we believe such bias to be small. This is, again, a subjective judgement based on our observations during the interviewing process and our checks on consistency between answers. When interpreting the results it is wise to allow for the possibility of a bias towards success.

Figure 48   How much modellers consider use of models has improved forecasts

	No. of companies
Very significantly	6
Significantly	30
Not very much	16
Not at all	6
Too early to comment	5
No reply	2
Total	65

Thirty modellers thought that forecasts had improved significantly and another six went even further and said they thought that forecasts had improved very significantly. The main reasons given were increased accuracy and a reduction in the time taken to prepare forecasts. *London Transport Executive* said that its forecasts had shown a significant improvement, because with the previous manual system, which took five days, the forecast was not available with sufficient speed to permit the evaluation of even minor amendments within a limited time-scale. With its computerised corporate model the forecasting can now be completed accurately and quickly (and a number of alternatives can all be evaluated in the same day).

The increase in accuracy as a result of the introduction of computers is more difficult to gauge. Seemingly small changes in assumptions may have chain reaction effects on clerical work. Extensions, sub-totals, summaries, net profit, tax calculations and even cash requirements must all be recalculated and rechecked. The planner will have to remain alert for long periods if mistakes are to be avoided, especially where there is a strict time limit for production of the plans. Errors may not be obvious, management may be unaware of them, and wrong decisions may ensue which can cost dearly.

In six companies the modellers did not consider that models had improved forecasts. Three of these modellers were mentioned in Section 36 as having come across obstacles which had proved insurmountable. In the other three companies the models were fully integrated into the total planning systems, but the modellers felt that there had been no improvement in forecasts since introduction of the modelling system. The previous manual system had been well developed and management were happier using the manual reports than the computer ones. They seemed to have a mistrust of the computer system which was seen, as is so often the case, as a mysterious 'black box'.

38. *Cost/benefit analysis*

We wished to determine whether corporate models had been successful in cost/benefit terms. Unfortunately, it is very difficult with a corporate model to measure the benefits. Few companies have been able to show, in tangible terms, that their use of corporate models has made a significant improvement to the profits of the company. To ascertain the true benefits of the model it would be necessary to measure the outcomes of decisions taken, against the outcomes of decisions that would have been taken without the use of the model. In most companies this is an impossible task. Consequently, we were forced to rely upon the subjective judgement of respondents in the sample companies.

Figure 49   Modellers' views on top management's assessment of modelling exercise (in terms of cost/benefits)

	No. of companies
Successful	36
Partly successful	12
Not successful	5
Too early	9
No reply	1
Others	2
Total	65

Modellers were asked whether directors in their company regarded the corporate model as a success in terms of benefits given the costs incurred. Their answers are shown in *Figure 49*. The comments made already, in Sections 35, 36 and 37, about the possibility of a bias to success and our belief that it is quite small apply equally here.

Figure 49 shows that most modellers thought top managers felt model building had been partly or completely successful in terms of cost/benefits. This will be welcome news to those potential modellers who have been worried that they will be unable to convince management that the expenditure on corporate modelling is warranted in these terms.

One company where the benefits have definitely exceeded the costs is *Yorkshire Imperial Plastics* where the Finance Director has built models specifically for those areas thought likely to provide quick pay-offs. His 'moulding model' which will be linked to the other models to form a complete corporate model has led to an improvement in plant capacity utilisation which has yielded a capital saving in the cost of new equipment of £70,000.

Only five modellers believed that the top management regarded corporate modelling as unsuccessful in terms of cost/benefits. One of these models was expensive because of the uneconomic use of consultants and the modellers felt that there was little improvement in forecasts to warrant this expense. With the second model the management did not accept the results possibly because they were presented in an unfamiliar manner, as the model was of the probabilistic type. In the third company the modeller had a continual struggle to obtain funds to continue modelling. The board was divided in its support of the model. Some board members had been antagonised by reports which had shown quite clearly that they were pursuing a course contrary to the stated objectives of the company. The fourth and fifth companies had models which had not been successfully implemented at the time of the survey.

39. *Top management support*

Support from senior executives is necessary if development and subsequent use of the corporate model are to occur. Consequently, modellers were asked who was the most senior person supporting modelling. Their answers are recorded in *Figure 50*. The reservations made earlier about the possibility of bias in the subjective answers, and the reasons for believing it to be limited, apply with equal force here, too.

Figure 50 Senior executives supporting corporate modelling

	No. of companies
Directors	55
Planners	6
Accountants	3
Computer specialists	1
Total	65

It would appear from *Figure 50* that, in most companies, support is given by at least one board member. From discussions during visits to companies modelling, though, it emerged that this support is often lukewarm. Many directors, whilst interested in the concept of corporate models, remain to be convinced that it is of major importance to the company. A number of modellers stressed the importance of early use of the corporate model to sustain the interest of top management.

Strong support from top management is obviously important. At *Lansing Bagnall* the support of board members has had a marked effect in accelerating development of corporate modelling. This support has stimulated the team who developed the corporate model and they are now putting the new skills they have developed to use in modelling subsidiary company activities. Elsewhere, strong support may be necessary to block attempts to discontinue modelling, as in one company with a widely publicised model where quite senior line managers have made regular suggestions that modelling should be discontinued.

40. *Ultimate responsibility for models*

Those ultimately responsible for use and updating of the corporate models are in the great majority of instances the original builders; in many cases they are also the users of the models. In many companies the model builders see the model as a mere tool to assist in their routine planning activities, i.e. as a sophisticated calculating machine, and accept responsibility for ensuring that it is properly used. The dangers are obviously greater where the computer model is concerned because there are so many additional things which might go wrong. The 'Others' included in the table are, Head of Management Services, Group Controller, Director General, and Systems Research Manager.

Figure 51 Personnel ultimately responsible for models

	No. of companies
Builders	45
Directors	6
Accountants	5
Planners	4
No reply	1
Others	4
Total	65

41. *Management reaction to models*

If corporate models are to be used for strategic decision-taking it is important that the board should react favourably to their use. Since this was the only means of gauging such reactions available during the survey, modellers were asked for their views on top management's reactions, and reasons for their answers were discussed with them in many of the sample companies. Results are tabulated in *Figure 52*. The possibility of a bias towards reporting a favourable reaction, due to a need to bolster self-esteem or desire to impress the interviewer, must again be taken into account when interpreting the significance of these figures. However, we would reiterate our belief that the bias, if it exists, is small, and refer the reader yet again to Sections 35 and 36 for the reasons. The perceptive reader will have noted that the subjective answers on various aspects of success are, on the whole, consistent. A detailed check on answers of the individual respondents, and of different respondents in the same company, suggests a similar consistency. Consequently, if a bias does exist, it is fairly general.

Figure 52 Top management reaction to use of corporate models

	No. of companies
Very favourable	11
Favourable	25
Unfavourable	7
Undecided	20
Other	2
Total	65

From *Figure 52* it may be seen that in 36 companies, that is 55 per cent of the total sample, it was thought by the modellers that the board had reacted either favourably or very favourably towards the use of the corporate model. Modellers in these companies displayed proselytising zeal. They seemed to have made a considerable effort to gain and retain management interest and support.

In 20 companies the modellers thought that top management had reserved its judgement. In some there were board members who were committed to corporate models, but others who thought them just expensive playthings. In others, models had not been sufficiently developed to permit informed opinion, as many as 15 of the 65 models having been started only in 1972 or 1973.

In only seven companies had management reaction been decidedly unfavourable. Even in these modellers have not been prohibited from further modelling activities. All 65 companies are continuing to model. However, we found instances of change in the approach to modelling as a result of management reaction. We estimate that approximately 10 per cent of the companies in our sample had tried optimisation or probabilistic simulation models which, although sophisticated, failed to gain management acceptance. Subsequently, they all built simple, deterministic simulation models. As already noted, there are few probabilistic models currently used, and the optimisation models are relatively rare outside the oil industry.

The two companies covered by the category 'Other' in *Figure 52* are intriguing. In each, the computer print-outs were interpreted and reproduced by planners before presentation to the board, who appeared to be happy with the result but unaware that a computer-run corporate model had been used to do the calculations. It was inappropriate, therefore, to talk of the board's reactions to use of their corporate model.

42. General problems encountered

42.1 Major problems
Modellers reported two major, general problems. The first was obtaining data in the form required, at the right time, and in the right place. The second was that of gaining management acceptance.

42.2 Management acceptance problems
Ten modellers stressed the difficulty of gaining management acceptance when talking of general difficulties and others mentioned it in connection with other questions. The reasons are varied. Some modellers suggested a general lack of knowledge of, and sympathy for, modern management techniques among their executive directors. This may be a valid observation in some companies. None the less, we gained an impression that in some companies the modellers had failed to recognise that most top managers cannot afford the time to get involved in the detail of corporate models, and indeed require output in the most easily assimilable form possible. Moreover, though many realised that corporate models touched upon only part, the quantifiable aspects, of strategic problems, not all recognised that there were many qualitative aspects which could sometimes be of overriding importance. The differences in terminology and experience of many modellers and the senior line executives they seek to serve also struck us as a contributory factor.

42.3 Data collection difficulties
Twenty-four modellers raised the problem of data collection. Where manual systems already exist, these problems may be less, but still occurred where the computer model was more complex and required more data than the manual calculations it replaced. Where there were no manual calculations, involving collection of planning data, for the computer model to replace, the problem was reported to be considerably greater because the entire system for data collection had to be designed and implemented *de novo*.

42.4 Need for team approach
The financial personnel who were involved in modelling often reported problems in data handling, programming, and computer file manipulation. On the other hand, many operational researchers/mathematicians and computer specialists found problems in understanding accounting logic, particularly where taxation and financing were concerned. There are difficulties here in that the accounting and taxation systems are in a constant state of flux. The advantages of the team approach, with the skills of the various team members complementing each other, can be readily appreciated.

42.5 Too much detail
Another problem mentioned frequently was that of getting the right level of aggregation of detail. If the relationships and detail were too gross the whole thing became a 'back-of-the-envelope'

exercise. However, where more detail is built into the model the possibility of it becoming too complex to be understood by management has to be considered. This problem was overcome by one company in the top 10 of 'The Times 1,000' which had one model for aggregative work and one for more detailed work. *Unilever Ltd*, too, has tended to use separate models for strategic planning and for more routine planning.

43. *What modellers have learned*

43.1 *A simple approach is best*
Modellers were asked what they would do differently if they were to start again from scratch. The most frequent answer was that a simpler approach would be taken. Many modellers attempted to build models which were unnecessarily complex, when viewed in the light of what management required and the data available. In retrospect many recognised that where the models are used for strategic planning, great detail on the company's operations are unnecessary. Many modellers had made the mistake of trying to include as much detail in their long-term as in their short-term plans.

43.2 *Advantages of modular models*
The modular approach was advocated as leading to better results. Only a handful of companies now favour the 'all singing all dancing' corporate model approach which is prevalent in much of the existing literature. Almost all of the advantages are with the modular approach, especially where it is flexible and individual modules may be run independently of others where necessary. Running and testing costs may be reduced where independent runs can be made. One snag, however, with the modular approach may be the difficulty in ensuring that inter-relationships are properly represented and that the modules are consistent with each other.

43.3 *Documentation is desirable*
Some modellers recognised that not enough attention had been paid to documentation. Modellers may get so deeply embroiled in their modelling work that documentation is put on one side. Often a decision is made by modellers to document the model completely only after it has been fully implemented. In a number of companies visited, key modellers were lost to the project, during development or on completion of model construction, before adequate documentation was produced. The problems of a newcomer picking up the task, and understanding the working and the full potential of the model from flow charts and someone else's computer programs, were such that in some of these the model was shelved and a new start made. Such difficulties would be avoided if documentation were updated on a continuing basis throughout model development.

43.4 *Speed of conversational mode of operation*
Many of the modellers favoured the use of conversational time-sharing computers. Whilst use of a terminal on-line to a time-sharing computer is relatively expensive, this is largely offset by the saving of executives' time. Programming, debugging and testing of models become much easier and quicker than with 'conventional' batch operation. There are various reasons for this. Keying errors normally show up immediately on the terminal and can be corrected immediately. Where it is obvious that the program is going awry it can be stopped to allow amendment. Another important point is that the modeller's thought process may be continuous; he does not have to wait hours for his output. A model in the batch mode has been found to take two to three times longer in terms of man-hours to program. In actual elapsed time the average batch model may be expected to take 10 times longer than the conversational model.

43.5 *Need to involve 'grass roots'*
A further comment was that 'grass roots' people should be involved earlier. By involving them at an earlier stage in the modelling process their acceptance should be easier to obtain as they would have more time to learn the new techniques involved; also they may feel a deeper involvement. If their ideas or suggestions could be included in the model they would probably feel better disposed towards its use. It has been found difficult to get 'grass roots' acceptance if involvement is not offered them until the implementation of the model is imminent.

Section E

Results of telephone survey

As indicated in the Section on Survey Methodology, it was recognised that the sample of companies covered by the main survey might be biased, and a survey was undertaken to check on this possibility. The broad details of this survey are:

(i) The sample of 100 companies was drawn at random from 'The Times 1,000'. Whilst this sample frame embraced only industrial companies it was thought adequate for our purposes.

(ii) The computer manager was approached by telephone in 96 of the random sample of 100. We were unable to contact two of the companies by telephone, however one of these answered by mail and the other company accorded us an interview. The remaining two firms had already completed a questionnaire during the main survey. Whilst there was a slight risk that the computer manager would not know about computer modelling, if a bureau was being used, this was regarded as small enough to ignore.

(iii) The computer manager was asked if the company had or was developing a corporate model. Where necessary, our definition of a corporate model was explained to him. Where the answer was affirmative, details on aspects of the model for which we thought our main survey might be biased were obtained from him, or another contact within the company given to us by him.

(iv) We were most impressed by the cordial and helpful reception given our enquiries. All 98 companies approached (it was not necessary to contact two since we already had full data on their models) answered our questions.

The same strict definition of corporate models as detailed on page 194 was adhered to in this random telephone survey. The result was that only 9 per cent of the sample can be categorised as having corporate models. Another 12 of the contacts said that modelling (other than corporate) was taking place somewhere within their organisations. Thus, our sample of 'The Times 1,000' revealed that at least 21 per cent of the companies were modelling in some respect.

One company contacted was *Brickwoods* which had been taken over by *Whitbread* and has been incorporated into the models of the parent company. Another one, which prefers to remain anonymous, stated: 'We used a modelling system in 1972 on a bureau basis. Only one accountant showed any interest in this area and he was called off to do "more important work". We are not prepared to build models for the accountants, but hope that it will not be too long before they show an interest in corporate modelling.'

The results of the survey are given in *Figure 53*. Use of the 'Chi-squared test' did not lead us to reject, at the 95 per cent level of confidence, our hypothesis that there was an association between the two survey samples.

235

Figure 53 Results of random telephone survey

Company No.	When companies began modelling	Language or system used	Class of models	Mode of operation	How models are run	Percentage of runs including probabilities
1	1972	PROSPER	Simulation	Conversational	Bureau	0
2	1969	FORTRAN TELCOMP ORACLE AS	Simulation	Conversational Remote batch	Bureau	10
3	1972	COBOL	Simulation	Remote batch	Bureau	0
4	1972	PROSPER	Simulation	Conversational	Bureau	0
5	1972	PROSPER	Simulation	Batch	In-house	5
6	1968	FORTRAN LP code	Simulation Optimisation	Conversational Batch	In-house	50
7	1972	FORTRAN	Optimisation	Conversational	Bureau	0
8	1970	COBOL PRINCE	Simulation Optimisation	Conversational	In-house Bureau	100
9	1969	FORTRAN PL/1	Simulation Optimisation	Conversational Batch	In-house Bureau	0

Figure 54 Comparison of main survey and telephone survey

	Main survey	Telephone survey	Total
General-purpose language	42	6	48
Modelling system	33	5	38
Total	75	11	86
Simulation – Deterministic	63	7	70
Probabilistic	16	4	20
Optimisation	14	4	18
Total	93	15	108
Batch	34	3	37
Remote batch	18	2	20
Conversational	39	7	46
Total	91	12	103
Bureau computer	45	7	52
In-house computer	40	4	44
Total	85	11	96

Section F

Copy of questionnaire

The City University Business School
Lionel Denny House
London EC1M 7BB

Confidential Questionnaire on Corporate Financial Models

Company code_____

Please tick where applicable.

Where there is insufficient space on questionnaire to give complete details please use blank sheets of paper and cross-reference to questionnaire.

The use of the word 'models' should be interpreted in the singular where the company has only one model.

SECTION A

1   *In which year did your company begin to develop or use computer models for corporate planning?*   _____

2   *In which of the following categories are your models?*

   (a) Built by your own staff in a general-purpose language, e.g. Fortran, Algol, without external assistance   _____

   (b) Built by your own staff in a general-purpose language, e.g. Fortran, Algol, with external assistance   _____

   (c) Obtained ready-made from a computer bureau   _____

   (d) Built by your own staff in a high-level special purpose modelling language from a computer bureau, e.g. Oliver, Prosper, Stratplan, without external assistance   _____

   (e) Built by your own staff in a high-level special purpose modelling language from a computer bureau, e.g. Oliver, Prosper, Stratplan, with external assistance   _____

   (f) Built specially for you by consultants   _____

3 *How do you run your models?*

(a) On your own computer _____ (b) On a bureau computer _____
(c) Other (please specify) _____
(d) Please give average turnaround time per run (batch models only)
_____

4 *What is the mode of operation?*

(a) Conversational _____   (c) Batch processing _____
(b) Remote batch processing _____   (d) Conversational remote
                                           batch _____
(e) Other (please specify) _____

5 *What are your models designed to do?*

Please state the major uses of each model, e.g. Financial planning (1—5 years),
Aid production or marketing decisions, Cash flow analysis

Model 1 _____
      2 _____
      3 _____
      4 _____
      5 _____
      6 _____
      7 _____
      8 _____

SECTION B

If you are using ready-made bureau models only, please proceed to Section C.

6 *Do you have a suite of models?* _____

If yes, please indicate which features are included
(a) Models may be interrogated singly
(b) Models must be interrogated sequentially _____
(c) Models may be integrated within computer run _____
(d) Models may be linked outside computer run i.e. direct input
     to one model from another (please specify) _____
_____

7   *Which of the following are represented in your models?*

Please tick appropriate item(s)
(a) Physical operations (i.e. non-financial)   ———
(b) Financial operations
        (i) At corporate level   ———
        (ii) At subsidiary level (if any)   ———
        (iii) At divisional level   ———
        (iv) At operating unit level   ———

8   *How large are your models?*

Please give approximate numbers of the following (if possible for each model)

	1	2	3	4	5	6	7	8
(a) Input variables								
(b) Output variables								
(c) Program statements								

9   *How would you class your models?*

(a) Optimising   ———   (c) Both   ———
(b) Simulation   ———
If (a) or (c) please tick the optimising techniques used
(a) Linear programming   ———   (d) Dynamic programming   ———
(b) Quadratic programming   ———   (e) Optimal search
                                                    procedures   ———
(c) Integer programming   ———   (f) Other (please specify)   ———

10   *Do your models have facilities for the following?*

(a) 'What if' questions   ———   (e) Queues   ———
(b) Backward iteration   ———   (f) Compound interest   ———
(c) Financial ratio analysis   ———   (g) Graph plotting   ———
(d) Discounted cash flows   ———   (h) Histogram plotting   ———
(i)   Sensitivity analysis (without input changes being necessary)   ———
(j)   Significance testing (please specify) ———

(k) Other (please specify) ———

11   *Do your models handle probability analysis?*   ———

If yes, please tick the distributions they can use
(a) Normal   ———   (e) Binomial   ———
(b) Uniform   ———   (f) Poisson   ———
(c) Exponential   ———   (g) Weibull   ———
(d) Log normal   ———   (h) Other (please specify)   ———

Please state approximate percentage of runs which are probabilistic   ———

12 *Do your models use forecasting techniques?* _____

If yes, please tick the techniques used
(a) Linear regression _____   (f) Geometric progression _____
(b) Multiple regression _____   (g) Arithmetic progression _____
(c) Exponential smoothing _____   (h) Step functions _____
(d) Curve fitting _____   (i) Power series _____
(e) Linear trend analysis _____   (j) Moving averages _____
(k) Other (please specify) _____
_____

13 *Flexibility of logic?*

Do your models allow for major changes in your business (e.g. acquiring
a new division) without additional programming being required? _____
(a) If yes, please specify how this has been achieved _____
_____

(b) If no, please specify approximately how many man-hours you think
would be required to make the necessary changes _____

14 *Flexibility of input?*

Has the user a choice as to the method by which data is input, e.g. may half-a-
million be input as .5 or 500,000? _____
(a) If yes, is this exercised by use of control parameters, or can user input at will, say,
absolute figures, annual absolute changes, or rates of change? (Please specify)
_____
_____

(b) Must the user input all data used in each run or can he merely change particular
items? (Applies only to conversational models) _____
_____

(i) If so, will the change be only temporary, so that the data base remains
unchanged, or does the change automatically become permanent? (Please
specify) _____
_____

15 *Flexibility of output?*

(a) Is there a choice of output report (e.g. Balance sheet, Profit and loss)?_____
If yes, how is this achieved?
(i) Control parameters input at outset of run _____
(ii) On call in interactive mode _____
(iii) Other (please specify) _____
_____
_____

(b) Has the user choice of output report format? _____

   If yes, how is this achieved? _____

   _____

   _____

(c) Is there a fixed sequence for reports chosen? _____

16 *Output reports by model?*

Report	Total company	Subsidiaries	Divisions	Operating units
	Organisational levels to which reports may refer			
Profit and loss	___	___	___	___
Balance sheet	___	___	___	___
Cash flow	___	___	___	___
Source and use of funds	___	___	___	___
Capital budgeting	___	___	___	___
Financial ratio analysis	___	___	___	___
Reports on production and distribution (please specify)				
___	___	___	___	___
___	___	___	___	___
Reports on marketing operations (please specify)				
___	___	___	___	___
___	___	___	___	___
Other (please specify)				
___	___	___	___	___
___	___	___	___	___
___	___	___	___	___

17 *How are time periods handled?*

(a) Maximum number of time periods which can be handled _____

(b) If models have specific time periods please specify, e.g. month, year

   _____

18 *In which languages are your models programmed?*

   _____

19 *How many calendar months (i.e. elapsed time) did it take to build your models?*

(a) First working model _____

(b) Present model (add'l) _____

   model number 1   2   3   4   5   6   7   8

241

20 *What have been the approximate costs involved in model building?*

Please provide the following data
(a)

		Man-weeks for first working model (excluding	Addit'l man-weeks for present model consultants)	Average cost to company of each man-week
(i) Feasibility study and determination of model inputs, outputs, and logical structure	Model 1			
	2			
	3			
	4			
	5			
	6			
	7			
	8			
(ii) Programming	Model 1			
	2			
	3			
	4			
	5			
	6			
	7			
	8			
(iii) Implementation (developing systems and data base to permit use as a planning tool; management education)	Model 1			
	2			
	3			
	4			
	5			
	6			
	7			
	8			

(b) What approximate total computer costs were incurred in developing models?

                      1   2   3   4   5   6   7   8

    (i) First working model _____

    (ii) Present model (addit'l)_____

(c) Consultancy costs and basis of charging? _____

_____

_____

_____

21. *What grades of staff are involved in model building?*

Will you please indicate the number and functional backgrounds of the model builders, e.g. accountant, operational researcher, programmer _____

_____

_____

_____

22. *Which aspects have deterred you from using a ready-made model or modelling language of a computer bureau?*

Please distribute 100 points to indicate the relative importance of factors that have deterred you from using (1) and (2) below. If you are using a modelling language of a computer bureau please answer (1) only

	(1) Ready-made model	(2) Modelling language
(a) Size restriction	_____	_____
(b) Inflexibility of		
(i) Logic	_____	_____
(ii) Inputs	_____	_____
(iii) Outputs	_____	_____
(c) Costs	_____	_____
(d) Insecurity of data	_____	_____
(e) Difficulties of data transfer	_____	_____
(f) Discontinuity of service	_____	_____
(g) Other (please specify) _____		
_____	_____	_____
_____	_____	_____
	100	100

23. *Did you come up against technical difficulties in building your models?* _____

If yes, please indicate the difficulties and explain how you overcame them _____

_____
_____
_____
_____
_____
_____
_____
_____
_____
_____

SECTION C

If you are not using a bureau package (i.e. modelling system or ready-made model) please proceed to Section D.

24. *Which ready-made model or modelling language are you using?* _____

_____

25. *What are bureau charges?*

    (a) Initial fee to access package _____

    (b) Annual support fee _____

    (c) Outright purchase price _____

    (d) If interactive

        (i) Connect time charge per hour _____

        (ii) CPU time charge per minute _____

        (iii) File storage charge _____

        (iv) Transmission charge _____

    (e) Other (please specify) _____

        _____

26. *What are the average annual fees paid to bureau in connection with your package?*

    _____

27. *Do you send staff on training courses provided by bureau?* _____

    If yes, please give details _____

    _____

28. *Does bureau provide after-sales support?* _____

    If yes, please give details _____

    _____

29. *Does bureau provide a consulting service?* _____

    If yes, please give details _____

    _____

30. *Would you care to comment on the service given by bureau?* _____

    _____

    _____

    _____

31. *What factors led you to adopt the package used by you?* _____

    _____

    _____

    _____

SECTION D

32. *Who initiated the proposal to develop or use your corporate financial models?*

    _____

    _____

33. *How are your models used?*

    (a) As *ad hoc* devices, e.g. for merger proposals   _____
    (b) In regular corporate and divisional planning   _____

34. *Who in the company uses the models?*

    _____

    _____

35. *How much reliance do you perceive top management place on the following?*

    Please distribute 100 points
    (a) Computer reports   _____
    (b) Manual reports   _____
    (c) Their own intuitive judgement   _____

           100
           _____

36. *How are your models integrated into the total planning system?* _____

    _____

    _____

37. *How much would you say that use of your models has improved forecasts?*

    (a) Very significantly   _____   (c) Not very much   _____
    (b) Significantly   _____   (d) Not at all   _____

38. *Do you think that top management feel that model building has been a success in terms of cost/benefits?* _____

    _____

    _____

39. *From which senior executive(s) in the company has support come for your corporate financial models?* _____

    _____

    _____

40. *Who is ultimately responsible for your corporate financial models?*

_____
_____
_____
_____

41. *How would you say that management have reacted to the introduction and use of corporate financial models?*

_____
_____
_____
_____
_____
_____
_____

42. *What general problems did you encounter in your model building?*

Please detail the problems and explain how you overcame them_____

_____
_____
_____
_____
_____
_____

43. *If you were to start from scratch again what would you do differently?*

_____
_____
_____
_____
_____
_____

Appendix 2

Financial modelling packages in the UK

Results of a survey conducted by
Professor Peter H. Grinyer
and
Jeff Wooller

Contents and notes

With so many packages around it is becoming increasingly difficult to sort out the wheat from the chaff. The checklists included in Chapter 7 may help in this respect. An analysis of packages available should also be of assistance.

We give here details of 38 of the financial modelling packages currently available in the UK. This information was provided by the bureaux themselves who also told us whether their modelling system could handle the bench-mark test used by Spicer and Pegler & Co to test modelling systems. Figures 1–3 show the print-outs produced by the test.

Care has been taken to ensure that the details are correct at the date of going to press. However, we recommend that potential users of any package should contact the bureau to confirm that the details are still correct, as this is a highly volatile and quick-moving market.

Figure 1 Calculation and cash flow from the bench-mark test

Calculation and Cash Flow

Pound 000s	1978	1979	1980	1981	1982	1983
Ave collection period	60	60	60	60	60	60
Ave payment period	60	60	60	60	60	60
Unit purchases	260	240	370	360	400	590
Cost price	100	100	100	100	100	100
Purchase value	26000	24000	37000	36000	40000	59000
Unit sales	200	250	350	350	450	600
Selling price	150	150	150	150	150	150
Cash receipts:						
Cash receipts	25068	36267	50034	52500	65034	86301
Equity issue	10000	0	0	0	0	0
Deb issue	12000	0	0	0	0	0
Total cash rec	47068	36267	50034	52500	65034	86301
Cash payments:						
Cash paid	21726	24329	34863	36164	39342	55877
Fixed assets cost	8000	14000	0	0	0	0
Period costs	1500	1620	1750	1890	2041	2204
Deb repayment due	0	0	0	0	0	2400
Div payment due	0	1900	1967	3310	3354	4886
Tax payment due	0	3799	3934	6620	6708	9771
Deb interest	1200	1200	1200	1200	960	720
Total cash payments	32426	46847	43713	49184	52405	75858
Cash bal before int	14642	5160	11869	16075	29909	42596
Interest received	1098	387	890	1206	2243	3195
Interest paid	0	0	0	0	0	0
Cash at bank	15741	5547	12759	17280	32152	45791
Bank overdraft	0	0	0	0	0	0

Figure 2 Revenue account from the bench-mark test

Pound 000s	1978	1979	1980	1981	1982	1983
Sales value	30000	37500	52500	52500	67500	90000
Cost of sales	20000	25000	35000	35000	45000	60000
Gross contrib	10000	12500	17500	17500	22500	30000
Period costs	1500	1620	1750	1890	2041	2204
Net op profit	8500	10880	15750	15610	20459	27796
Finance:						
Deb interest	1200	1200	1200	1200	960	720
Interest paid	0	0	0	0	0	0
Interest received	1098	387	890	1206	2243	3195
	102	813	310	−6	−1283	−2475
Profit before depr	8398	10067	15441	15616	21742	30271
Depreciation	800	2200	2200	2200	2200	2200
Profit before tax	7598	7867	13241	13416	19542	28071
Tax charge (Std)	3799	3934	6620	6708	9771	14035
Profit after tax	3799	3934	6620	6708	9771	14035
Dividend	1900	1967	3310	3354	4886	7018
Retained profit	1900	1967	3310	3354	4886	7018
Cum retention	1900	3866	7176	10530	15416	22434

Figure 3 Balance sheet from the bench-mark test

Pound 000s	1978	1979	1980	1981	1982	1983
Capital employed:						
Share capital	10000	10000	10000	10000	10000	10000
Cum retention	1900	3866	7176	10530	15416	22434
Shareholders' fund	11900	13866	17176	20530	25416	32434
Debentures	12000	12000	12000	12000	9600	7200
Total cap employed	23900	25866	29176	32530	35016	39634
Employment of capital:						
Fixed assets						
Fixed assets	8000	22000	22000	22000	22000	22000
Less depreciation	800	3000	5200	7400	9600	11800
	7200	19000	16800	14600	12400	10200
Current assets						
Stock at cost	6000	5000	7000	8000	3000	2000
Trade debtors	4932	6164	8630	8630	11096	14795
Cash at bank	15741	5547	12759	17280	32152	45791
	26672	16712	28389	33910	46248	62585
Current liabilities						
Deb repayment	0	0	0	0	2400	2400
Dividend	1900	1967	3310	3354	4886	7018
Tax charge (Std)	3799	3934	6620	6708	9771	14035
Trade creditors	4274	3945	6082	5918	6575	9699
Bank overdraft	0	0	0	0	0	0
	9973	9845	16013	15980	23632	33152
Net current assets	16700	6866	12376	17930	22616	29434
Net assets	23900	25866	29176	32530	35016	39634

Name of package	AS	BBL
Type of package	Modelling system General purpose	Modelling system General purpose
Owner of package	IBM	Core & Code, Wellesley, Mass.
Address to which interested potential user should write	IBM UK Ltd, 40 Basinghall Street, London EC2P 2DY	Tymshare (UK), Kew Bridge House, Kew Bridge, Brentford, Middlesex TW8 0EJ
Bureau on which package may be run	IBM CALL Timesharing Service	Tymshare (UK)
Hardware requirements where package available on user's computer	Not applicable	Not applicable
Mode of operation		
Batch	No	Yes
Remote batch	No	Yes
Conversational	Yes	Yes
Conversational remote batch	Yes	Yes
Purpose of model		
Financial planning (up to 1 year)	Yes	Yes
Financial planning (1 to 5 years)	Yes	Yes
Financial planning (over 5 years)	Yes	Yes
Project evaluation	Yes	Yes
Aid production decisions	Yes	Yes
Aid marketing decisions	Yes	Yes
Cash flow analysis	Yes	Yes
Time periods handled		
Maximum number	120	40,000
Specific periods	Optional	Optional
Maximum size of model		
Input variables	Maximum size of data	Maximum size of data
Output variables	matrix 120,000	matrix 40,000
Statements	1,000	No practical limit
Maximum number of characters per line of output	250	256
Model interlinking (via intermediate files)	Yes	Yes
Model integration (ability to transfer between models during computer run)	No	Yes
Facilities available		
Backward iteration	Yes	Yes
Graphical output	Yes	Yes
Histogram output	Yes	Yes
Discounted cash flows	Yes	Yes
Sensitivity analysis (automatic)	No	Yes
Significance testing	No	Yes
Consolidation	Yes	Yes
Forecasting techniques available		
Linear regression	Yes	*
Multiple regression	Yes	*
Curve fitting (least squares)	Yes	*
Arithmetic progression	Yes	Yes
Geometric progression	Yes	Yes
Moving averages	Yes	Yes
Exponential smoothing	Yes	Yes
Step functions	Yes	Yes *Available with compatible package
Risk analysis	Monte Carlo facilities available with compatible package	Monte Carlo facilities

BUDGET 6	CAPRI	COLYPLAN	DATAFORM III
Ready-made model Budgeting	Modelling system Corporate optimisation	Modelling system General purpose	Modelling system General purpose
Altergo Financial Management System Ltd	Metra Consulting Group Ltd	Coopers & Lybrand Associates Ltd	Comshare Ltd
Altergo Financial Management Systems Ltd, 38 Soho Square, London W1V 5DF	Metra Consulting Group Ltd, 23 Lower Belgrave Street, London SW1W 0NS	Coopers & Lybrand Associates Ltd, Abacus House, Gutter Lane, London EC2V 82H	Comshare Ltd, 32–34 Great Peter Street, London SW1P 2DB
(i) Atkins Computing (ii) Unilever Computer Services Ltd	Negotiable	(i) Honeywell Mark III Timesharing Service (ii) ADP Network Services	Comshare Timesharing Service
IBM 360/370, Series 1, PDP 11/35, ICL 1904 and 2903. Core requires 48k words	CDC 6600 with 65k words, IBM 370 (large), UNIVAC 1108 (Software must include mixed integer LP)	Not applicable	Not applicable
Yes	Yes	No	No
Yes	Yes	Yes	Yes
Yes	No	Yes	Yes
Yes	No	Yes	Yes
Yes	No	Yes	Yes
No	No	Yes	Yes
No	Yes	Yes	Yes
Yes	Yes	Yes	Yes
Yes	No	Yes	Yes
Yes	Yes	Yes	Yes
Yes	Yes	Yes	Yes
One year divided into 4, 12 and 13 periods	No practical limit Optional	No practical limit Optional – special facilities for periods of different lengths	No practical limit Optional
No practical limit	No practical limit	Maximum size of data matrix 6,000 No practical limit	Maximum size of data matrix 35,000 No practical limit
132	132	132	255
Yes	No	Yes	Yes
Yes	No	Yes	No
No	Yes	Yes	No
No	No	*	Yes
No	No	*	No
No	Yes	Yes	Yes
No	No	Yes	No
No	No	No	No
Yes	No	Yes	Yes
		*Available with compatible package	
No	No	Yes	No
No	No	*	No
No	No	*	No
Yes	No	Yes	Yes
Yes	No	Yes	Yes
Yes	No	*	No
No	No	Yes	No
Yes	No	Yes	No
		*Available with compatible package	
No	No	Monte Carlo facilities	No

Name of package	AS	BBL
Optimising techniques included	Linear programming and optimal search procedures	Yes
Column and row operation	Yes	Yes
Able to handle bench-mark (see page 249–251) easily	Yes	Yes
Flexibility of logic	Changes made easily in high-level language	Changes made easily in high-level language
Flexibility of input Ability of user to apply constants or parameter controlled growth rates to input data, without having to code in the model	Yes	Yes

Flexibility of output
  Choice of output report
  Choice of output report format
  Sequence of reports
	Yes
	Yes
	optional
		Yes
		Yes
		Optional

Provision of training course
  Length of course
 	
  Cost
	3 days
	
	£157 – free machine time
		3 days maximum
		
		£60 for first time user

Provision of consulting service e.g. building models for clients	Yes, but normally client would be expected to specify own models	Negotiable
After sales support	Free advice is constantly available at the IBM CALL Centre and country-wide branches	Usually free
Other points of interest	Modelling language is based on normal business language so that user can be closely associated in its construction. Additional forecasting facilities: Box Jenkins, adaptive filtering and other smoothing techniques	Many operational research functions

Cost aspects
  Outright purchase price
  Initial fee to access
  Annual support fee
  Royalties payable
	Not applicable
	None
	None
	None
		Not applicable
		None
		None
		Not disclosed

Basis of charging clients	Connect time CPU	Connect time CPU
Year first developed	1974	1970
Year first available in UK	1975	1974

Estimated number of users
  Worldwide
  UK only
	Over 100
	Over 100
		Over 50
		Below 10

BUDGET 6	CAPRI	COLYPLAN	DATAFORM III
No	Linear and integer programming	Linear programming available with compatible package	No
Yes	Row operation only	Yes	Yes
No	No	Yes	Yes
By special request to Altergo Systems	Changes made in general-purpose language	Changes made easily in high-level language or FORTRAN	Changes made easily in high-level language
Yes	No	Yes	No
Yes	Yes	Yes	Yes
Yes	No	Yes	Yes
Optional	Fixed	Optional	Optional
1 to 3 days	Courses designed specifically for client	Introductory 1 to 3 days, advanced 1 to 3 weeks	2 days (public course)
Included in price	£200/course day	Negotiable	Free
Negotiable	Normally done on fixed price basis. Daily rates charge would be £120–£200	Negotiable	Support as part of COMSHARE service. Larger consultancy jobs by negotiation
Support inclusive in price	At normal consultancy rates	Technical queries normally answered free. Fuller assistance at consultancy rates	Technical support as part of COMSHARE service
Specific tool for budgeting for profit and cash flow by accountants in industry and commerce. No knowledge of computers necessary	Desirable for clients to have expertise and experience in linear programming. Typical clients would be oil or mining companies	Models written in numeric codes designed to speed model development and modification. Extensive facilities for complex financial calculations	Sophisticated report generator containing some modelling capabilities. Well interfaced with other COMSHARE systems (e.g. data management, statistics). Available internationally
£10,000			Not applicable
£500 on bureau			None
£500 on bureau	Negotiable	Negotiable	None
Not disclosed			None
Connect time	Depends on computer	Connect time	Connect time
CPU	used	CPU	CPU
1975	1968	1970	1968
1975	1970	1972	1971
8	15	21	Over 100
8	0	14	75

Name of package	DATASOLVE	EIS
Type of package	Modelling system General purpose	Modelling system General purpose
Owner of package	Enhanced IBM package	Boeing Computer Centres Ltd
Address to which interested potential user should write	APL BDU, BOC Datasolve, 99 Staines Road West, Sunbury, Middlesex	Boeing Computer Centres Ltd, St Martin's House, 31–35 Clarendon Road Watford, Herts WD1 1JA
Bureau on which package may be run	BOC Datasolve	Boeing Computer Centres Ltd
Hardware requirements where package available on user's computer	IBM 370 with APL SV	IBM 360/370
Mode of operation		
Batch	No	Yes
Remote batch	No	Yes
Conversational	Yes	Yes
Conversational remote batch	Yes	Yes
Purpose of model		
Financial planning (up to 1 year)	Yes	Yes
Financial planning (1 to 5 years)	Yes	Yes
Financial planning (over 5 years)	Yes	Yes
Project evaluation	Yes	Yes
Aid production decisions	Yes	Yes
Aid marketing decisions	Yes	Yes
Cash flow analysis	Yes	Yes
Time periods handled		
Maximum number	60	No practical limit
Specific periods	Optional	Optional
Maximum size of model		
Input variables	Maximum size of	
Output variables	data matrix 600,000	No practical limit
Statements	No practical limit	
Maximum number of characters per line of output	132	Limited only by printing device
Model interlinking (via intermediate files)	Yes	Yes
Model integration (ability to transfer between models during computer run)	Yes	Yes
Facilities available		
Backward iteration	No	Yes
Graphical output	Yes	Yes
Histogram output	Yes	Yes
Discounted cash flows	Yes	Yes
Sensitivity analysis (automatic)	No	Yes
Significance testing	No	Yes
Consolidation	Yes	Yes
Forecasting techniques available		
Linear regression	Yes	Yes
Multiple regression	Yes	Yes
Curve fitting (least squares)	Yes	Yes
Arithmetic progression	Yes	Yes
Geometric progression	Yes	Yes
Moving averages	No	Yes
Exponential smoothing	Yes	Yes
Step functions	No	Yes
Risk analysis	No	No

EMS	EVALU8	EXPRESS	FCS
Modelling system	Modelling system	Modelling system	Modeling system
General purpose	General purpose	General purpose	General purpose
Economic Sciences Corp	OLS Computer Services (UK) Ltd	MDS Inc, Boston, Mass.	EPS Consultants
CSS International (UK) Ltd, 142 Vauxhall Bridge Road, London SW1V 1AU	OLS Computer Services (UK) Ltd, 6/24 Southgate Road, London N1 3JJ	Tymshare (UK), Kew Bridge House, Kew Bridge, Brentford, Middlesex TW8 0EJ	EPS Consultants, 8 South Ridge, Odiham, Hants RG25 1NG Tel. 025671 2343
CSS International (UK) Ltd	OLS	Tymshare (UK)	COMSHARE Timesharing Service
Not applicable	Not applicable	Not applicable	IBM 370, ICL 2900, Univac, Burroughs, DEC, Xerox, H-P, Honeywell, etc and some mini-computers
Yes	No	Yes	Yes
No	No	Yes	Yes
Yes	Yes	Yes	Yes
No	No	Yes	Yes
Yes	Yes	Yes	Yes
Yes	Yes	Yes	Yes
Yes	Yes	Yes	Yes
Yes	Yes	Yes	Yes
Yes	Yes	Yes	Yes
Yes	Yes	Yes	Yes
No practical limit	2,500	No practical limit	255
Optional	Optional except that must be for at least one month	Optional	Optional
No practical limit	Maximum size of data matrix 2,500 150 rules	Maximum size of data matrix 2,000,000 No practical limit	Maximum size of data matrix 20,000 3,000
32	72	256	255
Yes	No	Yes	Yes
Yes	No	Yes	Yes
No	No	Yes	Yes
Yes	No	Yes	Yes
No	No	Yes	Yes
Yes	Yes	Yes	Yes
Yes	Yes	Yes	Yes
Yes	No	Yes	Yes
Yes	No	Yes	Yes
Yes	No	Yes	Yes
Yes	No	Yes	Yes
Yes	No	Yes	Yes
No	No	Yes	Yes
No	No	Yes	Yes
Yes	No	Yes	Yes
Yes	No	Yes	Yes
No	No	Yes	Yes
No	No	Monte Carlo facilities	Monte Carlo facilities

Name of package	DATASOLVE	EIS
Optimising techniques included	No	No
Column and row operation	Row operation only	Yes
Able to handle bench-mark (see pages 249–251) easily	Yes	Yes
Flexibility of logic	Changes made easily in high-level language	Changes made easily in high-level language
Flexibility of input Ability of user to apply constants or parameter controlled growth rates to input data, without having to code in the model	No	Yes
Flexibility of output Choice of output report Choice of output report format Sequence of reports	Yes Yes Optional	Yes Yes Optional
Provision of training course Length of course Cost	1 day Free	3 days Free
Provision of consulting service e.g. building models for clients	Fixed price contract or per diem charge	Negotiable
After sales support	Free advice, system updates, manuals charged for	Readily available – free
Other points of interest	Has over 50 operators. System written in APL which means modifications are very easy and quick to program. Package marketed as FPS	Has its own data base system specially designed for handling time spread data, enabling models to have direct and efficient access to data bases in excess of 200m bytes. Special emphasis on time series data and graphics
Cost aspects Outright purchase price Initial fee to access Annual support fee	Not applicable None None	Negotiable None None
Royalties payable	None	None
Basis of charging clients	Connect time CPU	Connect time CPU
Year first developed	1974	1971
Year first available in UK	1974	1978
Estimated number of users Worldwide UK only	Not known Not known	Over 100 No details

MS	EVALU8	EXPRESS	FCS
Ability to solve simultaneous equations	No	Yes	No
Yes	Yes	Yes	Yes
Yes	No	Yes	Yes
Changes made easily in high-level language	Changes made easily in high-level language	Changes made easily in high-level language	Changes made easily in high-level language
Yes	Yes	Yes	Yes
Yes	Yes	Yes	Yes
Yes	Yes	Yes	Yes
Optional	Optional	Optional	Optional
1 to 3 days as required. Computer resources only are charged	Individual tuition. Free	4 days maximum. £90 for first time user	2 days (public course). £50 per head
Limited free consultancy	Negotiable	Negotiable	Fixed price contract or per diem charge
Free advice and back-up	Technical support service normally free	Usually free	Free advice, system updates etc
Gives access to econometric databases	Intended to be a simple yet powerful aid for the non-computer specialist	Ease of use for management. Complete information processing environment	Language has over 70 operators and functions with practically no constraints. System has 70 commands. Available in USA, Canada, Europe etc.
Not applicable	Not applicable	Not applicable	Negotiable
None	None	None	None
None	None	None	None bureau, negotiable in-house
None	None	Not disclosed	Not disclosed
Connect time. CPU	Connect time only	Connect time. CPU	Connect time. CPU
Not known	1972	1973	1972
1977	1972	1975	1973
Not known. 1	20. 15	Over 100. Over 100	Over 100. Over 100

Name of package	FORESIGHT	FORPLAN
Type of package	Modelling system General purpose	Modelling system General purpose
Owner of package	Foresight Systems Inc, Los Angeles	Unilever Ltd
Address to which interested potential user should write	Foresight Systems Inc, Linkside West, Hindhead, Surrey (for in-house package). Cybernet and LUCS (for bureau use)	U I Management Consultants Ltd, St. Bridget's House, Bridewell Place, London EC4B 4BP
Bureau on which package may be run	Cybernet Time Sharing, London United Computing Systems	Unilever Computer Services Ltd
Hardware requirements where package available on user's computer	IBM computers with 106k bytes OS, 54k bytes DOS. ICL 1900 with 23k words. Available on other systems	IBM 360/370 OS
Mode of operation		
Batch	Yes	Yes
Remote batch	Yes	Yes
Conversational	Yes	Yes
Conversational remote batch	Yes	Yes
Purpose of model		
Financial planning (up to 1 year)	Yes	Yes
Financial planning (1 to 5 years)	Yes	Yes
Financial planning (over 5 years)	Yes	Yes
Project evaluation	Yes	Yes
Aid production decisions	Yes	Yes
Aid marketing decisions	Yes	Yes
Cash flow analysis	Yes	Yes
Time periods handled		
Maximum number	Normally 30 but can be extended	104
Specific periods	Optional	Optional
Maximum size of model		
Input variables	'Standard' matrix size	
Output variables	is 200 × 30 periods, but extended version to 600 × 30 periods	No practical limit
Statements	600	
Maximum number of characters per line of output	132	132
Model interlinking (via intermediate files)	Yes	Yes
Model integration (ability to transfer between models during computer run)	Yes	Yes
Facilities available		
Backward iteration	No	Yes
Graphical output	Yes	No
Histogram output	Yes	No
Discounted cash flows	Yes	Yes
Sensitivity analysis (automatic)	No	Yes
Significance testing	Partial	No
Consolidation	Yes	Yes
Forecasting techniques available		
Linear regression	Yes	No
Multiple regression	No	No
Curve fitting (least squares)	Yes	No
Arithmetic progression	Yes	No
Geometric progression	Yes	No
Moving averages	Yes	No
Exponential smoothing	Yes	No
Step functions	No	No
Risk analysis	No	No

FPS	GPOS 2	ICMS	INFOTAB
Modelling system General purpose	Modelling system General purpose	Modelling system General purpose	Modelling system General purpose
RTZ Computer Services Ltd	On-Line Decisions International	Inbucon/AIC Management Consultants Ltd	Capex Corporation, 2613 North Third Street, Phoenix, Arizona
RTZ Computer Services Ltd, PO Box 19, 1 Redcliff Street, Bristol BS99 7JS	On-Line Decisions Inc, Suite 18, Claridge House, 32 Davies Street, London W1Y 1LG	SIA Ltd, Ebury Gate, 23 Lower Belgrave Street, London SW1W 0NW	CSS International (UK) Ltd, 242 Vauxhall Bridge Road, London SW1V 1AU
RTZ Time Sharing	Atkins Computing	SIA Ltd	CSS International (UK) Ltd
Any computer with at least 56k bytes and FORTRAN compiler	XDS Sigma 5/6/7/9 operating under all current operating systems, IBM 360/370 etc	HP 2000 series, CDC 6000, Cyber 70 series with 20k words/time-sharing partition	Not known. Refer to Capex Corp.
Yes	Yes	No	Yes
Yes	Yes	No	No
Yes	Yes	Yes	Yes
Yes	Yes	No	No
Yes	Yes	Yes	Yes
Yes	Yes	Yes	Yes
Yes	Yes	Yes	Yes
Yes	Yes	Yes	Yes
Yes	Yes	Yes	Yes
Yes	Yes	Yes	Yes
Yes	Yes	Yes	Yes
No practical limit	No practical limit	999	1,500
Optional – may be mixed	Optional	Optional	Optional
Matrix size limited only by hardware available	Basic 5,000 words of data; more can be paged in the model if needed. Output matrix 1,080 × 6.	Maximum size of data matrix 99,000	Maximum size of data matrix 62,500
No practical limit	No practical limit	No practical limit	No practical limit
132	132	Normally 72 but can be extended	132
Yes	Yes	Yes	Yes
Yes	Yes	Yes	Yes
No	Yes	Yes	No
Yes	Yes	Yes	No
Yes	Yes	Yes	No
Yes	Yes	Yes	Yes
No	Yes	Yes	No
No	Yes	Yes	No
Yes	Yes	Yes	Yes
Yes	Yes	Yes	No
No	Yes	Yes	No
No	Yes	Yes	No
Yes	Yes	Yes	No
Yes	Yes	Yes	No
Yes	Yes	Yes	No
Yes	Yes	Yes	No
No	Yes	Yes	No
Monte Carlo facilities	Yes – optional extra	No	No

Name of package	FORESIGHT	FORPLAN
Optimising techniques included	No	Available with compatible package
Column and row operation	Yes	Yes
Able to handle bench-mark (see pages 249–251) easily	Yes	Yes
Flexibility of logic	Changes made easily in high-level language	Changes made easily in high-level language or a general-purpose language
Flexibility of input Ability of user to apply constants or parameter controlled growth rates to input data, without having to code in the model	Yes	Yes
Flexibility of output Choice of output report Choice of output report format Sequence of reports	Yes Yes Optional	Yes Yes Optional
Provision of training course Length of course Cost	2 days Negotiable	3 to 5 days Negotiable
Provision of consulting service e.g. building models for clients	Negotiable	Full facilities of UIMC
After sales support	Provided free	Full facilities of UIMC
Other points of interest	Plain English instruction. Extensive consolidation powers. Widespread business application. Calls to special purpose user routines, such as matrix inversion functions, can easily be inserted (in own installation)	Used extensively in Unilever Companies and others
Costs aspects Outright purchase price Initial fee to access Annual support fee Royalties payable	$25,000 None None Owners receive approx. 50% of bureau charges	Negotiable None None Not stated
Basis of charging clients	Connect time CPU	Connect time CPU
Year first developed	1968	1975
Year first available in UK	1969	1975
Estimated number of users Worldwide UK only	Over 100 70	Over 10 Over 10

FPS	GPOS 2	ICMS	INFOTAB
No	Model applications have been developed using linear and integer programming	No	No
Yes	Yes	Yes	Yes
Yes	Yes	Yes	Yes
Changes made in FORTRAN	Changes made easily in high-level language or FORTRAN	Changes made easily in high-level language or BASIC	Changes made easily in high-level language
Yes	Yes	Yes	Yes
Yes	Yes	Yes	Yes
Yes	Yes	Yes	Yes
Optional	Optional	Optional	Optional
3 days	3 days	3 to 5 days as required	1 to 3 days as required
Usually free	Negotiable	Negotiable	Computer resources only are charged
Negotiable	Negotiable	Fixed price contract or per diem charge	Limited free consultancy
Full after sales support normally free	One man-day per month free consulting support	Technical support service normally free	Free advice and back-up
Extremely flexible. Accounting logic specified by user. Very economical for multiple runs with same model logic. Also available in Canada, USA, Australia and South Africa	Other facilities include parametric analysis i.e. multi-dimensional sensitivity with automatic output editing. Additional data space may be coded into model without practical limit	A flexible and comprehensive system providing economical and simple modelling. Backed by major international business consultancy	System can read external data files generated by other systems
£7,000+	Negotiable	Negotiable	Negotiable
None	None	None	None
Negotiable	Variable depending on modules selected; minimum £3 connect hour	None	None
None		Not disclosed	Not disclosed
Connect time	Connect time	Connect time	Connect time
CPU	CPU	CPU	CPU
1970	1968	1972	Not known
1972	1971	1972	1973
Over 100	Over 100	30	Over 100
20	23	30	15

Name of package	INTERSIM	LOP
Type of package	Modelling system General purpose	Ready-made model Life office profitability
Owner of package	Arthur Andersen & Co	Computations (Pty) Ltd, Sydney, Australia
Address to which interested potential user should write	Arthur Andersen & Co, 1 Surrey Street, London WC2R 2PS	Pensions & Insurance Computer Services, 43 Dean Street, London W1V 5AP
Bureau on which package may be run	Honeywell Mark III Timesharing Service	Negotiable
Hardware requirements where package available on user's computer	Not applicable	CDC 6000 Series, IBM 360 (256k bytes core), ICL 1900 (48k words core). Available on comparable systems too
Mode of operation		
Batch	No	Yes
Remote batch	Yes	Yes
Conversational	Yes	No
Conversational remote batch	Yes	No
Purpose of model		
Financial planning (up to 1 year)	Yes	No
Financial planning (1 to 5 years)	Yes	No
Financial planning (over 5 years)	Yes	Yes
Project evaluation	Yes	Yes
Aid production decisions	Yes	No
Aid marketing decisions	Yes	Yes
Cash flow analysis	Yes	No
Time periods handled		
Maximum number	4,225	40
Specific periods	Optional	Years
Maximum size of model		
Input variables	Approx. 2,200 per period	Not applicable to ready-made
Output variables	Approx. 1,500 per period	model
Statements	Approx. 2,000 per period	
Maximum number of characters per line of output	132	132
Model interlinking (via intermediate files)	Yes	Yes
Model integration (ability to transfer between models during computer run)	Yes	No
Facilities available		
Backward iteration	No	No
Graphical output	*	No
Histogram output	*	No
Discounted cash flows	*	Yes
Sensitivity analysis (automatic)	No	No
Significance testing	*	No
Consolidation	Yes	Yes
	*Available if run on Honeywell Mark III Timesharing Service	
Forecasting techniques available		
Linear regression	*	No
Multiple regression	*	No
Curve fitting (least squares)	*	No
Arithmetic progression	No	No
Geometric progression	No	No
Moving averages	No	No
Exponential smoothing	*	No
Step functions	Yes	No
	*Available if run on Honeywell Mark III Timesharing Service	
Risk analysis	Monte Carlo facilities available if run on Honeywell Mark III Timesharing Service	No

MAPS	ORACLE	PAMMOD	PASTON/PASFOR
Modelling system	Modelling system	Modelling system	Ready-made model
General purpose	General purpose	General purpose	Inflation accounting
Ross Systems Inc,	ADP Network Services Ltd	PA Computers and	PA Computers and
California		Telecommunications Ltd	Telecommunications Ltd
RTZ Computer Services Ltd,	ADP Network Services Ltd,	PACTEL,	PACTEL,
PO Box 19,	179–193 Gt Portland Street,	Rochester House,	Rochester House,
1 Redcliff Street,	London W1N 5TB	33 Greycoat Street,	33 Greycoat Street,
Bristol BS99 7JS		London SW1P 2QF	London SW1P 2QF
RTZ Time Sharing	ADP Network Services	Various	Various
DEC PDP 11 under RSTS/E	DEC System 10	Mini or micro computer system	Mini or micro computer system
Yes	Yes	No	No
Yes	Yes	No	No
Yes	Yes	Yes	Yes
Yes	Yes	No	No
Yes	Yes	Yes	Yes
Yes	Yes	Yes	Yes
Yes	Yes	Yes	Yes
Yes	Yes	Yes	Yes
Yes	Yes	Yes	Yes
Yes	Yes	Yes	Yes
Yes	Yes	Yes	Yes
No practical limit	1,000	61	6
Optional – may be mixed	Optional	Optional	Optional
Matrix size limited only by hardware available	Total of 2,000 per period	1,000⎱ Regardless of	Not applicable to ready-made model
		1,000⎰ number of periods	
No practical limit	No practical limit	No practical limit	
132	132	132	80
Yes	Yes	Yes	No
Yes	Yes	Yes	Yes
No	Yes	Yes	No
No	Yes	Yes	No
No	Yes	Yes	No
Yes	Yes	Yes	No
No	Yes	Yes	No
No	Yes	No	No
Yes	Yes	Yes	No
No	Yes	*	*
No	Yes	*	*
No	Yes	*	*
Yes	Yes	Yes	Yes
Yes	Yes	Yes	Yes
Yes	Yes	*	*
No	Yes	*	*
No	Yes	Yes	Yes
		*Available in an associated program	*Available in an associated program
No	Monte Carlo facilities (on request)	No	No

Name of package	INTERSIM	LOP
Optimising techniques included	Linear programming available if run on Honeywell Mark III Timesharing Service	No
Column and row operation	Yes	Not applicable
Able to handle bench-mark (see pages 249–51) easily	Yes	No
Flexibility of logic	Changes made in FORTRAN	No
Flexibility of input Ability of user to apply constants or parameter controlled growth rates to input data, without having to code in the model	Yes	Yes

Flexibility of output
    Choice of output report
    Choice of output report format
    Sequence of reports
	Yes
	Yes
	Optional
		Yes
		No
		Fixed

Provision of training course
    Length of course
    Cost
	As required
	Negotiable
		No

Provision of consulting service e.g. building models for clients	£80–£100 per day	Negotiable hourly charges
After sales support	Minor queries normally free but otherwise consultants charged out on normal hourly basis	Full support (free for first 12 months)
Other points of interest	Extensive validation on conversational input (commands and data values). Multiple versions of data values permanently on file. Recovery procedures included for each stage in running the model	Model can be tailored to a limited extent. Applies solely to projections of a life assurance fund

Cost aspects
    Outright purchase price
    Initial fee to access
    Annual support fee
    Royalties payable
	£575
	Negotiable
	None
	None
		£4,500
		None
		None
		None

Basis of charging clients	Connect time CPU Input/output	CPU only (batch model)
Year first developed	1970	1969
Year first available in UK	1973	1972

Estimated number of users
    Worldwide
    UK only
	11
	3
		20
		4

MAPS	ORACLE	PAMMOD	PASTAN/PASFOR
No	Maximise and minimise commands incorporated. Linear programming links can be arranged	Optimal search procedures (general purpose heuristic)	No
Yes	Yes	Row operation plus summary columns	Not applicable
Yes	Yes	Yes	No
Changes made easily in high-level language	Changes made easily in high-level language or FORTRAN	Changes made easily in high-level language or BASIC	No
Yes	Yes	Yes	Yes
Yes	Yes	Yes	Yes
Yes	Yes	Yes	No
Optional	Optional	Optional	Optional
2 days	2 days	As required	As required
Usually free	£60	Negotiable	Negotiable
Negotiable	£30–£80 per day, plus machine time	Negotiable	Negotiable
Full after sales support normally free	Full ADP Timesharing support normally free	Minor queries normally free. Otherwise consulting charged at normal daily rates	Minor queries normally free. Otherwise consulting charged at normal daily rates
English-type instruction. Logic specified by user. Extremely flexible and easy to use. Also available in USA. Shortly to be released in Australia	User written FORTRAN subroutines may be included. FORTRAN or BASIC programs may be incorporated. Close links to information management, statistical and graphical facilities. Available in USA, Europe	Extensive conversational input checking. Conversation tailored to suit both expert and novice users. Virtually unlimited size of model but can operate on most mini and many micro processor based computer systems	Both packages have been designed with sufficient input flexibility to cater for a wide range of companies and can be run using conventional historic cost accounting logic and also the main proposed inflation accounting methods
£5,000	Negotiable	Negotiable	Negotiable
None	None	None	
Negotiable	None	None	
Not disclosed	None	Negotiable	
Connect time	Connect time	Used so far on bureaux charging connect time only	Used so far on bureaux charging connect time only
CPU	CPU		
1974	1970	1972	1975
1977	1971	1972	1975
50	Over 100	Over 100	40
10	Over 100	Over 100	40

Name of package	PAMMOD	PAUS
Type of package	Modelling system General purpose	Modelling system Risk analysis
Owner of package	PA Management Consultants Ltd	Bonner & Moore Associates, Houston, Texas
Address to which interested potential user should write	PA Management Consultant Ltd, Sundridge Park, Bromley, BR2 3TP, Kent	CSS International (UK) Ltd, 242 Vauxhall Bridge Rd, London, SW1V 1AU
Bureau on which package may be run	Various	CSS International (UK) Ltd
Hardware requirements where package available on user's computer	Not applicable	Not known. Refer to Bonner & Moore Associates
Mode of operation		
Batch	No	Yes
Remote batch	No	Yes
Conversational	Yes	Yes
Conversational remote batch	No	Yes
Purpose of model		
Financial planning (up to 1 year)	Yes	Yes
Financial planning (1 to 5 years)	Yes	Yes
Financial planning (over 5 years)	Yes	Yes
Project evaluation	Yes	Yes
Aid production decisions	Yes	Yes
Aid marketing decisions	Yes	Yes
Cash flow analysis	Yes	Yes
Time periods handled		
Maximum number	61	No practical limit
Specific periods	Optional	Optional
Maximum size of model		
Input variables	1,000 } Regardless of	No practical limit
Output variables	1,000 } the No. of periods used	
Statements	No practical limit	
Maximum number of characters per line of output	132	132
Model interlinking (via intermediate files)	Yes	Yes
Model integration (ability to transfer between models during computer run)	Yes	Yes
Facilities available		
Backward iteration	Yes	No
Graphical output	No	Yes
Histogram output	No	Yes
Discounted cash flows	Yes	Yes
Sensitivity analysis (automatic)	Yes	Yes
Significance testing	No	No
Consolidation	Yes	No
Risk analysis	No	Monte Carlo facilities
Forecasting techniques available		
Linear regression	*	No
Multiple regression	*	No
Curve fitting (least squares)	*	No
Arithmetic progression	Yes	No
Geometric progression	Yes	No
Moving averages	*	No
Exponential smoothing	*	No
Step functions	Yes	No

* Available in an associated program

PLANMASTER	PROPHIT II	PROSPER	PROSPER (VDU version)
Modelling system General purpose	Modelling system General purpose	Modelling system General purpose	Modelling system General purpose
Planmaster Systems Ltd	Control Data Corporation, USA	ICL	ICL-Dataskil
Comshare Ltd, 32–34 Great Peter Street, London SW1P 2DB	CDC Data Services/UK, 153 East Barnet Road, East Barnet, Herts EN4 8RA	ICL, ICL House, Putney, London SW15	ICL-Dataskil, Reading, Berks RG1 2DB
COMSHARE Timesharing Service	CALL/CDC	(i) Baric, Manchester (ii) Computel, Bracknell (iii) Redac, Tewkesbury	(i) Baric (ii) Computel
Not applicable	Not applicable	ICL 1900 Series, ICL System 4, ICL 2903 Series	ICL 1900 Series, ICL 2903 Series and VDU hardware. 24k words core store required
No Yes Yes Yes	No No Yes No	Yes Yes Yes Yes	No No Yes No
Yes Yes Yes Yes Yes Yes Yes	Yes Yes Yes Yes Yes Yes Yes	Yes Yes Yes Yes Yes Yes Yes	Yes Yes Yes Yes Yes Yes Yes
60 Optional	75 Optional	60/104 Optional	60 Optional
Maximum size of data matrix 15,500 No practical limit	Maximum size of data matrix 9,300 1,500	No practical limit	No practical limit
255	255	160	80
Yes Yes	Yes Yes	Yes No	Yes Yes
Yes Yes Yes Yes Yes No Yes	Yes Yes Yes Yes Yes Yes Yes	No Yes Yes Yes Yes No Yes	Yes Yes Yes Yes Yes No Yes
No No No No No No No No	Yes Yes Yes Yes Yes Yes Yes Yes	Yes No No Yes Yes Yes Yes Yes	Yes No Yes Yes Yes Yes Yes Yes
Yes	Monte Carlo facilities available on compatible package	Monte Carlo facilities	Monte Carlo facilities

Name of package	PAUS	PLANCODE
Optimising techniques included	No	Available as an extra
Column and row operation	Row operation only	Yes
Able to handle bench-mark (see pages 249–51 easily)	No	Yes
Flexibility of logic	Changes made easily in high-level language or FORTRAN	Changes made easily in high-level language or a general-purpose language
Flexibility of input Ability of user to apply constants or parameter controlled growth rates to input data, without having to code in the model	No	Yes
Flexibility of output Choice of output report Choice of output report format Sequence of reports	Yes Yes Optional	Yes Yes Optional
Provision of training course Length of course	1 to 3 days as required	As required
Cost	Computer resources only are charged	£200
Provision of consulting service e.g. building models for clients	Limited free consultancy	Hourly or contract basis
After sales support	Free advice and back-up	Usually free advice
Other points of interest	Risk analysis system which works mainly in terms of statistical output. Virtually unlimited model size. Sophistication and complexity of models also virtually unlimited. User's own subroutines can be included	Particularly appropriate for use in budgetary control and consolidations
Cost aspects Outright purchase price Initial fee to access Annual support fee Royalties payable	Negotiable None None Approximately 10% of normal charges based on variables in the model	Not applicable None £320–£340 per month None
Basis of charging clients	Connect time CPU	Not applicable
Year first developed	1968	1975
Year first available in UK	1972	1975
Estimated number of users Worldwide UK only	Over 100 15	No details

PLANMASTER	PROPHIT II	PROSPER	PROSPER (VDU version)
Limited hill-climbing	No	No	No
Yes	Yes	Yes	Yes
Yes	Yes	Yes	Yes
Changes made easily in high-level language	Changes made easily in high-level language	Changes made easily in high-level language	Changes made easily in high-level language
Yes	Yes	Yes	Yes
Yes	Yes	Yes	Yes
Yes	Yes	Yes	Yes
Optional	Optional	Optional	Optional
2 days	2 days	2 days or 1 week	2-day conversion from standard PROSPER or 1 week
Usually free	Free to CALL/CDC clients	£75–£180	Negotiable
Support as part of total service. Major consultancy by arrangement	No	£300–£500 per week	£300–£500 per week
Free advice, updates, technical assistance	Free advice to all users	Complete systems support; some free assistance in model-building	Complete systems support
Strong on consolidation. Data scrambling. File compression. Flagging of bad or doubtful data. Automatic currency conversion. Inflation facilities	A very general package having a wide range of functions and very easy to use. Can be integrated with other CALL/CDC packages to provide management information	Can be used by accountants/managers not having previous programming or modelling experience. Free format input available from Computel and Redac	A faster, more powerful version of standard PROSPER. Sophisticated editing facilities available from VDU. Reports sent to VDU screen for interrogation. Hard copy available. Works at up to 600 characters/second
Not applicable	Not applicable	Standard version supplied free	Approx. £4,000
None	None		None
None	None		Approx. £400 (free first year)
Not disclosed	None		None
Connect time	Connect time	Connect time	Connect time
CPU	CPU	CPU (Where applicable)	CPU (Where applicable)
1972	1971	1967	1973
1973	1974	1968	1973
50	Over 100	Over 100	80
40	Over 100	Over 100	50

Name of package	PWBPS	RAMIS II
Type of package	Modelling system	Modelling system
	General purpose	General purpose
Owner of package	Price Waterhouse & Company	Mathematica Inc
Address to which interested potential user should write	Price Waterhouse Associates, Southwark Towers, 32 London Bridge Street, London SE1 9SY	Mathematica Inc, Roxburghe House, 273 Regent Street, London W1R 8BX
Bureau on which package may be run	Honeywell Mark III Timesharing Service	CSS International (UK) Ltd Unilever Computer Services Ltd Any other IBM based bureau if rights are purchased or rented
Hardware requirements where package available on user's computer	FORTRAN compiler	IBM 360/370 OS, VM, CMS, CSS, DOS/VS
Mode of operation		
Batch	Yes	Yes
Remote batch	Yes	Yes
Conversational	Yes	Yes
Conversational remote batch	No	Yes
Purpose of model		
Financial planning (up to 1 year)	Yes	Yes
Financial planning (1 to 5 years)	Yes	Yes
Financial planning (over 5 years)	Yes	Yes
Project evaluation	Yes	Yes
Aid production decisions	Yes	Yes
Aid marketing decisions	Yes	Yes
Cash flow analysis	Yes	Yes
Time periods handled		
Maximum number	99	No practical limit
Specific periods	Optional	Optional
Maximum size of model		
Input variables		
Output variables	No practical limit	No practical limit
Statements		
Maximum number of characters per line of output	120	Limited only by printing device
Model interlinking (via intermediate files)	Yes	Yes
Model integration (ability to transfer between models during computer run)	Yes	Yes
Facilities available		
Backward iteration	No	No
Graphical output	No	Yes
Histogram output	No	Yes
Discounted cash flows	Yes	Yes
Sensitivity analysis (automatic)	No	No
Significance testing	No	No
Consolidation	Yes	No
Forecasting techniques available		
Linear regression	No	No
Multiple regression	No	No
Curve fitting (least squares)	No	No
Arithmetic progression	No	No
Geometric progression	No	No
Moving averages	No	No
Exponential smoothing	No	No
Step functions	No	No
Risk analysis	No	No

REPORT	SIMSTRAT	STRATEGY	TABAPL
Modelling system General purpose	Modelling system General purpose	Modelling system General purpose	Modelling system General purpose
OLS Computer Services (UK) Ltd	Unilever Ltd	Unilever Ltd	Boeing Computer Centres Ltd
OLS Computer Services (UK) Ltd, 6/24 Southgate Road, London N1 3JJ	Atkins Computing Services Ltd, Epsom Unilever Computer Services Ltd, Wembley	Unilever Computer Services Ltd, Wembley or UI Management Consultants Ltd (see FORPLAN)	Boeing Computer Centres Ltd, St Martin's House, 31–35 Clarendon Road, Watford, Herts WD1 1JA
OLS	As above	Unilever Computer Services Ltd	Boeing Computer Centres Ltd
Not applicable	IBM 360 OS/DOS with 110k bytes minimum partition	Bureau service and a subset available for IBM/OS installations	IBM 360/370
No	Yes	Yes	Yes
No	Yes	Yes	Yes
Yes	Yes (Atkins)	Yes	Yes
No	Yes (With Atkins batch print-out is available from conversational runs)	Yes	Yes
Yes	Yes	Yes	Yes
Yes	Yes	Yes	Yes
Yes	Yes	Yes	Yes
Yes	Yes	Yes	Yes
Yes	Yes	Yes	Yes
Yes	Yes	Yes	Yes
Yes	Yes	Yes	Yes
600	Atkins – No practical limit	No practical limit	No practical limit
Optional	UCSL 36 Optional	Optional	Optional
Maximum size of data matrix 1,200 No practical limit	Maximum size of data matrix 25,000 No practical limit	No practical limit	No practical limit
144	132	132	Limited only by printing device
Yes	Yes	Yes	Yes
Yes	Yes	Yes	No
No	Yes	Yes	Yes
No	Yes	Yes	Yes
No	No	Yes	Yes
No	Yes	Yes	Yes
No	Yes	Yes	No
No	No	Yes	No
Yes	Yes	Yes	Yes
No	Yes	Yes	*
No	Yes	Yes	*
No	Yes	Yes	*
No	Yes	Yes	Yes
No	Yes	Yes	Yes
No	No	Yes	Yes
No	No	Yes	*
No	No	Yes	Yes *Available with compatible package
No	Non-Monte Carlo approach; standard PERT approach, i.e. sum of individual optimistic/pessimistic estimates to produce total distribution	Monte Carlo facilities available with compatible package	No

Name of package	PWBPS	RAMIS II
Optimising techniques included	No	No
Column and row operation	Yes	Yes
Able to handle bench-mark (see pages 249–51) easily	Yes	Yes
Flexibility of logic	Changes made easily in high-level language	Changes made easily in high-level language
Flexibility of input Ability of user to apply constants or parameter controlled growth rates to input data, without having to code in the model	No	Yes

Flexibility of output
    Choice of output report
    Choice of output report format
    Sequence of reports
	Yes
	Yes
	Optional
		Yes
		Yes
		Optional

Provision of training course
    Length of course
 	
    Cost
	As required
	
	Negotiable
		3 days
		
		£120

Provision of consulting service e.g. building models for clients	Negotiable weekly rate	Negotiable
After sales support	Negotiable	Free 'hot-line' service, system enhancements and manuals
Other points of interest	Simple and economical to operate	Essentially a database management system with business option operating in a high-level language. Hence large volumes of data are easily handled and much historical data can be used as a basis for future forecasts

Costs aspects
    Outright purchase price
 	
    Initial fee to access
    Annual support fee
    Royalties payable
	Negotiable	Negotiable

Basis of charging clients	Charge normally part of an overall consultancy charge	Negotiable
Year first developed	1975	1967
Year first available in UK	1975	1973

Estimated number of users
    Worldwide
    UK only
	12
	0
		Over 100
		15

REPORT	SIMSTRAT	STRATEGY	TABAPL
No	No	Available with compatible package	No
Yes	Yes	Yes	Yes
Yes	Yes	Yes	Yes
Changes made easily in high-level language	Changes made easily in high-level language	Changes made easily in high-level language or a general-purpose language	Changes made easily in high-level language or APL
No	Yes	Yes	Yes
Yes	Yes	Yes	Yes
Yes	Yes	Yes	Yes
Optional	Optional	Optional	Optional
As required	Regular 1- and 2-day training courses (Atkins)	2 days	As required
Free	Normally free	£50	Free
Negotiable	Atkins Simple models often built free. Also free advice on modelling system. UCSL Fixed price quotation	Estimate number of days × daily rate but price then fixed (including computer and expenses)	As required
Technical support service normally free	Free support	Free advice, but if excessive at daily consultancy rate	Readily available – free
Suitable for preparing tables of data from limited numerical input and predefined rules, e.g. accountants' spread sheets	Multi-product modelling facilities. Automatic depreciation and tax facilities for project evaluation. Report definitions may be stored. Complete sets of run commands may be stored	System developed out of SIMSTRAT and FORPLAN continuing a 10-year period of development	Based on the powerful general-purpose language APL. Designed to handle tables of predefined size
Not applicable	Negotiable	FORPLAN subset available – see FORPLAN entry	Negotiable
None	None	None	None
None	None	None	None
None	25% of CPU charge when running model (Atkins)	Not disclosed	None
Connect time only	Connect time CPU	Connect time CPU	Connect time CPU
1970	1971	1978	1976
1970	1971	1978	1976
Over 100	Over 100	Previous versions over 100	No details
20	Over 100		

275

Name of package	TABOL	TYMTAB
Type of package	Modelling system General purpose	Modelling system General purpose
Owner of package	General Electric Company (USA)	Tymshare Inc
Address to which interested potential user should write	Honeywell I.S. Ltd, 114/118 Southampton Row, London WC1B 5AB	Tymshare (UK), Kew Bridge House, Kew Bridge, Brentford, Middlesex TW8 0EJ
Bureau on which package may be run	Honeywell Mark III Timesharing Service	Tymshare (UK)
Hardware requirements where package available on user's computer	Not applicable	Not applicable
Mode of operation		
Batch	No	No
Remote batch	No	No
Conversational	Yes	Yes
Conversational remote batch	Yes	Yes
Purpose of model		
Financial planning (up to 1 year)	Yes	Yes
Financial planning (1 to 5 years)	Yes	Yes
Financial planning (over 5 years)	Yes	Yes
Project evaluation	Yes	Yes
Aid production decisions	Yes	Yes
Aid marketing decisions	Yes	Yes
Cash flow analysis	Yes	Yes
Time periods handled		
Maximum number	10,000	310
Specific periods	Optional	Optional
Maximum size of model		
Input variables		Maximum size of
Output variables	No practical limit	data matrix 3,000
Statements		No practical limit
Maximum number of characters per line of output	Normal 158. System maximum much greater	256
Model interlinking (via intermediate files)	Yes	Yes
Model integration (ability to transfer between models during computer run)	Yes	Yes
Facilities available		
Backward iteration	Yes	Yes
Graphical output	Yes	*
Histogram output	Yes	*
Discounted cash flows	Yes	Yes
Sensitivity analysis (automatic)	Yes	Yes
Significance testing	*	*
Consolidation	Yes	Yes
	*Available with compatible package	*Available with compatible package
Forecasting techniques available		
Linear regression	*	*
Multiple regression	*	*
Curve fitting (least squares)	*	*
Arithmetic progression	*	Yes
Geometric progression	*	Yes
Moving averages	*	*
Exponential smoothing	*	*
Step functions	*	*
	*Available with compatible package	*Available with compatible package
Risk analysis	Monte Carlo facilities available with compatible package	Monte Carlo facilities available with compatible package

Name of package	TABOL	TYMTAB
Optimising techniques included	Optimal search procedures available with compatible package	No
Column and row operation	Yes	Yes
Able to handle bench-mark (see pages 249–51) easily	Yes	Yes
Flexibility of logic	Changes made easily in high-level language or FORTRAN	Changes made easily in high-level language
Flexibility of input Ability of user to apply constants or parameter controlled growth rates to input data, without having to code in the model	No	Yes
Flexibility of output Choice of output report Choice of output report format Sequence of reports	Yes Yes Optional	Yes Yes Optional
Provision of training course Length of course Cost	1- and 2-day courses Free	2 days followed by support as required £30 for new user
Provision of consulting service e.g. building models for clients	Limited free user support, extensive support negotiable	Negotiable
After sales support	Standard Timesharing Service support	Usually free
Other points of interest	Standard financial rules. Spread, Interpolation, Growth, Difference (absolute and %), Depreciation, Amortisation, Loan, Payback, Future Value, Tax	Ease of use for management. Part of total information processing environment
Costs aspects Outright purchase price Initial fee to access Annual support fee Royalties payable	Not applicable None None None	Not applicable None None None
Basis of charging clients	Connect time CPU	Connect time CPU
Year first developed	1970	1971
Year first available in UK	1970	1974
Estimated number of users Worldwide UK only	Over 100 Over 100	Over 50 Over 10

APPENDIX 3

General-purpose and simulation programming languages

I.   *Introduction*

This appendix gives a brief, introductory account of general-purpose and simulation languages for computer programming.

Computer programming is the process whereby instructions are coded in a manner that can be implemented by the computer. The earliest programs used a code that was followed directly by the computer, known as machine code, but this required considerable programming skill, was error prone because of its complexity, and was costly. Consequently, special mnemonics and devices to facilitate programming were developed, these being very close to machine code, normally being restricted to single makes of computer, and still being difficult to learn and use. The limitations of these 'low-level' languages led to the development of 'high-level' languages in which a single statement may lead to a whole series of computer operations. These languages are usually transferable, with minor modifications, between different makes of computers. Moreover, they are closer to business English in some cases, COBOL, or to mathematical notation in others. Thus they are orientated towards the needs of the user rather than towards the operations of the computer.

High-level languages are possible because of the use of special programs called compilers. These instruct the computer to undertake operations whereby the high-level language program ('source program') is translated into a machine code program ('object program') which the computer can understand directly. This process of translation is called 'compiling'.

The most commonly used high-level languages may be applied to a wide range of different problems. For example, PL/1 can be used to program payroll or other business systems, as well as almost any model using mathematical notation. Such languages have been called 'general-purpose languages' for obvious reasons.

Some other high-level languages have been developed for much narrower ranges of applications. Modelling systems, dealt with in Chapter 7, are an obvious example. Among the earliest were simulation languages but, because they were designed specifically for mapping physical flows, general-purpose languages are eminently more suitable than simulation languages for corporate models. This is especially so where the models concentrate on financial aspects at an aggregative level. Simulation languages tend to be more suitable for models at the shop-floor or operating unit level of the organisation, and concerned, for example, with machines producing a flow of manufactured goods.

Figure 1 is useful in that it shows the degree of flexibility of the various languages to be discussed. In this context flexibility is defined as the range of applications for which the language may be used without difficulty. PL/1 is the most flexible, closely followed by FORTRAN, whereas at the other end of the scale is DYNAMO.

Figure 1 Various levels of flexibility

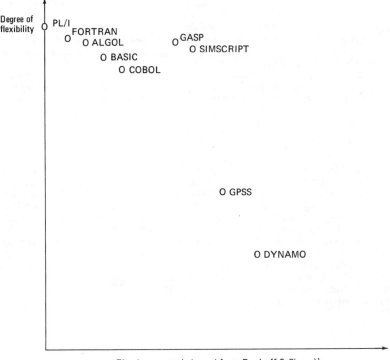

Fixed structure (adopted from Emshoff & Sisson)[1]

2. *General-purpose languages*

There are five well-known, widely used, general-purpose languages which we shall discuss here:

A FORTRAN
B COBOL
C ALGOL
D PL/1
E BASIC

A *FORTRAN* – (FORmula TRANslator)
FORTRAN is the most widely used for scientific applications of all programming languages which brings its own advantages and disadvantages. The fact that FORTRAN software is included on most computers provides an almost universal language in which any mathematical problem can be stated. Its main disadvantages arise from attempts to use it for programming that it was never intended to handle, for example, alpha-numerical data handling. So many people know and like FORTRAN that they want it to do everything for them and no language will do that.

FORTRAN programmers become irritated when they try and use their FORTRAN programs on different computers as the programs will often not be accepted without programming changes. There are two basic reasons for this lack of uniformity between computers. The first reason is that FORTRAN is a language that has gradually evolved since 1954, changing in the light of users' experiences. The second reason for FORTRAN's lack of uniformity is that it has been designed for all sizes of computers. But storage capacity, for instance, can be a severe constraint with small computers, and the FORTRAN compilers differ accordingly.

B   *COBOL* – (COmmon Business Oriented Language)
COBOL is designed for use in the batch mode. The word 'common' indicates that an attempt has been made to produce a language which is reasonably compatible from computer to computer. This has not been fully achieved, because of the differences between computers, but COBOL has probably been more successful than FORTRAN in this respect.

COBOL caters for data structures and systems found in typical businesses. It has tried to be as close to 'Business English' as possible to facilitate programming and also ease of reading and comprehension. The advantages of such a language for modellers who are not professional programmers can readily be appreciated. It is not a language which endears itself to professionals, but it is possible to reduce programming by use of a 'short-hand' program which itself produces normal COBOL programs, easily read by others. This readability aspect of COBOL is extremely useful should management be interested in the program and want to see exactly what it is designed to do.

C   *ALGOL* – (ALGOrithmic Language)
ALGOL is in many ways similar to FORTRAN. The two languages were, in fact, developed at the same time, ALGOL in Europe and FORTRAN in the USA. ALGOL has been accepted more in this country than in the USA, where FORTRAN is the generally accepted language. In some respects ALGOL is superior to FORTRAN which now incorporates some of the better points of ALGOL. It was intended and has turned out to be more of a mathematical language than FORTRAN which is more scientifically based. The advocates of ALGOL maintain that it is superior in almost all respects, certainly easier to learn and more flexible.

ALGOL, like FORTRAN and COBOL, has been designed primarily for use in the batch mode. However, even in the UK, FORTRAN is more readily available than ALGOL which is one good reason for us to recommend the use of FORTRAN. There are many more FORTRAN programmers around, which means that it should be easier to get replacement programmers at short notice to continue work on the model, although FORTRAN programmers normally find little difficulty in converting to ALGOL and vice-versa.

D   *PL/1* – (Programming Language 1)
PL/1 is suitable for programming jobs involving both numerical, scientific problems and also business data processing. It was built subsequent to the development of FORTRAN and COBOL and has tried to adopt the best points of both languages.

PL/1 is the most general of all languages. It has been designed so that new programmers can write simple PL/1 programs, whilst remaining suitable for the professional programmer who wishes to use the full range of the computer's capabilities. It was designed primarily as a batch language, but may be used in conversational mode on some bureaux computers. It differs from COBOL in that it is succinct rather than verbose.

E   *BASIC* – (Beginner's All-purpose Symbolic Instruction Code)
BASIC was developed in 1965 to provide a language which is relatively simple to learn and also easy to read. The designers hoped that it would become a stepping-stone for students wishing to go on eventually to join the main stream of FORTRAN and ALGOL users. The BASIC compiler has a large number of error messages which facilitate speedy development of programs. It is now generally considered as a conversational programming language for use on computers ranging from minicomputers to the largest computer systems.

Although PL/1 has been developed to combine the best features of FORTRAN and COBOL there is very little evidence to suggest that it will take over from FORTRAN. If anything, FORTRAN seems to be gaining in strength at the expense of the other general-purpose languages. It is more or less accepted as the standard language and it will require a very good language indeed to dislodge it from its position of supremacy.

Simulation languages

A simulation language is designed to reduce programming effort by providing routines to perform simulation operations which would otherwise have to be programmed in detail in a general-purpose language. One distinguishing feature of simulation languages is the mechanism for moving the model ahead in small time intervals. They also provide error checking techniques superior to the ones generally found in use with general-purpose languages. These 'diagnostics' can detect logical errors and are a boon as far as debugging the program is concerned. Another objective of a simulation language is to produce a generalised structure for model building that will facilitate model design and thus reduce the time spent at this stage of the model development.

In practice the model builder may be restricted in his choice of simulation language by limitations of time and funds. These constraints act to reduce the alternatives to languages that can be obtained easily for available computer equipment. Where there are alternatives it is important to pick the language most appropriate to the problem on hand. However, experience in the use of a language may outweigh other considerations.

The reduction in model development time has to be offset against a reduction in flexibility and increased computer run time. The benefits to a company of using a simulation language will normally only accrue where the programmer is already thoroughly familiar with the simulation language. If the programmer is not experienced in using the language it will obviously take time for him to become accustomed to it, and to take advantage of all the facilities offered by it. More time-wasting will occur if the programmer is unable to complete the program and it has to be handed over to another programmer who may have to go through the same learning process. Unless there is a programmer experienced in the use of the particular simulation language, a general-purpose language will often be more suitable.

We did not come across a single use of a simulation language in our survey of corporate modelling, and very few modellers thought these languages suitable for largely financial models. In view of the general lack of enthusiasm for simulation languages and the fact that there are many books currently available dealing specifically with these languages, we do not think it wise to go into great detail. Particulars are given here of only four of the better known simulation languages:

    A SIMSCRIPT
    B GPSS
    C GASP
    D DYNAMO

A   *SIMSCRIPT*

SIMSCRIPT is one of the older simulation languages and resembles FORTRAN to quite an extent. It is so general that anything that can be done in FORTRAN can also be done in SIMSCRIPT. Unfortunately with a language that is so general a lot of programming is required.

B   *GPSS* – (General Purpose Systems Simulator)

GPSS is another of the older simulation languages being first publicly described in 1961. GPSS differs from other simulation languages because its programs are based on block diagrams drawn by the user to represent the systems he wishes to simulate. Each block is built separately and joined together to form the program. The transactions are shunted around from block to block until all the sequences have been completed. Users have found it easier to learn than the normal statement-orientated simulation languages, although it is somewhat less flexible.

281

C   *GASP*

GASP is essentially a set of sub-programs connected via a main program called the GASP executive. Its modular characteristics make it quite easy to expand and alter simulation programs to suit the needs of any given system. GASP represents a completely different concept in simulation languages from that offered by GPSS and SIMSCRIPT because it is written in FORTRAN. It is widely available because all that is required to run GASP simulation programs is a computer which has facilities for FORTRAN. Naturally, using FORTRAN the usual problems of input and output formatting are encountered. However, as far as debugging is concerned it is a great improvement on FORTRAN in that it provides three very powerful automatic error detection features. However, where the latest versions are available users tend to prefer GPSS or SIMSCRIPT.

D   *DYNAMO*

DYNAMO is probably the best known of the continuous type of simulation languages. For general usage it is being superseded by other newer types of simulation languages. However, as it is a language which is especially tailored for one type of user, it is likely that it will continue to be used by them. The notation is relatively simple and users generally find that writing programs in DYNAMO is really quite straightforward.

These languages are quite widely used in the USA and it may be only a matter of time before they become more prevalent in this country.

Reference

1.   Emshoff, J. and Sisson, R. L.; *Design and use of computer simulation models*. Collier-Macmillan, 1971.

Further reading

Buxton, J. N. (ed.); Simulation programming languages.
Proceedings of the IFIP working conference on simulation programming languages, Oslo, 1967.

Fisher, F. P. and Swindle, G. F.; *Computer programming systems*. Holt Rinehart Winston, 1964.

Higman, B.; *A comparative study of programming languages*. MacDonald, 1967.

Naylor, T. H.; Balintfy, J. L.; Burdick, D. S. and Chu, K.; *Computer simulation techniques*. Wiley 1966.

Sammet, J. E.; *Programming languages: history and fundamentals,* Prentice Hall, 1969

Appendix 4

A select bibliography

(Prepared with the assistance of Gerry Smith, Librarian/Information Officer of The City University Business School.)

Monographs

Bonini, C. P.; *Simulation of information and decision systems in the firm*. Markham, 1967.

Boulden, J. B.; *Computer-assisted planning systems – management concept, application, and implementation*. McGraw-Hill, 1975.

Burrill, C. W. and Quinto, L.; *Computer model of a growth company*. Gordon and Breach, 1972.

Dearden, J.; *Computers in business management*. Dow Jones-Irwin, 1966.

Donaldson, G.; *Strategy for financial mobility*. Harvard University, Graduate School of Business, Division of Research, 1969.

Emshoff, J. and Sisson, R. L.; *Design and use of computer simulation models*. Collier-Macmillan, 1971.

Flower, J.; *Computer models for accountants*. Haymarket, 1973.

Gershefski, G. W.; *The development and application of a corporate financial model*. Planning Executives Institute, Oxford (Ohio), 1968.

Hertz, D. B.; *New power for management: computer systems and management science*. McGraw-Hill, 1969.

Hull, J. *et al*; *Model building techniques for management*. Saxon House, 1976.

Jones, G. T.; *Simulation and business decisions*. Penguin, 1972.

Kotler, P.; *Marketing decision making: a model building approach*. Holt, Rinehart & Winston, 1971.

McKinsey and Company Inc., 1968, pp. 1–38. Reprinted in McRae, T. W. (ed.), *Management information systems*. Penguin Books, 1971.

McRae, T. W.; *Computers and accounting*. Wiley, 1976.

Martin, F. F.; *Computer modelling and simulation*. Wiley, 1968.

Mattessich, R.; *Simulation of the firm through a budget computer program*. Irwin, 1964.

Meier, R. C. *et al*; *Simulation in business and economics*. Prentice-Hall, 1969.

Meyer, H. I., *Corporate financial planning models*. Wiley, 1977.

Miller, E. C.; *Advanced techniques for strategic planning*. American Management Association, 1971.

Mize, J. H. and Cox, J. G.; *Essentials of simulation*. Prentice-Hall, 1968.

Mulvaney, J. E. and Mann, C. W.; *Practical business models*. Heinemann, 1976.

National Economic Development Office: *Investment in the chemical industry*. A Report by the Investment Working Party of the Chemicals EDC, 1972.

Naylor, T. H.; *Computer simulation experiments with models of economic systems*. Wiley, 1971.

Rivett, P.; *Principles of model building: the construction of models for decision analysis*. Wiley, 1972.

Smith, J. U. M.; *Computer simulation models*. Griffin, 1968.

Stewart, R.; *How computers affect management*. Macmillan, 1971.

Journal articles

Anthony, T. F. and Watson, H. J.; Probabilistic financial planning. *Journal of Systems Management*, Sept. 1972.

Archer, W. R. V.; The RTZ financial modelling program. *Long Range Planning*, June 1971.

Barkdoll, G. L.; Using financial models to improve communications. *Managerial Planning*, May–June 1971.

Bhaskar, K. and Morris, R.; Computer based budgets. *Accountancy Age*, 13 June 1975.

Boodman, D. M.; Profit prophets: computer-based planning models for managers. *Data Processing Magazine*, Winter 1971.

Boulden, J. B.; Computerised corporate planning. *Long Range Planning,* June 1971.

Boulden, J. B.; Multinational planning systems. *Long Range Planning,* Sept. 1972.

Boulden, J. B.; A systems approach to corporate modelling. *Journal of Systems Management,* June 1973.

Boulden, J. B. and Buffa, E. S.; Corporate models: on-line, real-time systems. *Harvard Business Review,* July–Aug. 1970.

Boulden, J. B. and McLean, E. R.; An executive's guide to computer-based planning. *California Management Review,* Fall 1974.

Bryant, J. W.; A simulation model of retailer behaviour. *Operational Research Quarterly.* Vol. 26, No. 1, 1975.

Burnham, P.; Evaluating options in corporate growth plans. *Accountants Weekly,* 26 Jan. 1973.

Canning, R. G. (ed.); Using corporate models. *EDP Analyzer,* Jan. 1971.

Carruthers, J. A. and Greggains, D. J. K.; Simulation under focus. *Computer Management,* Sept. 1971.

Carson, I.; How ICL uses its company model. *International Management,* Jan. 1971.

Carter, A. J. T.; Bringing the computer into financial planning. *Method,* June–July 1972.

Chambers, A.; Users can cut costs by computing for managerial tasks. *Computer Weekly,* 12 April 1973. (Related articles appeared in *Computer Weekly,* 26 April and 3 May.)

Chambers, D. J. *et al*; Developing dividend and financing policies with a computer terminal. *Accounting and Business Research,* Autumn 1971.

Chambers, J. C. *et al.*; How to choose the right forecasting technique. *Harvard Business Review,* July–Aug. 1971.

Churchill, M. and Ward, B.; How BMW computerised cash planning. *Accountancy,* June 1976.

Clarke, B. J.; The principles of simulation as a management aid. *Accountants' Journal* (New Zealand), Oct. 1970.

Clutterbuck, D.; Do-it-yourself approach to five-year planning. *International Management,* Sept. 1973.

Cooke, J. E.; Principles of simulation. *Cost and Management* (Canada), Jan. 1968. (Related articles appeared in *Cost and Management,* Feb. and March 1968.)

Cookson, J. S.; Financial modelling – a practical application. *Public Finance & Accountancy,* Feb. 1975.

Cooper, J. and Jones, P.; The corporate decision. *Data Processing,* March–April 1972.

Davall, B. M. and Wilkinson, J. W.; Simulating an accounting information system model. *Management Accounting* (USA), Jan. 1971.

285

Engberg, R. E. and Moore, R. L.; A corporate planning model for a construction materials producer. *Management Adviser*, Jan.–Feb. 1974.

Forrington, C. D. V.; Business modelling. *Data Processing*, July–Aug. 1973.

Furey, C.; Scanning corporate planning. *Accountancy Age*, 27 May 1977.

Gershefski, G. W.; Building a corporate financial model. *Harvard Business Review*, July-Aug. 1969.

Gershefski, G. W.; Corporate models: the state of the art. *Management Science* (Application), Feb. 1970.

Gilligan, K.; Computer-aided budgeting at IPC. *Data Processing*, Jan.–Feb. 1975.

Gorman, T. J.; Corporate financial models in planning and control. *Price Waterhouse Review*, Summer 1970.

Grinyer, J. R.; Financial planning models: incorporating dividend growth elements. *Accounting and Business Research*, Spring 1973.

Grinyer, P. H.; Corporate financial simulation models for top management. *Omega,* Vol. 1, No. 4, 1973.

Grinyer, P. H. and Batt, C. D.; Some tentative findings on corporate financial simulation models. *Operational Research Quarterly*, March 1974.

Hall, W. K.; Strategic planning models: are top managers really finding them useful? *Journal of Business Policy*, Winter 1972.

Hammond, J. S.; Do's and don'ts of computer models for planning. *Harvard Business Review*, March–April 1974.

Harrison, F. B. and Baker, A.; The accountant takes to models – some experiences in NCB Coal Products Division. *Operational Research Quarterly*, Vol. 25, No. 1, 1974.

Harrison, F. L.; Computer modelling in practice. *The Accountants' Magazine*, June 1976.

Hayes, R. H. and Nolan, R. L.; What kind of corporate modelling functions best? *Harvard Business Review*, May–June 1974.

Hertz, D.; Management science and the chief executive. *Management Decision,* Winter 1972.

Higgins, J. C. and Finn, R.; Managerial attitudes towards computer models for planning and control. *Long Range Planning*, Dec. 1976.

Higgins, J. C. and Finn, R.; Planning models in the UK: a survey. *Omega*, Vol. 5, No. 2, 1977.

Higgins, J. C. and Whitaker, D.; Computer aids to corporate planning. *The Computer Bulletin*, Sept. 1972.

Hull, J. and Alexander, B.; The impact of inflation on corporate financial performance. *Management Decision*, Vol. 14, No. 1, 1976.

Jackson, A. S. *et al*; Financial planning with a corporate financial model. *The Accountant,* 27 Jan. 1968. (Related articles appeared in *The Accountant*, 3, 10, 17 Feb. 1968.)

Kingston, P. L.; Concepts of financial models. *IBM Systems Journal*, Vol. 12, No. 2, 1973. (This issue also contains five other intersting articles.)

McRae, T. W.; Financial computer models. *Management Decision*, Vol. 15, No. 1, 1977.

Mallinson, A. H.; A risk analysis approach to profits forecasts. *Accounting and Business Research*, Spring 1974.

Marsh, P. J.; Financial modelling. *Managerial Finance*, Vol. 1, No. 2, 1975.

Moss, K.; Is your company set for growth? *Computer Management*, Nov. 1972.

Naylor, T. H.; A conceptual framework for corporate modelling and the results of a survey of current practice. *Operational Research Quarterly*, Vol. 27, No. 3, 1976.

Nobbs, R. A.; Applying an organisation model for corporate planning in a small maufacturing firm. *Management Informatics*, Vol. 2, No. 3, 1973.

Power, P. D.; Computers and financial planning. *Long Range Planning*, Dec. 1975.

Precious, J. R. and Wood, D. R.; Corporate modelling: when success can be a long-term forecast. *Accounting and Business Research*, Autumn 1975.

Sherwood, D.; Business computer models – dispelling the myths. *Accountancy*, Dec. 1977. (A related article appeared in *Accountancy*, Jan. 1978.)

Stephenson, G. G.; A hierarchy of models for planning in a division of ICI. *Operational Research Quarterly*, Vol. 21, No. 2, 1970.

Tyran, M. R.; Simulator model applications. *Management Accounting* (USA), Oct. 1972.

Wagner, J. and Pryor, L. J.; Simulation and the budget: an integrated model. *Sloan Management Review*, Winter 1971.

Warren, J. M. and Shelton, J. P.; A simultaneous equation approach to financial planning. *Journal of Finance,* Dec. 1971.

Weber, J. P.; The corporate model applied to a general insurance office. *Journal of the Chartered Insurance Institute,* 1973.

Conference proceedings, Research reports, Theses

Agin, N. I. and Junkune, C.; Corporate planning models: what level of abstraction? In: *Fifth Conference on Applications of Simulation, New York, 1971. Proceedings.* New York: Association for Computing Machinery.

Brown, D. E.; Stages in the life cycle of a corporate planning model. In: Schriebei, A. N. (ed.); *Corporate simulation models.* University of Washington Graduate School of Business Administration, 1970.

Deam, R. J. *et al*; *Firm: a computer model for financial planning.* Institute of Chartered Accountants in England and Wales. (Research Committee occasional paper No. 5, 1975.)

Gershefski, G. W.; The design and use of computer assisted financial planning systems in the petroleum industry. In: *National Petroleum Refiners Association Computer Conference, Philadelphia 1972. Proceedings.*

Goldie, G. H.; *Simulation and irritation.* Published in Schrieber, A. N. (ed.) (*op. cit.*).

Hall, W. K.; *The implications and implementation of explanatory modelling in corporate planning.* University of Michigan, Bureau of Business Research. (Working paper No. 50, Oct. 1971.)

Neild, P. G.; Mathematical models as a tool for financial management; Financial modelling in UK industry. In: *European Federation of Financial Analysts Societies VIIth Congress, Torremolinos, 1972. Proceedings.* (A shortened version of the second paper appears in *Journal of Business Policy.* Spring 1973.)

Reilly, D. N. and Jenkins, P. M.; *Conversational planning systems.* IBM Peterlee, Research report UKSC–0038, Jan. 1974.

Schrieber, A. N. (ed.); *Corporate simulation models.* University of Washington, Graduate School of Business Administration, 1970.

Slade, C. D.; *The selection of a financial modelling language.* The Fourth Annual Symposium on Corporate Planning and Modelling. SSI, P.O. Box 2809. Chapel Hill, NC 27514.

Wagle, B. V. and Jenkins, P. M.; *The development of a general computer system to aid the corporate planning process.* IBM Peterlee, Research report UKSC–0024.

Wagner, W. H. *et al*; *Telecommunications earnings estimation model (TEEM): an evaluation.* Published in Schrieber, A. N. (*op cit.*).

Wooller, H. J.; *Survey of corporate modelling in the UK with special reference to cost variations and conditions associated with success.* Ph.D. thesis, The City University Business School, June 1977.

Glossary

ACCESS
(i) The way in which the user enters data or program statements into the computer.
(ii) With time-sharing systems, and as a verb, following steps that connect the terminal to the computer.
(iii) Used as a verb describing the process of obtaining data from a peripheral unit or retrieving it from a storage device. See ACCESS TIME.

ACCESS TIME
The time taken to retrieve data from a storage device or from a peripheral unit. The expression is commonly used in time-sharing applications to denote the time that elapses between the user transmitting data to the computer and the computer accepting it. Compare with TURNAROUND TIME.

ACCOUNTING CONVENTIONS
Generally accepted procedures of accounting.

ALGOL
ALGOrithmic Language. A problem-orientated high-level computer programming language for mathematical and scientific use. (Fuller description page 280.)

ALGORITHM
A systematic sequence of instructions or procedural rules used to solve specific business and other problems. Algorithms are usually expressed mathematically.

ALPHA-NUMERICAL DATA
Data containing letters of the alphabet as well as numbers.

APL
A Programming Language. One of the newer high-level programming languages, and not yet in widespread business use. The language is intended specifically for terminal use, but it does require a special terminal.

ARITHMETIC MEAN
The simple average as used in, say, cricket for determining the batsman's average, i.e. total runs divided by total completed innings.

ARITHMETIC PROGRESSION
A sequence in which each term is equal to the sum of the preceding term and a constant,
e.g. 1, 1 + 2, 3 + 2, 5 + 2, 7 + 2, etc.
i.e. 1, 3, 5, 7, 9, ,,
where the starting term is 1 and the constant is 2.

AUXILIARY STORE
See BACKING STORE.

BACKING STORE
A supplementary store to the main core of the computer. It will often hold more data than the main core, but access time is longer. Backing store generally takes the form of magnetic tapes, drums, or discs or a combination of these. Also known as back-up store or auxiliary store.

BACKWARD ITERATION	A facility used to find the combinations of input variables which will result in a specified output. The technique relies on automatically searching the available range of inputs until the desired result is obtained. For example, what level of sales will have to be reached if the company's target of a 10 per cent return on capital employed is to be reached and prices, fixed investment, etc. are to remain unchanged.
BASE PERIOD	The first period (e.g. month, quarter, year) in the series of time periods for each of which the corporate model produces a set of results. Normally, historical figures are input for the period, and the last period for which they are available is used. Where future values of, say, sales are assumed to follow a regular pattern the figures for the base period may be used in estimating them.
BASIC	Beginners' All-purpose Symbolic Instruction Code. A general-purpose high-level language that is particularly easy to learn and is suitable for batch as well as conversational operation. (Fuller description page 280.)
BATCH MODE	An approach to processing data whereby jobs are 'batched' and put in a queue for submission to the computer, usually via punched cards or tape. Once accepted, the jobs normally stay on the computer until completed, and output is usually delivered to the ultimate user as reports typed by the line printer. This mode is in contrast to the conversational mode.
BENCH-MARK	A standard against which performance can be evaluated.
BINOMIAL DISTRIBUTION	A mathematical function describing the chance of any given number of successes in a given number of trials, where the chances of success and of failure remain constant between consecutive trials, e.g. as when tossing a coin.
BIT	A BInary digiT. A single digit in binary notation, i.e. 0 or 1, which is the smallest possible unit of information that the computer can store.
BLOCK DIAGRAM	A chart setting out the sequence of operations to be performed in handling a particular application. It consists mainly of rectangular 'boxes' linked by lines which show the logical relationship between the boxes. A detailed diagram drawn up by programmers, prior to coding a particular program, which uses a fuller set of computer orientated symbols is called a flowchart.
BOUGHT-IN	A package from a bureau which is ready-made for use (i.e. requires no computer programming by the user).
BREAK FACILITIES	A term used by us to signify that the user is able to interrupt the normal sequence of operation to allow, say, changes in data held on files to be made, but such that the operation can be picked up again from the 'break-point'.
BUFFER STORE	A storage area used to retain data for transmission between different units, e.g. between a central processor and its input/output peripherals. The main purpose is to compensate for the different speeds with which units handle data.
BUREAUX	A term used by us to embrace computer bureaux, consultants, and computer hardware manufacturers who offer special computer software for corporate modelling.
BYTE	Often contains eight 'bits' of information and represents either one letter of the alphabet or two numbers.

Glossary

CARD READER An input device that reads information from punched cards into the computer by 'sensing' the holes in the cards.

CASE STUDY A selection of facts drawn from a practical environment and used for illustrative or teaching purposes.

CHAINING The process of organising an application program into segments which can be run serially such that each segment uses the output of the previous one. Chaining is used to run very large programs that would otherwise exceed the fast storage capacity of the machine in use.

CHI-SQUARED TEST A test used to find the statistical significance of experimental results.

COBOL COmmon Business Oriented Language. A widely available high-level programming language developed for general commercial use. (Fuller description page 280.)

COLUMN OPERATION Modelling systems usually store data in a large matrix in which columns represent successive years and rows different items of information (similar to conventional balance sheets). A column operation calculates all values in one column of the matrix before proceeding to the next. This operation corresponds to that usually adopted by accountants when preparing financial statements.

COMMANDS Instructions to the computer. For example the words PRINT, RUN, SAVE control the functioning of the computer.

COMMENT STATEMENT Explanatory text embedded in a computer program which explains a particular operation. Comment statements are non-executable; that is they are ignored by the computer.

COMPILER A complex program that converts statements written in a programming language into machine code, which can be executed directly by the computer.

COMPUTER ROUTINES A synonym for program but often used to mean a subdivision of a program. Standard routines, such as calculation of the present value, are often programmed by a bureau and may be incorporated directly in a user's program.

CONNECT TIME The time a terminal is connected to the computer.

CONSOLI-DATION A word used to denote the consolidation of data into an aggregate, for the purpose of expressing it in summary form, e.g. divisional profit and loss accounts may be added to obtain a corporate profit and loss account.

CONSTANT An item which remains unchanged for each run.

CONSTRAINT A limiting condition; sometimes expressed mathematically.

CONTINUOUS SIMULATION A technique of simulation modelling which describes systems in terms of continuous flows, e.g. flows of liquids, rather than discrete events. Corporate models only very rarely use continuous simulation.

CONTROL FILE A file of high-level statements used to control the overall logical sequence of a computer run. This file is not a program but rather a set of instructions to a program which determines its operation.

CONTROL PARAMETERS Alphabetical or numerical characters used to control the logical flow within a program during a particular run.

CONVER-SATIONAL MODE The method of access in which the user and computer communicate in a 'conversational' or 'interactive' manner via a terminal. (Fuller description page 194.)

CONVER-SATIONAL REMOTE JOB ENTRY CRJE involves accessing the computer in conversational mode via a terminal (possibly remote from the location of the CPU) to set up a control file. This file is then placed in the queue of jobs for batch processing.

CORE STORE A form of computer memory using 'cores' of magnetised material that can hold a single bit of information. Often referred to as core memory, or magnetic store.

CORPORATE MODEL A set of expressions representing the key operations of an organisation; the simplest comprise accounting statements linked in a straightforward way. (Fuller description page 194.)

CPU Central Processing Unit. This is the 'nerve centre' of the computer which performs the arithmetic and effects all the data transfers within the computer.

CSL A high-level programming language designed specifically for certain kinds of simulation models using Monte Carlo techniques, but is inappropriate for corporate models.

CURVE FITTING Use of techniques to find the mathematical function that best represents historical or experimental data. A straight line may be fitted in this way. Because it may be used to determine the trend implicit in a series of past values (say sales in each of the past 10 years), curve fitting may be an aid to forecasting.

DATA Syntactically data is the plural of datum. However, we use it to represent both singular and plural, in accord with common usage.

DATA BASE Data files held on appropriate storage devices which may be accessed by different programs (models).

DEBUGGING The process of locating and correcting 'bugs' (errors) in a computer program.

DETERMIN-ISTIC MODEL One which is based on single point estimates of each important variable. For example, only one estimate is given for future sales in each year up to a planning horizon.

DIAGNOSTIC ROUTINE A computer routine to assist in the debugging process by tracing program errors.

DISCRETE Separate; discontinuous.

DIVISION A division is used by us as an arbitrary level of the company hierarchical structure located between subsidiary company level and operating unit level.

DOCUMEN-TATION The orderly, written presentation of details of the purpose, functions and operational aspects of a program.

DOS Disc Operating System. A collection of programs stored on disc, provided by computer manufacturers to control the execution of all other programs.

DUAL (SHADOW) PRICE A term used in mathematical programming to mean the marginal value of a scarce resource, e.g. how much additional profit would be made if an additional hour of labour was available.

DYNAMIC PROGRAMMING A mathematical technique for optimising a set of decisions which must be made sequentially, with subsequent decisions depending on the results of preceding stages.

DYNAMO A special-purpose high-level programming language used for continuous simulation models. (Fuller description page 282.)

ECONOMIC FEASIBILITY One aspect of a feasibility study should cover economic feasibility. This implies that as full an analysis as possible of financial benefits and costs should be undertaken. If the results of cost/benefit analysis are not positive the project is likely to be rejected unless there are overriding, non-economic considerations in favour.

ELAPSED TIME Calendar time from the start to the finish of a job.

EMPIRICAL DISTRIBUTION A probability distribution based on frequencies observed in practice.

EQUITY The risk-bearing capital of a company. Also known as ordinary share capital.

EQUITY ASSETS The net assets of a company belonging to the ordinary (equity) shareholders. On a going-concern basis the equity assets will be equal to the ordinary share capital plus reserves. On a winding-up the equity assets are those assets available for distribution to the ordinary shareholders after all liabilities and prior claims have been satisfied.

ERROR REPORTING FACILITIES A set of instructions which instructs the computer to check for and then report any errors to the user.

EXECUTE To carry out an instruction.

EXPONENTIAL DISTRIBUTION A term often applied to the negative exponential distribution $(f(t) = \lambda e^{-\lambda t})$

EXPONENTIAL SMOOTHING A short-term forecasting technique.

EXTRA-POLATION Extension of a trend. All automatic, mathematically based forecasting techniques extrapolate trends, and therefore rest on the assumption that the underlying tendencies will remain unchanged in the future.

FAST STORE Store with relatively rapid access time.

FEASIBILITY STUDY An initial examination to ascertain the advantages and disadvantages of undertaking or continuing with a particular project or plan.

FILE An organised collection of records stored or handled as one unit, e.g. payroll records.

FILE COMPRESSION Techniques for packing data onto files with the object of reducing the storage space requirement.

FILE HANDLING	The manipulation of files and associated data.
FILE – MASTER OR PERMANENT	A file of data which it is intended to keep unchanged during the computer runs and which is held intact on backing store. To permit temporary changes during the run, a copy of the file may be made, which can then be either erased or substituted for the master file.
FILE TAPPING	Obtaining unauthorised access to computer files.
FILE – TEMPORARY	A file onto which data is put on a temporary basis pending a decision as to its future status.
FINANCIAL FLOWS	A sequence of events traced in financial terms, e.g. sales in consecutive periods expressed in £.
FINANCIAL RATIOS	Quantitative relationships between selected financial data, e.g. return on capital employed.
FINANCING	Ascertaining where the finances required by the organisation are to be acquired: whether from issues of ordinary shares, preference shares, debentures, unsecured loans or overdraft.
FIXED FORMAT	Where data must occupy set character positions in punched card or tape; in free format the positioning requirement is less rigorous.
FLAG	An indicator to draw attention to a specific condition – such as an error. Synonymous with a marker or tag.
FLEXIBILITY OF INPUT	The freedom to input data in a number of different ways, e.g. fixed or free format.
FLEXIBILITY OF LOGIC	Within any single model, the logic must be fixed, but it may have been designed to accommodate major changes in the structure of the company without reprogramming. The extent to which this is possible is the degree of flexibility of logic.
FLEXIBILITY OF OUTPUT	Different users of reports have different needs. Planning staff require detailed output to study, whereas directors often only require summaries. A model with full flexibility of output gives choice of reports, choice of report formats and choice of the sequence of reports.
FORECASTING ROUTINES	Standard programs for predicting values on the basis of historical data. A variety of mathematical techniques may be available and a choice be offered among them.
FORMAT	A predetermined layout of data on a document or in a file. It is often used to describe the exact form in which data is to be read or written by an input/output statement. (See also FIXED FORMAT and FREE FORMAT.)
FORTRAN	FORmula TRANslation. A high-level general-purpose scientific programming language, which is widely used for corporate modelling. (Fuller description on page 279.)
FREE FORMAT	With free format, data is punched onto cards or tape for reading into the computer in the right order but without attention to precise spacing. The opposite of 'fixed format'.

294

FREQUENCY DISTRIBUTION	A table showing the classes into which data have been grouped and the number of items falling into each class, i.e. the frequency of occurrence.
FUNCTION	A function is an algebraic expression of the relationship between variables, e.g. $z = a - b$ may express profit (z) as a function of revenue (a) and costs (b). The word function is also used to denote a particular subset of management; financial, production, marketing and personnel being normally regarded as the main 'functions' or 'functional areas'.
GASP	A simulation language based on FORTRAN but with more powerful error detection features. (Fuller description page 282.)
GEARING	Proportion of a company's capital made up of other than equity capital. Also known as 'leverage'.
GENERAL-PURPOSE LANGUAGE	A programming language which has a wide range of applications and may be used (with at most very minor modifications) on computers from different manufacturers. For instance, FORTRAN is appropriate for a wide range of scientific and mathematical applications and COBOL for many commercial applications. (Fuller description pages 278–82.)
GEOMETRIC PROGRESSION	A sequence of numbers in which the ratio of successive terms is constant, e.g. $1, \ 1 \times 2, \ 2 \times 2, \ 4 \times 2, \ 8 \times 2$, etc. i.e. $1, \quad 2, \quad\quad 4, \quad\quad 8, \quad\quad 16, \quad ,,$
GPSS	General Purpose Systems Simulator is one of the oldest simulation languages (not to be confused with a general-purpose programming language). It is not suitable for corporate modelling applications. (Fuller description page 281.)
HARD COPY	A printed copy of computer output, e.g. printed reports, listings, documents and summaries.
HARDWARE	The physical parts that go to make up a computer system.
HARMONIC ANALYSIS	A forecasting method using trigonometric functions to fit seasonal or cyclical variations.
HEURISTIC	A trial-and-error approach in seeking a particular goal. Compare with ALGORITHM.
HIGH-LEVEL LANGUAGE	A language in which each instruction corresponds to several machine code instructions. It allows programming in a code similar to that used in the logic describing the application, e.g. FORTRAN is similar to algebra, COBOL to English.
HILL CLIMBING	A term popularly applied to 'the method of steepest ascent'. It is useful for finding optimum solutions for sets of non-linear equations too complex to allow solution by analytical methods. This method determines the direction of maximum improvement around a given trial value, follows this to reach a new trial value, and then continues to repeat the operation until no further improvement can be effected.
HISTOGRAM	A graph of a frequency distribution obtained by drawing rectangles whose bases coincide with the class intervals. The areas of the rectangles are proportional to the number of items falling into each class.
IN-HOUSE	Facilities internal to the company.
INPUT/OUTPUT	Input is data fed to the computer by means of appropriate equipment. Output is data produced by the computer run for the user.

INPUT VARIABLE
A value fed into a computer model and which can vary from run to run, e.g. the number of items in stock. The opposite of a variable is a constant, which is a figure input once and for all and not intended to be changed frequently, e.g. warehouse size.

INTEGER PROGRAMMING
A method of linear programming in which the solutions are derived in whole numbers.

INTEGRATION OF MODELS
Allows models to be linked together in a single computer run.

INTERACTIVE
See CONVERSATIONAL MODE.

INTER-LINKING
Models are run independently of each other and results (output) stored. Other models can then call for these results and use them as their own input as required.

INTER-POLATION
The estimation of the value of a variable at a particular point which lies between two known points.

INTERPRETERS
Synonymous with interpretive routines. These translate program statements into machine code instructions, which are used immediately to process data. The interpreter performs the same function as a compiler, but whereas a compiler translates the entire program before processing of data, the interpreter does so statement by statement during the run.

INTER-QUARTILE MEAN
This is a term applied in this book to the arithmetic average of all items contained in the inter-quartile range: this range excludes the top and bottom 25 per cent of values.

INTERRUPT
See BREAK FACILITIES.

ITERATE
To repeatedly execute a succession of steps until a desired end-point is reached; each step is based on results obtained in the preceding step.

JEAN
A general-purpose programming language suitable for conversational models.

JUMP
A departure from the regular sequence of program steps. Synonymous with transfer and branch.

K
An abbreviation of kilo which is often used among computer specialists to mean 1,000. Strictly it is $2^{10} = 1,024$.

KEY IN
The act of inserting data into the systems via a keyboard printer or VDU.

KEYBOARD PRINTER
Colloquially termed a teletype terminal because of the widespread use of the equipment of the Teletype Corporation. It allows the user to input data to the computer via a keyboard and to receive messages and output from the computer via a printing head. (See photograph on page 42.)

LABEL
A group of characters assigned to a particular line, or statement, in the program as an identifying or reference point.

LEAST SQUARES
A method of curve fitting based on the principle that the curve which fits best is that for which the sum of the squares of the deviations from the observed values is a minimum.

LEVEL OF AGGREGATION	The hierarchical level in the company at which detail is accepted. For instance, input may be at the operating unit level, in the form of weekly production data. If this is the case it will normally be converted into financial terms and aggregated up to corporate level, perhaps incorporating detail from divisional and subsidiary levels, before its use in reaching truly corporate decisions.
LINE PRINTER	A printer which prints a line, rather than a character, at a time, and is faster than a keyboard printer.
LINEAR PROGRAMMING	A set of algorithms to determine the 'best' or optimal solution of a problem expressed in terms of linear equations.
LINEAR PROGRAMMING CODE	Specially designed high-level computer code/language used with linear programming packages.
LINEAR REGRESSION	A statistical technique to determine the line which best represents the relationship between two variables. Best is here expressed in terms of minimising the sum of squared deviations. Where there are more than two variables it is called multiple linear regression.
LINEAR TREND ANALYSIS	In time series analysis a trend which is reasonably represented by a straight line. It is usually calculated by the least squares method.
LOG NORMAL DISTRIBUTION	A probability distribution. Where the logarithms of the values of a random variable have a normal distribution, then the random variable is said to have a log normal distribution.
LOGIC	The principles of reasoning. Where computer programs are concerned the logic describes the relationships between elements in the program.
LOGISTICS	Activities concerned with the location and movement of goods and personnel.
LOW-LEVEL LANGUAGE	A programming language in which each instruction corresponds to a single machine code instruction. Sometimes called assembler or mnemonic code.
MACHINE CODE/LANGUAGE	The basic instruction code which a computer is capable of recognising and executing. All languages must be translated into this code before the computer is capable of executing them. Such translation is called compilation.
MAGNETIC CASSETTE	A small lightweight magnetic tape cassette used for storing data; similar to those in domestic use.
MAGNETIC DISC	A storage device on which data is recorded on the magnetised surface of a rotating disc. Each disc is capable of holding in the order of a million bytes of information.
MAGNETIC DRUM	A storage device on which data is stored on a rotating magnetic cylinder.

MAGNETIC TAPE	Closely resembling the tapes used on tape recorders, it consists of a plastic tape coated with a magnetic surface on which data can be stored. Computer access to data stored on tape is slow compared with that on discs and drums, but tape is much cheaper for bulk data storage.
MARGINAL COSTING	The increase in cost following an increase in the number of items being processed, e.g. the cost of the marginal item is the cost of producing 50,001 less the cost of producing 50,000. In practice an approximation to this may be used.
MATHEMATICAL PROGRAMMING	Algorithms used to obtain an 'optimal' or 'best' solution to problems stated in mathematical terms. These include linear programming, integer programming, quadratic programming, and dynamic programming. Application of these is limited by the fact that many problems cannot be stated in the appropriate mathematical form.
MATRIX	Strictly defined it is a rectangular array of numbers on which mathematical operations may be undertaken by following specified rules for addition, multiplication, etc. The term is used loosely to refer to any rectangular table of figures.
MINI-COMPUTER	A small, low-cost computer sometimes dedicated to specific tasks, but often capable of a limited amount of general-purpose use.
MNEMONICS	Words and groups of letters devised to be remembered easily, e.g. MULT could be the mnemonic code for 'multiply'.
MODE	A particular method of operation of the computer. The two most common are the batch and conversational modes.
MODEL	A representation of the subject of interest. In the case of corporate models, the representation is by means of logical and mathematical expressions, usually converted into a form suitable for computer operation. Use of such a model allows a variety of operating conditions to be tested, without affecting the actual situation.
MODEL DEVELOPMENT	The process of building a model from inception to implementation. Where models are regularly improved and updated after implementation, as in many cases, model development never really ends.
MODEL IMPLEMEN-TATION	The task of ensuring that the model is used as an aid to decision-taking. Implementation includes the training of staff who will use the model, development of systems to collect required information, documentation, and demonstration and other early model runs for users.
MODEL TESTING	Once the model has been debugged, tests are carried out to ensure that the model really does simulate the accounting logic and other company operations adequately. This testing is also known as 'model validation' or 'validity testing'.
MODELLING SYSTEM	A high-level language especially designed for corporate modelling and normally available from a bureau. (Fuller description page 195.)
MODULE	A module is a sub-model. A corporate model may comprise a number of modules and is then modular. If it has only one module, i.e. its parts cannot be used separately, but must be run as a unified whole, the model is non-modular.
MONOLITHIC MODEL	A model comprising one module only that is also very large.

MONTE CARLO   This term is popularly applied to use of simulated sampling. The actual population of items is assumed to be described by a probability distribution. By use of random numbers, samples are then drawn from the theoretical population described by this probability distribution.

MOVING AVERAGE   The average of a fixed number of immediately past values. For instance, the moving average of sales may be calculated in 1974 as the average of sales in years 1965 to 1973, and in 1975 as that of sales in years 1966 to 1974. This provides a simple basis for forecasts.

MULTIPLE REGRESSION   See LINEAR REGRESSION.

NORMAL DISTRIBUTION   A probability distribution which produces a bell-shaped curve, symmetrical about the mean. Also known as the Gaussian distribution, it is an important distribution, and is widely used.

OBJECT PROGRAM   A machine code program which the computer can execute directly.

OPERATING FEASIBILITY   One of the aspects of a feasibility study. Here the question being asked is 'If the model is developed, will it be used successfully?'

OPERATING SYSTEM   OS is a set of computer software to control the running of user programs.

OPERATING UNITS   Organisational units that are at the shop-floor level or its equivalent. Some physical activity is implied as in the production process.

OPERATIONAL RESEARCH   The application of the methods of science to complex problems arising in direction and management in industry, business and government. Its distinctive aspect is the development of models with which to predict and compare the outcomes of alternative decisions, strategies or controls.

OPERATOR (MATHEMAT-ICAL)   An operator relates two variables to produce a third variable, e.g. REVENUE = UNIT SELLING PRICE × UNIT SOLD. Here × is the 'multiplication' operator.

OPPORTUNITY COST   The term used by economists to denote the maximum value foregone by use of resources. By contrast with the historical cost, e.g. the interest on money invested, the opportunity cost is the return that the company would have obtained if the resources had been invested in the best available alternative.

OPTICAL CHARACTER RECOGNITION   OCR is the automatic identification of printed characters by light-sensitive devices.

OPTIMISATION   The process by which a mathematical optimal or 'best' solution is obtained for a problem by means of appropriate mathematical routines. For instance, optimisation may yield solutions which minimise expected costs or maximise profit.

OPTIMISATION CODES   Special codes used in conjunction with linear programming packages.

OPTIMUM SEARCH PROCEDURES   A term applied by some to a group of mathematical methods which search for the highest value in the immediate vicinity of an initial trial value.

ORGANIS-ATIONAL LEVEL	The level in the company hierarchy. In our main survey the successive levels in the companies were called corporate, subsidiary, division and operating unit levels, to avoid problems of different nomenclature in the different companies.
OUTPUT VARIABLE	A value (e.g. rate of return) produced by operation of a model. Although it is possible to feed in an input variable and to reproduce this as an output variable, generally an output variable is calculated by operation of the model.
PACKAGE	A software product designed to facilitate a particular application. Both modelling systems and ready-made models are packages.
PAGING	A system which enables a programmer to write programs which require more core storage than is available on his computer. Program segments (pages) are stored on fast backing store, each segment being called in as required.
PAPER TAPE	A reel of paper onto which data is punched in the form of holes which can be read by paper tape readers. It has the advantage of being less bulky and cheaper than punched cards.
PAPER TAPE READER	A device that converts data punched on paper tape into signals readable by the computer.
PARAMETER	An item of information or a quantity which is used in a mathematical calculation or in a program and which may be varied between calculations or runs respectively. In a program a parameter has a name. For example the parameter RATE has a value of 0.5 in: RATE = 0.5 TAX = RATE × NET PROFIT. Apart from their use in calculations parameters may also be used to control the logic followed in a batch-processed model (see CONTROL PARAMETERS).
PARTITION	A segment of a computer's fast store.
PASSWORD	A sequence of characters which allow access to particular computer files. Some files cannot be read without the correct password or key. In time-sharing systems the password is usually given in an initial dialogue with the computer as a user number.
PERIPHERAL UNITS	Units of equipment other than the CPU, but under its control. Thus all input, output and storage devices are peripherals.
PERT	Program Evaluation and Review Technique is a project planning and control system which focuses attention on critical activities.
PHYSICAL FLOWS	A sequence of events traced in physical terms, e.g. sales in consecutive periods expressed in tons.
PL/1	Programming Language 1. A high-level language orientated towards both commercial and scientific applications. (Fuller description page 280.)
POISSON DISTRIBUTION	A probability distribution for the number of occurrences of an event in a period of time.
POPULATION	The set of items from which samples are drawn and to which statistical inferences refer.

Glossary

PRESENT VALUE	The PV or NPV (Net Present Value) of cash flows occurring at specified future times is found by discounting at a sometimes arbitrary interest (discount) rate.
PRICE/ EARNINGS RATIO	The ratio: $\dfrac{\text{Price of share}}{\text{Earnings per share}}$.
PROBABILITY DISTRIBUTION	A mathematical function, or expression, that assigns a probability to each value within its range.
PRODUCT MIX	The set of products, as defined by their major characteristics, marketed by the company.
PRO FORMA	A mock-up of an actual report, balance sheet, etc. For example, a forecast profit and loss account may be produced by inserting estimates of future performances on a standard layout (pro forma) profit and loss account.
PROGRAM	A comprehensive list of instructions which a computer must follow in sequence to solve a problem. Programs are written using a defined set of conventions known as a programming language.
PROGRAMMING LANGUAGE	A set of conventions which allows the writing of programs.
PUNCH OPERATOR	A person who prepares punched card or tape input to computer.
QUADRATIC EQUATION	An equation in which some of the variables are squared, e.g. $ax^2 + bx + c = 0$.
QUADRATIC PROGRAMMING	An optimising method involving quadratic equations with linear constraints.
QUANTUM	The term applied on some time-sharing systems to the standard unit of time allowed to a user.
QUEUING THEORY	A topic of advanced mathematics developed to assist the analysis of situations where waiting lines occur.
RANDOM ACCESS	A technique for entering or retrieving data from various parts of a file in a random manner rather than sequentially.
RANDOM NUMBER	A number calculated in such a way that there is the same probability of its occurrence as for each of a large set of numbers within a predefined range.
RANDOM SAMPLING	A method of taking a sample which ensures that individual members of the population from which it is drawn have the same chance of selection.
READY-MADE MODEL	A model which is immediately ready for use without the need for programming. (Fuller description page 195.)
REDUNDANT ITEMS	These may be thought of as items deliberately left blank to allow for specific contingencies. For instance, a firm with three existing subsidiaries might program for four to allow for expansion.
REMOTE BATCH	Generally, the use of a punched card terminal at a location different to the central processing unit. The term is extended in this book to include both remote job entry and conversational remote job entry.

REMOTE JOB ENTRY	Method of accessing a computer via a terminal. A characteristic is that the job is run in the batch mode.
REPORT GENERATOR	A software package that allows convenient print-outs of selections of data held on computer files. The user is normally required to specify the format of the files, the format and content of the report to be printed, and any special rules for consolidation, etc.
RERUN FACILITIES	Instructions included in system software so that in the case of an interruption, or error, the program can be restarted from the point at which it occurred, rather than the whole program having to be rerun.
RESEARCH TOOL	A model is classed, in this book, as a research tool when it has been built to aid an *ad hoc* investigation rather than for routine use as part of the total planning procedures.
RESPONSE TIME	A term used in time-sharing to mean the elapsed time between the sending of a message to the computer and the receipt of the computer response.
RISK	The probability, greater than zero but less than one, that an event will occur. This may also be measured on a percentage scale by multiplying the probabilities by 100, e.g. there may be 10 per cent chance of a loss of over £10,000 next year.
RISK ANALYSIS	Risk analysis or probabilistic models recognise that sales, costs and so on are not certain, and may assume a sometimes large number of different values. Consequently for each set of assumptions, the routines of the model are repeated many times, each time with values generated in such a way that, overall, their relative frequencies reflect those expected to occur in practice.
ROW OPERATION	If the computer is restricted to row operation it will calculate all values in one row of the matrix before proceeding to the next row. In a corporate model this can restrict balances being carried from one period to another. Contrast with COLUMN OPERATION.
SCRAMBLING	Data retained on files is deliberately 'jumbled' or 'scrambled' so as to appear incomprehensible to any unauthorised person who may access the files.
SENSITIVITY ANALYSIS	Analysis of the sensitivity of results obtained to errors in the estimates used to calculate them. In the case of a deterministic simulation model this is done by systematically varying the estimates used to see what effects, either singly or in combination, they have on the results.
SERIES	A set of terms in succession the value of each of which is determined by prescribed rules.
SET	A collection of items having some common property.
SIGNIFICANCE TESTS	Statistical procedures that provide bases for deciding whether a difference between observations and expected results are significant, i.e. cannot be attributed to chance. Such tests are used in research to test hypotheses.
SIMSCRIPT	A high-level simulation language, designed by Rand Corporation. (Fuller description page 281.)
SIMULATION LANGUAGE	A language designed to reduce programming effort by providing routines to perform simulation. (Fuller description page 281–2.)

SINGLE-VALUE ESTIMATE	Synonymous with point estimate. Single figure estimates used in deterministic models that assume certainty. These models may be contrasted with probabilistic (risk analysis) models.
SOFTWARE	Generally used to refer to all items in a computer system which do not come in the hardware category, including user programs.
SOURCE PROGRAM	A high-level language program. This has to be translated by the computer into machine code before being processed by it. See COMPILER.
SPECIAL PROGRAMMING LANGUAGE	A language, capable of being read by and followed by a computer, that has been developed for a particular application, e.g. planning (in which case it is known as a modelling system).
STATEMENT	An instruction in a computer program.
STATISTICAL ANALYSIS	The application of mathematical methods pertaining to the collection, classification and use of numerical facts.
STEADY-STATE POSITION	A position of stability reached following a period of fluctuations.
STEP FUNCTION	A function which describes the manner in which a variable changes its value in discrete steps, e.g. if the cost per cruise of a liner steward is £40, a decision to take more stewards will lead to step increases in costs of £40. Wage costs may therefore be a step function of number of passengers.
STORE	A device that can accept and hold data, and from which it may be retrieved.
STRATEGIC DECISION	A decision fundamental to the future of the firm; decisions on the products to be produced, market distribution channels, the acquisition of major productive plants, and methods of financing would normally be regarded as strategic.
STRUCTURAL FLEXIBILITY	A corporate model has structural flexibility if the individual modules of a suite can be run individually in the order requested by the user.
SUB-ROUTINE	A set of instructions within a computer program designed to perform a specific function which may be required several times in the model as a whole.
SUBSIDIARY	Although strictly the term should be applied only to companies legally subsidiary to a holding company, we apply it in this book to the hierarchical position between the 'corporate level' and 'division'.
SUITE OF MODELS	A collection of models (modules) which together constitute a corporate model.
TACTICAL DECISION	A decision made in support, or implementation, of company strategies. Most marketing, production and financial decisions are of this nature, e.g. decisions on the recruitment and deployment of a sales force are tactical decisions in support of the strategic decisions on products and markets.
TAILOR-MADE MODEL	A model incorporating logic unique to one company. It may be developed either in a general-purpose language or by use of a modelling system.
TECHNICAL FEASIBILITY	That part of the feasibility study which ascertains whether the proposed model would be within the limits of available technology and physical resources.

TELCOMP   A general-purpose language designed for use on a time-sharing system.

TELETYPE   The trade mark of the Teletype Corporation often used generally, when referring to a keyboard terminal. (See photograph on page 42.)

TERMINAL   A device capable of sending and/or receiving data from a computer over a communications system. In some cases, like a remote batch terminal, the terminal cannot be used to control operation of the computer, whilst in some others, like the time-sharing system terminal, it can.

TIME SCALE   A time dimension of a graph. The unit of measurement in many corporate models is a year. Values of sales, etc. may then be extended for each period.

TIME SERIES ANALYSIS   The analysis of any series of data collected, observed or recorded at discrete time intervals, e.g. daily FT closing prices, as a function of time. The objective is to separate the time series into individual components (trend, seasonal variation, cyclical variation and residual variation).

TIME SERIES ANALYSIS USING SHISHKIN'S METHOD   A mathematically complex, and rarely used, method of analysing a time series. The method may involve more than one process, e.g. first a preliminary smoothing (approximating to seasonal effects), next a more refined trend fitting, followed by successive approximations until the required accuracy is obtained.

TIME-SHARING   A technique which allows a central computer to be shared among many users often geographically remote from each other and from the computer. Response is usually sufficiently fast for each user to feel that the computer is dealing with his program only.

TRANSMISSION CHARGES   The cost of transferring data from one location to another.

TREND ANALYSIS   An extrapolation of data using standard statistical procedures.

TURNAROUND TIME   The time between despatch of input data and receipt of output (printed reports) in batch processing system and between accessing the system and completion of a model run in a time-sharing system.

UNCERTAINTY   The condition in which there is inadequate knowledge to assign probabilities to possible future events.

UNIFORM DISTRIBUTION   A probability distribution which assigns equal chances of occurrence to each of its values.

USER-SPECIFIED DISTRIBUTION   A probability distribution based on subjective estimates made by users.

VALIDITY TESTING   See MODEL TESTING.

VARIABLE   A quantity capable of assuming different numerical values in a given range.

VARIANCE   A measure of dispersion of values around their mean. (The arithmetic mean of the squares of deviations from the distribution mean.)

VDU   Visual Display Unit. A device for presenting information television-type screen.

Glossary

VDU
Visual Display Unit. A device for presenting information on a television-type screen. (See photograph on page 41.)

VENN DIAGRAM
A diagram in which events are represented by circles or ellipses; overlaps between these indicate the concurrence of the events. In this book, by attaching absolute or percentage figures to the events represented by circles, Venn diagrams have been used to illustrate the relative importance of different classes which can overlap. For instance, the use of months, quarters and years in runs of the corporate model.

VIRTUAL MEMORY
A system enabling a computer to adopt dynamically to problem size without user intervention.

WEIBULL DISTRIBUTION
A probability distribution often used in analysing reliability of industrial equipment.

'WHAT IF' QUESTIONS
An abbreviated version of '**What** would happen **if**', etc., e.g. **What if** advertising is cut by 50 per cent?

WORD
A basic unit of data in a computer memory.

Subject index

Manual interlinking 47-8, 201
    report 2, 150, 227-30
    system 64, 124-7, 142, 228-30, 233
Manuals 83, 104, 220, 223
Marketing 3-4, 183, 200-1, 210, 217
Mathematical programming 24, 107, 110, 120-3, 203-4
Mathematician 16-8, 218
Matrix generator 196
Merger 1, 84, 147, 180-2, 207
Minicomputer 280
Mnemonics 278
Mode of operation 40-9, 172-9, 194-5, 198-9, 236
Model builder 16-8, 64, 112-3, 142, 217
    definition 194
    development 61-2, 144, 155-71, 174-5, 281
    testing 61, 82-3, 156, 234
    use 147-9, 174
Modelling system 10-8, 172-9, 195, 222-5, 236
    acquisition 10-1, 196-8
    advantage 11-4, 57-60, 85-107, 195-8
    cost 43, 156-71
    disadvantage 13-4, 42-3, 57-60, 86-107
Modular approach 37-8, 142, 201, 203, 213
    advantage 85, 112-3, 144-6, 183, 234
    disadvantage 234
Module 37, 104, 135, 144-6, 194
Monolithic model 37-8, 47-9, 144, 201
Monte Carlo 205
Motor industry 5, 27-9, 109-13, 128-32, 193
Moving average 107, 206
Multiple regression 107, 206

Nature of model 1-3, 62

Oil industry 5, 24, 193, 204-5, 233
On-line 220, 234
Operating feasibility 62-3
    manuals 83, 104, 220, 223
    unit level 3-5, 34-6, 62, 202, 210-2
Operation of model 40-9
Operational feasibility 62-3
    researcher 16-8, 147-8, 217-8, 226-7
Opportunity cost 157
Optical character recognition 42
Optimisation 107-8, 203-4, 211, 222, 236
    advantage 24, 122-3
    code 14-5, 170-1, 196-8, 236
    cost 123, 156, 170-1
    disadvantage 19-24, 109-13
Optimum search procedure 107, 110, 204
    solution 19, 203-4
Organisational level 34-6
Output flexibility 50, 57-60, 94-5, 209, 219
    report 4-5, 80-1, 209-11, 227-8
    format 50, 58-9, 98, 105, 209
    sequence 50, 59, 105, 202, 209
    variable 37, 106, 142-5, 156, 203

Package 174, 195, 222-5
    choice of 101-8, 174, 224-5
    cost 108, 223-4

312

Companies index